About Island Press

Island Press is the only nonprofit organization in the United States whose principal purpose is the publication of books on environmental issues and natural resource management. We provide solutions-oriented information to professionals, public officials, business and community leaders, and concerned citizens who are shaping responses to environmental problems.

In 2004, Island Press celebrates its twentieth anniversary as the leading provider of timely and practical books that take a multidisciplinary approach to critical environmental concerns. Our growing list of titles reflects our commitment to bringing the best of an expanding body of literature to the environmental community throughout North America and the world.

Support for Island Press is provided by the Agua Fund, Brainerd Foundation, Geraldine R. Dodge Foundation, Doris Duke Charitable Foundation, Educational Foundation of America, The Ford Foundation, The George Gund Foundation, The William and Flora Hewlett Foundation, Henry Luce Foundation, The John D. and Catherine T. MacArthur Foundation, The Andrew W. Mellon Foundation, The Curtis and Edith Munson Foundation, National Environmental Trust, The New-Land Foundation, Oak Foundation, The Overbrook Foundation, The David and Lucile Packard Foundation, The Pew Charitable Trusts, The Rockefeller Foundation, The Winslow Foundation, and other generous donors.

The opinions expressed in this book are those of the author(s) and do not necessarily reflect the views of these foundations.

The Western
Confluence

The Western Confluence

A *Guide to* Governing Natural Resources

Matthew McKinney *and*
William Harmon

Island Press

Washington • Covelo • London

Library of Congress Cataloging-in-Publication data.

McKinney, Matthew.
  The western confluence : a guide to governing natural resources /
Matthew McKinney and William Harmon.
    p. cm.
  Includes bibliographical references and index.
  ISBN 1-55963-962-8 (cloth : alk. paper) — ISBN 1-55963-963-6 (pbk. : alk. paper)
  1. Natural resources—West (U.S.)—Management. 2. Natural
resources—Government policy—West (U.S.) 3. Natural resources—Law
and legislation—West (U.S.) I. Harmon, Will. II. Title.
  HC103.7.M35 2004
  333.7'0978—dc22

                                                                    2004002134

British Cataloguing-in-Publication data available.

Printed on recycled, acid-free paper ✪

Design by Sans Serif, Inc.

Manufactured in the United States of America
10 9 8 7 6 5 4 3 2 1

To citizens and leaders who participate
in governing natural resources

Contents

List of Tables, Boxes, Figures, and Maps

Foreword

The American West has long been characterized by deep currents of individualism and contentiousness. All too often, the old adage "whiskey is for drinking, water is for fighting" has been reality, not homily.

Yet there are other currents. The wagon trains and barn-raisings were community efforts, as were the informal arrangements where senior water rights holders made adjustments that allowed junior irrigators to get water, even in dry years. We smile at the colorful tales of the rough-hewn mining camps, but those societies installed laws and customs that made claim-jumping and shoot-outs the exception, not the rule. In more recent times, Governor Tom McCall inspired people to pull together to begin the cleanup of the Willamette River, Governor Bruce Babbitt convened stakeholders to address Arizona's sinking groundwater levels, and tribes and states continue to work together, however fitfully, to complete negotiated water right settlements.

This other, less heralded, tradition impelled Wallace Stegner to write that when the West "fully learns that cooperation, not rugged individualism, is the pattern that most characterizes and preserves it, then it will have achieved itself and outlived its origins. Then it has a chance to create a society to match its scenery." The same impulse drives the authors of *The Western Confluence* and the upswelling of cooperative enterprises that forms the stuff of this book.

Collaborative efforts can encounter all manner of obstacles. Out in the field, a forest supervisor or BLM district manager may be imbued with the old-style desire to "manage" a landscape—a mindset that might allow consultation but hardly welcomes true negotiation with the interested parties. Washington, D.C., has sabotaged collaboration by ramrodding set-in-concrete development agendas, off-limits to negotiations out West. Irrigators with senior water rights, holding all the cards, may refuse to budge. Environmental groups, unwilling to trust locals in the rural West, may go straight to court. And let it be clear that negotiating is not always an option: Whether you operate the coal-fired power plant or love to the depths of your being the vivid, stretched-out vistas, there may come a point where you simply must fight rather than talk.

Nonetheless, over the past generation westerners increasingly have turned to collaboration. Some of the reasons have to do with a growing and changing citizenry, while others involve an evolution in the ways government does business.

When the first census was taken in 1790, the nation held 3.9 million people. Today my home state of Colorado accounts for that many. In the West, most of the growth has been recent as the region has boomed to 60 million residents, four times the population half a century ago. The results have been writ in the urban strips from the Denver Front Range to the megalopolises of the Pacific Coast and in many of the cities and towns in between.

In addition to the changes wrought by sheer numbers, we now take a different view of the two categories of natural resources that together have always been so central to the West's societies and economies: the federal public lands, still 50 percent of the region, and our rivers, coveted for their rarity in this dry terrain. The might of the California Gold Rush and Manifest Destiny engraved—in stone, it seemed—a panoply of laws and traditions that handed subsidies and control over the public lands and rivers to water developers, ranchers and farmers, and mining and timber companies. Then in the 1950s, industry, responding to the growth in the nation generally and the West in particular, devised big plans for the Missouri River basin, the surging rivers and deep forests of the Northwest, and the coal deposits and rivers of the Southwest. Development winched up all across the region. The immensity of the projects began to set in, and changes in our attitudes toward the lands and waters of the West gradually took hold. Although the laws have not fully caught up, by the early twenty-first century westerners—all of us—now know what we have and what we have to lose: sweeping, sacred expanses of space that inflame the mind and salve the soul.

Over the course of the nation's history, two structural trends in government have addressed the burgeoning size and complexity of society. The modern federal bureaucracy traces to the turn of the century with the creation of early agencies such as the Interstate Commerce Commission and the Forest Service. The administrative sector then mushroomed during the New Deal when Congress, knowing it could no longer do all the lawmaking, established a raft of new agencies—"little legislatures" with broad authority to make laws and regulate activities. State agencies developed more slowly but the basic story was the same because state lawmakers also needed to delegate authority to address the rising number of people and disputes on the ground.

The second experiment with dispute resolution involved the courts. Since *Brown v. Board of Education,* the 1954 school desegregation case, judges have increasingly addressed public issues, including environmental and natural resources conflicts. Today, Congress regularly leaves key terms in statutes ambiguous, knowing that they will be refined in the agencies or the courts.

Now, of course, the agencies and courts have themselves been overwhelmed by the scale of societal problems. Administrative processes have too often become inflexible, formalized, and interminable. As for the judiciary, citizens can get answers there, but only if they have a good deal of time and even more money. Justice delayed, or justice too dear, is justice denied. Further, the statutes often force judges to give a yes-or-no, up-or-down answer when the dispute may cry out for a nuanced solution tailored to the specifics of communities and watersheds. Needless to say, legislatures, administrative agencies, and courts will always be important forums for resolving disputes, but in recent years the search for alternatives has intensified.

These powerful historical and contemporary forces, much elaborated upon in the pages that follow, have caused collaboration to emerge as a useful approach for addressing natural resource disputes in the American West. The watershed groups now found in every western state (with a dozen or more each in California, Colorado, Idaho, Montana, Oregon, and Washington) provide perhaps the leading example. These groups have in common several basic beliefs: that a problem or problems on a particular river can best be resolved by open, frank discussion and negotiation among all the affected interests; that, in the West, the lay of the land usually directs that decisions can best be made by using the watershed as the geographic reference point; and that working cooperatively can search out the full range of options and, when it works, will craft solutions at once practical and creative—solutions that can last because they are bred of agreement, not coercion.

Beyond that, as is the case of the broader collaboration movement, it is hard to make generalizations about watershed groups. They are large and small, informal and process-laden, penniless and well funded (the promise of these new institutions has attracted federal, state, and foundation funding). Some direct their energies toward a specific conflict, such as Endangered Species Act compliance, while others do ongoing work on a range of watershed problems. Some disbanded early, some have lasted. Of those, some have accomplished little, others have achieved modest successes, and some have made significant breakthroughs. We have seen river conditions improve through better grazing and logging practices, reductions in industrial and agricultural pollution, modified release schedules from dams, and conservation easements on key acreages. The toughest issue has been stream flows, since senior diverters understandably strive to protect their water rights. To date, on a West-wide basis the accomplishments have been encouraging but hardly revolutionary.

Of one thing I am sure. As one who has followed these developments for a generation and has recently attended statewide gatherings in California, Montana, and Oregon, I am convinced that the determination within watershed groups runs deep, and the spirit is high. These are people, environmentalists and ranchers alike, who love their rivers and are willing, usually on a volunteer basis, to commit their valuable time to healing them.

The western movement toward collaboration is still young. It is too early to predict that this approach will become a mainstay in resolving disputes over land and water. Yet the history and modern case studies offered up in *The Western Confluence* suggest that something significant is afoot here. Let us hope so. After all, the issue is not to win but to do right by the extraordinary natural systems that give us so much.

Charles Wilkinson
Distinguished University Professor
Moses Lasky Professor of Law
University of Colorado–Boulder

Preface

Since the earliest days of settlement, the American West has been shaped (perhaps more than any other region in North America) by persistent conflicts over natural resources. Miners and farmers arguing for their share of water; cattle barons and sheepherders dividing the open range with fences and bloodshed; loggers and conservationists vying for the same stand of old-growth trees.

Today, despite 150 years of hard-won experience, we're no better off. Debates over natural resources and land use are marked by acrimony and gridlock. Resource managers, decision makers, and citizens alike are adrift in a sea of conflicting demands over water, land, wildlife, and energy resources. No action seems safe, and decisions that satisfy the majority (or the side with the most clout) too often leave fundamental issues unresolved and key interests unmet. Disputes drag on or recur with little hope for resolution. In short, public policy on natural resources has become a mix of art and weather—everyone knows what they like, but no one can do anything about it.

To cope with this stream of disputes, people who care about the West have developed a number of strategies over the years—prior appropriation, scientific expertise, public participation, citizen ballot initiatives, public interest litigation, devolution, and negotiation. The West's hardscrabble landscape has taught us to never throw anything away, so the old strategies were never retired—each new strategy was simply added to the rest. Most of these strategies are now deeply embedded in western policies and institutions, and all of them are still in play, providing various mechanisms for public decision making and dispute resolution. To one degree or another, each also either encourages or restricts citizen participation in the decision-making process. In short, the various strategies that have emerged over the past 150 years offer different—sometimes competing—approaches to governance and who decides how western resources should be used.

Despite this apparent wealth of ways to resolve conflict, the West is still locked in a tug-of-war over natural resource issues. In fact, as we'll see in the following chapters, the problem-solving strategies have themselves become a source of conflict. When irrigators and fisheries advocates fight over water, for example, they also pit the doctrine of "first in time, first in right" against the "best available science." If they disagree over whether the water should stay in the stream or be sprayed on the crops, they also cannot agree on which method to use to resolve the dispute.

This book proposes a way out of the gridlock. To effectively resolve disputes over the West's natural resources, we must first understand the array of available strategies, how they evolved over the past 150 years, and how they continue to shape the legal, institutional, and cultural fabric of natural resource decision making. Drawing on several disciplines, *The Western Confluence* examines the evolution and history of the ideas that have shaped the policies, institutions, and strategies used to resolve natural resource disputes in the American West.

In the course of western settlement and development, each strategy emerged in response to the shortcomings of the preceding approaches to decision making and dispute resolution, and each incorporated the best ideas at the time. While each strategy began at a different time and place in the history of western resource policy, they have braided together at the beginning of the twenty-first century, creating a roiling, often turbid confluence of ideas. This metaphor of "confluence" can help us understand the interaction of the dominant strategies available to resolve natural resource disputes in the West. Imagine tracing a river to its source—to know it in all its complexity—by exploring each of its tributaries to their many different beginnings. We take the same approach in this book. Each chapter explores a different dispute resolution strategy, beginning at a pivotal moment in the history of western resource policy and then moving forward to the present to show how that strategy has evolved. Rather than following a single time line in chronological order, each succeeding chapter then takes the reader back in time—up a different tributary—to understand the origins and evolution of the next dispute resolution strategy.

The confluence analogy helps us understand the past and present but also gives us a vision for the future. Our basic proposition and prescriptive framework is that the best way to sustain communities and landscapes in the West—that is, to promote livable communities, vibrant economies, and healthy landscapes—is to create forums where people with diverse viewpoints or interests can work together on common problems. As a dispute resolution strategy, such a process might take the form of negotiation, collaboration, or consensus building.

Regardless of the label, or the particular procedures and tactics used, we contend that interest-based strategies are more effective when they are inclusive, informed, and deliberative. By inclusive participation, we mean that an effort is made to meaningfully engage all viewpoints and interests, including unaffiliated citizens and national interests. It also suggests that participants are empowered by the presumption that their input and advice will be considered by the decision makers and will influence the outcome. An informed process is one that offers an equal opportunity to share views and information. The process fosters mutual learning, common understanding, and consideration of a variety of options. It enables participants to jointly develop and rely on the best available information, regardless of the source. A deliberative dialogue occurs when people listen to one another, consider the rationale or reason for competing viewpoints (that is, the interests that underlie the positions), and seek solutions that integrate as many interests as possible.[1] Such processes, we believe, hold the most promise for a livable, sustainable West.

The validity of this proposition and prescriptive framework is a matter of historic record. Interest-based problem solving represents the most recent response to the limitations of all the other decision-making and dispute resolution strategies that have emerged during the past 150 years. While it is not a panacea, it does provide a vision for improving the other strategies and charting new ways to engage citizens and leaders in the process of shaping public policy to sustain the communities and landscapes of the West. Integrating interests also tends to be less costly than determining who is right, which in turn is less costly than determining who is more powerful. We cannot say that integrating interests is always better than focusing on rights and power, but it does tend to result in greater satisfaction with outcomes, less recurrence of disputes, less strain on relationships, and lower transaction costs.

Assuming that the different approaches to decision making and dispute resolution will continue to be around for the foreseeable future, we offer suggestions in each chapter on how the values of interest-based problem solving can be integrated into the various dispute resolution strategies. Just as one dispute resolution strategy may be more appropriate than another in a given situation, so too our suggestions in each chapter are meant to be suggestive, not definitive. No single model of governance is likely to effectively resolve the myriad of natural resource disputes in the West. Over time, through a process of experimentation and learning, the best ideas and approaches will emerge, and the people who engage in this process will jointly develop the theory and practice of adaptive governance.

Before we head upstream to explore the first tributary, it's important to understand the nature and complexity of western resource disputes. The introduction sets the stage with a story about a complex, ongoing, multiparty dispute in the Klamath River basin of Oregon and California. In many ways, the Klamath case typifies western resource disputes, and we'll return to it in subsequent chapters to illustrate how specific dispute resolution strategies are applied in the real West.

NOTE

1. See Daniel Yankelovich, *The Magic of Dialogue: Transforming Conflict into Cooperation* (New York: Simon & Schuster, 1999), for other ways to define deliberation and dialogue.

Introduction

When newcomers first visit the upper Klamath Basin, they are most often struck by its apparent emptiness—a sprawling lake rimmed by sharp escarpments, few buildings or even fences, and a highway that runs arrow-straight to the horizon. This first impression has some merit. Upper Klamath Lake has the largest surface area of any lake in Oregon, varying seasonally from 60,000 to 90,000 acres. The upper basin is part of a watershed that covers about 16,000 square miles, an area larger than Massachusetts and New Jersey combined.[1] It stretches from the high desert northeast of Crater Lake National Park in Oregon to the Pacific Ocean just north of Redwood National Park in northern California. Beyond a scattering of small towns, humans are not a prominent feature of the landscape—rural population densities average fewer than five persons per square mile.

The people who do live here, however, see a relatively crowded landscape, one rich in resources—water, arable land, fish, timber, and hydropower—and cluttered with competing demands for those resources, entangled laws, and cultures in conflict (Old West versus New West, commodity production versus conservation, and nontribal versus tribal). Competition is perhaps fiercest for the basin's water supply—a limited resource stretched to meet a diversifying and growing demand.

As with most lakes in the basin, Upper Klamath Lake has shrunk about 30 percent since the late 1800s due to diking and draining to create more arable land. Wetlands in the basin are now 20 percent of their historical size. Through a network of headgates, canals, and ditches, the U.S. Bureau of Reclamation (USBR) manages the Klamath Project in the upper basin,

1

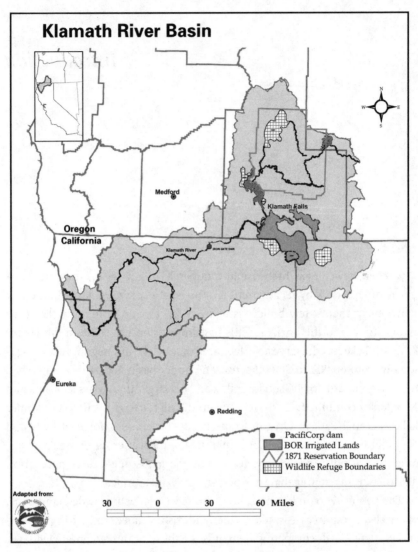

MAP I.1. Klamath River Basin. (Adapted from Oregon Water Resources Department.)

providing irrigation water to about 1,400 farms. Annual on-farm crop revenues exceed $100 million.

Many smaller lakes and reservoirs are scattered across Klamath County in Oregon and Modoc and Siskiyou counties in northern California. Together, these waters are the lifeblood of the basin's economy and environment, sustaining nearly 150,000 people, 540,000 acres of irrigated land, hydroelectric power generation, a complex of six national wildlife refuges, the largest seasonal gathering of bald eagles in the lower forty-eight states, more than 80 percent of the seasonal habitat for Pacific Flyway waterfowl, and four fish species listed as threatened or endangered under the Endangered Species Act.

Even with the dams and natural lakes and wetlands, the basin has little capacity to store surplus water in wet years for later use. The water that comes in is used, evaporates, or flows out. There is little margin for drought—and great potential for conflict among those who claim a stake in Klamath waters.

A Collision of Interests

The Klamath Tribes—the Klamath, Modoc, and Yahooskin—say the Creator placed them in the upper basin when the world was first being populated.[2] Anthropologists estimate that the Klamath people have lived here for at least 14,000 years. Either way, say the tribes, they were the basin's first human inhabitants, and their continuous presence testifies to the success of their relationship with the land, waters, and other resources of the basin.

For generations, the Klamath people sustained themselves on wild foods in the basin, surviving winters on reserves stored from the previous fall. Those reserves dwindled toward spring, and the March spawning runs of the *c'wam* (TCH-wam), or Lost River sucker, and the *qapdo* (KUP-doh), or shortnose sucker, were celebrated—as they still are today—as a sacred gift from the Creator, a bounty of food in a season of need. For most of the twentieth century, the suckers were a popular and important food fish for native and nontribal people alike.

In an 1864 treaty, the tribes ceded 20 million acres (an area the size of Maine) to the U.S. government, reserving a tribal homeland of 2 million acres and the right to continue to fish, hunt, trap, and gather food.[3] For the next ninety years, the tribes prospered alongside nontribal newcomers through a commercial fishery based in part on suckers, ranching, freight hauling, and sustained-yield logging of the largest remaining stand of ponderosa pine in the West. By 1950, the Klamath Tribes were one of the most economically successful in the nation. Then in 1954, under a misguided policy to assimilate tribes into mainstream society, Congress dissolved the Klamath Tribes and paid individuals for their shares of the remaining tribal lands, which then became national forest and wildlife refuge. Despite its severe terms, the Termination Act protected tribal water rights, asserting that "nothing in this [Act] shall abrogate any water rights of the tribe and its members."[4] Nevertheless, the Klamath, Modoc, and Yahooskin fell into poverty, and outsiders contested tribal rights to fish, hunt, and use the basin's waters. Late in the twentieth century, an enlightened Congress reversed its stance on assimilation policies and restored federal recognition to the Klamath Tribes. Although the Klamath Restoration Act of 1986 did not return any tribal lands, it affirmed once again the tribes' water rights. Twice during the drought in 2001, irrigators in the Klamath Project went to court challenging the U.S. Department of the Interior's legal authority to reduce the project's water allocation for the sake of tribal *c'wam* and *qapdo* fisheries and other endangered species. In both cases, federal courts ruled that tribal rights were senior and held precedence over any rights claimed by the irrigators.[5]

The earliest European claims on Klamath waters came from homesteaders, who began staking them in earnest not long after the Treaty of 1864. Completion of the Klamath Project in 1907 (the second-oldest USBR project in the country) ensured water for farmers attracted to the area by the government's offer of free, recently reclaimed, irrigable land. After World War I, the government gave preference to veterans over other homestead applicants, awarding groups of homesteads in the basin five times between 1922 and 1937.[6] The program continued after World War II with three lottery-style drawings awarding more than 200 homesteads between 1946 and 1949. To "prove up" and gain clear title, winners had to farm the land for five years. The farmers who succeeded relied on the dependable delivery of water from the Klamath Project and subsequent reclamation and irrigation projects.

While basin irrigators now work to protect their water rights claims in the Oregon adjudication process, a few have considered selling out. Without assurances of water, they say, they can't get buyer contracts for their crops, and they've worked too hard for too long to farm on speculation.

The farmers rely on the U.S. Bureau of Reclamation to manage the Klamath waterworks for the benefit of irrigation. USBR was a newborn agency when it began building the Klamath Basin Project in 1905. Nearly 100 years later, its role in the basin has not substantially changed, though project management is vastly more complicated today because many more interests and agencies have a stake in or jurisdiction over resources within the project boundaries. Accordingly, USBR has tried to protect the water supply it manages for project irrigators, while accommodating, when feasible, fish and wildlife, tribal, hydropower, and other demands for water.

But USBR often finds itself in conflict with another federal agency, the U.S. Fish and Wildlife service (USFWS), which manages the six wildlife refuges in the Klamath Basin. In 1908, shortly after the initial Klamath Reclamation Project was completed, President Theodore Roosevelt designated Lower Klamath Lake and surrounding marshes as the nation's first wildlife refuge for waterfowl. USBR continued to drain wetlands and open them to agricultural development and settlement. After a century of such development, less than 25 percent of the historic wetlands remain, much of it held in six national wildlife refuges: Lower Klamath, Tule Lake, and Clear Lake refuges in California; and Bear Valley, Upper Klamath, and Klamath Marsh refuges in southern Oregon. Most of these refuges rely on a complex system of ditches, gates, and other "plumbing" for their water supply, which in some cases comes primarily from irrigation return flows.

The mission of the National Wildlife Refuge System is "to administer a national network of land and waters for the conservation, management, and where appropriate, restoration of fish, wildlife, and plant resources and their habitats within the United States for the benefit of present and future generations of Americans."[7] Refuges in the Klamath Basin protect a variety of habitats and serve as a migratory stopover for about 80 percent of the Pacific Flyway waterfowl. Peak concentrations in the fall total more than 1 million birds. Agricultural and water programs in the basin are coordinated under an agreement between USFWS and USBR.[8] The U.S. Fish and Wildlife Service is also the federal agency responsible for listing species under the Endangered Species Act.

According to the Klamath Basin Wildlife Refuge office in Klamath Falls, managers are currently faced with three major concerns.[9] First, the Klamath Basin has lost 80 percent of its original wetlands, a significant loss of habitat for a wide range of migratory and resident waterfowl, fish, and other species. Second, water quality in the basin has been degraded by agricultural and timber practices. And third, during drought years, water quantity is insufficient to balance wildlife needs with basin agricultural demands. Some feel that water in the basin is simply overallocated—that there is not enough water to satisfy fish and wildlife needs and agricultural demand. Refuge managers are watching the ongoing water rights adjudication process in Oregon, with the refuges caught between senior rights for irrigation and a court-ordered priority to leave water in the system for fish protected under the Endangered

Species Act. The adjudication process must also consider tribal water rights, which may gain legal seniority as the earliest water rights in the basin.

Drought Brings the Klamath to the Brink

Despite occasional dry years and intensifying discord among irrigators, the tribes, and wildlife management agencies, basin residents saw little incentive to engage in preemptive drought planning. In fact, after decades of antagonism, the different factions in the basin apparently preferred to plan through litigation, filing no fewer than fifteen water-related lawsuits during the 1990s.[10] The stage was set—awaiting a drier than usual year—for a major battle over water in the Klamath Basin.

From 1995 through 1998, the basin enjoyed the wettest consecutive four years ever recorded. But in 2001, precipitation in the basin reached only 55 percent of average, and April snowpack (the most critical indicator of total local snow accumulation) was a mere 21 percent of normal. Spring runoff never came, and Upper Klamath Lake began to shrink. On March 27, 2001, Governor John Kitzhaber declared a state of drought emergency in Klamath County. He requested a coordinated response from state and federal agencies and urged all interests in the basin to work cooperatively to share the shortage, seeking to balance the demands of the basin's irrigators, wildlife refuges, fish protected under the Endangered Species Act, and tribal water rights. Unfortunately, the rules in place for allocating resources did not encourage such sharing.

That same month, the USFWS released its biological opinion on shortnose and Lost River suckers, endangered fish native to Upper Klamath Lake. To help sucker populations recover, the USFWS said, the U.S. Bureau of Reclamation would have to increase Upper Klamath Lake levels above the previous year. The National Marine Fisheries Service then recommended in its own biological opinion that USBR spill more lake water to increase flows in the lower Klamath River to protect habitat for threatened coho salmon. As the drought worsened, the two wildlife agencies told USBR to stop all water deliveries to basin irrigators and wildlife refuges.

Farmers also demanded their allocations. When a federal judge ruled against them, farmers drove out to the ditches and forced open headgates. They also lobbied decision makers at every level, from county officials and local state legislators all the way up to President George W. Bush. They circulated a petition asking government officials to allow full delivery of water for irrigation, cede the Klamath Project to the State of Oregon, and strip all funding for enforcement of the Endangered Species Act. Farmers told the story of their plight to newspaper and television reporters, hoping to garner widespread public support.[11] Farmers and refuge managers hoped USBR would ignore the order. Then they asked local political leaders to appeal for a review of the biological reports. The appeal eventually reached Vice President Dick Cheney, who asked eighty federal biologists to review the decision. Based on that review, and taking advantage of welcome spring rains, Cheney authorized the release of 75,000 acre-feet of water to farmers east of Klamath Falls.[12] The majority of farmers within the federal Klamath Project (and the wildlife refuges), however, remained without water. After ninety-four years of receiving water from USBR ditches, some 200,000 acres of cropland were doomed to go dry.

The farmers refused to accept the decision. They filed suit in federal court against the three agencies, claiming that shutting off their water was a breach of the USBR project trust agreement. The judge upheld the agencies' decision, however, and on April 4, 2001, ruled that USBR would violate the Endangered Species Act if it delivered any additional water.

Angry farmers organized protests on the streets of Klamath Falls, denouncing the suckers as trash fish and calling for repeal of the Endangered Species Act. Then on July 4, 2001, protesters forced open irrigation headgates. USBR responded by posting armed federal guards to keep the headgates closed, spending $900,000 through the summer to enforce the closure.[13] Also in July, three local men were arrested and charged with felony intimidation after they drove through a small tribal town yelling, "Sucker lovers, come out and fight!" and blasting signs and buildings with a shotgun, at one point asking a group of children if they were Indians and then shooting over their heads.[14] In August, a convoy of more than 100 trucks from around the West rolled into Klamath Falls for a rally in front of the county courthouse to show support for area farmers.[15]

Also in August, a conservation group filed suit to force USBR to deliver water to a wildlife refuge to sustain waterfowl migration, a significant food source for bald eagles.[16] The responsible federal agencies met in Sacramento to develop long-range plans for improving water management in the Klamath Basin. At the same time, a federal judge in Eugene, Oregon, mediated a dialogue among farmers, salmon fishermen, conservationists, and government agencies to seek mutually satisfying solutions. An outgrowth of an ongoing dispute resolution effort coordinated by the Oregon

Department of Water Resources, parties were ordered by federal court to engage in the mediation in response to a lawsuit brought by Klamath Basin irrigation districts against USBR. After the mediation failed, the original dispute resolution working group resumed its monthly meetings but has yet to produce any major solutions.[17] Despite exploration of many avenues for resolving the problem, the irrigation headgates remained closed as the drought continued through the summer. Economic losses in the basin were estimated at over $250 million.

In early 2002, USBR released its proposed ten-year operations plan for the Klamath Project and an assessment of the plan's impacts on fish and wildlife in the basin. Just three months later, the National Marine Fisheries Service and USFWS published their separate biological opinions, concluding that USBR's proposed operations would jeopardize the coho and sucker populations and "result in an increased risk to the continued existence" of these threatened and endangered species.[18] USBR immediately agreed to comply with the wildlife agencies' recommendations but also criticized their research and questioned the validity of USFWS and Marine Fisheries Service data and conclusions. The USBR regional director fired off memoranda to both wildlife agencies, citing a report on the Klamath situation drafted by the National Research Council (NRC).[19] He wrote: "We believe that the NRC Report, which has received extensive peer review through an established process in the science community, represents the best available science."[20]

During the 2002 irrigation season, USBR delivered water to basin irrigators, reducing flows in the Klamath River. To address concerns about suckers and salmon, USBR worked with project irrigators to set aside an additional 20,000 acre-feet of water in USBR's water bank. In cooperation with basin tribes, this water was managed over the summer to provide flows intended to protect coho salmon populations. Irrigators also voluntarily provided pulse flows from groundwater and left some fields fallow to save water. But in September, California state biologists discovered more than 33,000 dead salmon and steelhead in the lower Klamath River.[21] As of this writing, USFWS and the National Marine Fisheries Service deny that the decision to send water through irrigation canals rather than down the river was responsible for the death of the fish, but they are still investigating the fish die-off. Many fisheries advocates, however, blame USBR's operation of the Klamath Project. In January 2002, the California Department of Fish and Game submitted a report to the federal government claiming that low flows in the

Klamath River trapped salmon and exposed them to disease.[22] It emphasizes that there is a substantial risk of future fish kills in the river.

Understanding Natural Resource Conflicts in the West

On the surface, much of the conflict in the Klamath centers on water and intensifies in dry years. But to see the Klamath Basin conflict solely as a "water war" seriously understates the nature and scope of the dispute. In fact, the conflict in this situation stems from the confluence of the four forces that shape nearly every western resource dispute:

1. *Competing demands for a limited resource.* Everyone wants a share of the water, but in dry years there isn't enough to go around. Some say the Klamath Basin has been overallocated—rights have been given to more water than exists. The same holds true in many places throughout the West.

2. *Confusion and conflicting interpretations regarding complex information.* The hydrology and ecology of the Klamath Basin are complex, intertwined systems, and even the experts disagree in their interpretations of studies and information. Perhaps the clearest example of this is the dispute over how much water is needed to sustain the various fisheries in the basin—each agency's biologists favor their own data, draw their own conclusions, and distrust the others' interpretations.

3. *Overlapping decision-making authority among government agencies with often contradictory missions and legal mandates.* At least three federal agencies have jurisdiction over water use in the Klamath. USBR is legally bound to support project farms and agriculture. The National Marine Fisheries Service must protect the salmon that spawn in the lower river. And USFWS juggles internally conflicting mandates—one arm dedicated to managing the upper basin wildlife refuges and another arm protecting endangered species, including downstream fish that sometimes need the water being held for other species in the refuges.

4. *The collision of largely incompatible strategies, ones deeply embedded in the history and cultures of the West, for resolving natural resource disputes.* This is a central theme of this book. In one piece of the Klamath situation, the dispute between irrigators and fishery advocates may center on who gets water, but it also pits

100-year-old water rights against scientific expertise and a broader sense of the public good. In short, this dispute is about the strategies we use to govern natural resources—in this case, the three strategies of first in time, first in right; scientific management; and the public trust doctrine.

Further crisis in the Klamath was forestalled when winter snowpack and overall precipitation returned to higher levels, but the 2001 drought refuses to fade in the memories of the Klamath Basin residents and resource managers who lived through it. The dispute continues—in contested claims in the ongoing Oregon water rights adjudication process, in debates over new scientific data, in media headlines, and among neighbors in the basin. To date, attempts to resolve the Klamath situation—relying on existing laws, scientific expertise, citizen petition, litigation, and even collaboration—have not comprehensively addressed the four issues described above.

How these diverse interests will resolve their predicament in the Klamath Basin remains to be seen. The only certainty is that no one interest—and no single decision-making approach—can address the multiplicity of societal, legal, economic, and environmental demands being placed on the system. This is true in the Klamath, and in the West as a whole.

NOTES

1. Much of this snapshot of the basin, its waterways, and competing demands for water is based on "Meeting Growing and Competing Demands for Water: The Klamath Basin Experience," by Paul R. Cleary, director, Oregon Water Resources Department (paper prepared for the Western Governor Association's Environmental Summit on the West II, Salt Lake City, Utah, April 25, 2002); on Rebecca Clarren, "No Refuge in the Klamath Basin," *High Country News*, August 13, 2001; and on the Web site for the Mid-Pacific Region, Klamath Basin Area Office of the U.S. Bureau of Reclamation, http://www.usbr.gov/mp/kbao/.
2. Information on the Klamath Tribes obtained from the tribes' Web site, http://www.klamathtribes.org.
3. Treaty of 1864, 16 *Statutes at Large of the United States of America, 1789–1873* 707.
4. *Termination Act of 1954*, 25 *U.S. Code* 564m.
5. *Klamath Water Users Association v. Patterson*, 15 F. Supp. 2d 990, 996 (D. Or. 1998), 204 F.3d 1206 (9 Cir. 2000); *Kandra v. United States*, Civ. No 01-6124-AA, Opinion and Order of April 30, 2001 (D. Or.).

6. Jeff Stoffer, "Sucker Punched," originally published in *American Legion Magazine*, reprinted at http://www.klamathbasincrisis.org/articles/suckerpunchedjeffstoffer.htm.

7. *National Wildlife Refuge System Improvement Act of 1997*, Public Law 105-57, 16 *U.S. Code* 668dd et seq.

8. U.S. Fish and Wildlife Service (USFWS), Klamath Basin Wildlife Refuge Web site, http://klamathbasinrefuges.fws.gov/.

9. USFWS, Klamath Basin Wildlife Refuge Web site; personal phone call with staff at Lower Klamath National Wildlife Refuge, January 15, 2003.

10. Cleary, "Meeting Growing and Competing Demands for Water."

11. "Convoy Protests Water Shutoff," AP Newswire, August 22, 2001.

12. Committee on Endangered and Threatened Fishes in the Klamath River Basin, National Research Council, *Scientific Evaluation of Biological Opinions on Endangered and Threatened Fishes in the Klamath River Basin: Interim Report* (2002), http://www.nap.edu.

13. Cleary, "Meeting Growing and Competing Demands for Water."

14. Jeff Barnard (Associated Press), "Anger Boils Over: Shooting Raises Issue of Racism in Water Wars of Klamath Basin," *Helena Independent Record*, January 14, 2002.

15. Associated Press, "Convoy Protests Water Shutoff," *Helena Independent Record*, August 22, 2001.

16. Jeff Barnard (Associated Press), "Groups Sue to Get Water for Eagles on Oregon Wildlife Refuge," *Helena Independent Record*, August 8, 2001.

17. Stephen E. Snyder, "Reflections on the Klamath Water Crisis."

18. National Marine Fisheries Service, "Biological Opinion, Klamath Project Operations" (May 31, 2002); U.S. Fish and Wildlife Service, "Biological Opinion, Klamath Project Operations," (May 31, 2002).

19. Committee on Endangered and Threatened Fishes in the Klamath River Basin, National Research Council, *Scientific Evaluation of Biological Opinions on Endangered and Threatened Fishes in the Klamath River Basin.*

20. "Decision Regarding the Proposed Action Addressed in the National Marine Fisheries Service's May 31, 2002, *Biological Opinion on the Proposed Operation of the Klamath Project*" (memorandum from Kirk Rodgers, regional director, U.S. Bureau of Reclamation, to Rodney R. McInnis, acting regional administrator, National Marine Fisheries Service, June 3, 2002), http://www.usbr.gov/mp/kbao/.

21. Michael Milstein, "Salmon Die-off Blamed on Klamath Diversion," *Oregon Live.com*, January 4, 2003, http://www.oregonlive.com.

22. Laura Paskus, *High Country News*, January 30, 2002, 3.

The Nature of
Western Resource Disputes

The Klamath Basin situation is a dramatic illustration of the type of disputes common throughout the West at the beginning of the twenty-first century. A quick scan of any local newspaper or one of the West's regional news media, such as *High Country News* or *Headwaters News*, provides a bird's-eye view of an endless parade of disputes similar in tone to the Klamath debate. Despite the variety of natural resource issues, and the vastness of the West, these disputes tend to share a number of common characteristics. But to understand the interplay of these characteristics, it helps to first understand something of the nature of the West itself.

Nature of the West

Wallace Stegner, one of the more astute observers of the region, said that the two most compelling factors shaping society in the West are its aridity and its high concentration of federal public lands.[1] With the exception of a few areas along the Pacific Coast, most of the region receives less than twenty inches of rain each year, making it a semi-arid to arid environment.

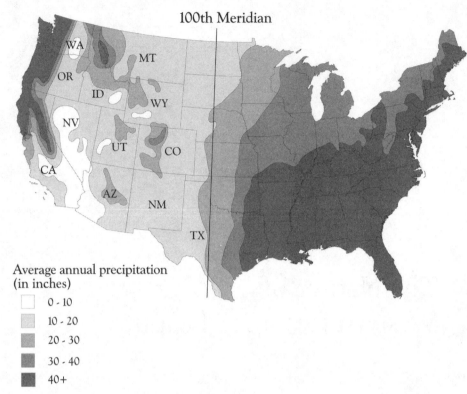

100th Meridian

Average annual precipitation
(in inches)

- [ ] 0 - 10
- 10 - 20
- 20 - 30
- 30 - 40
- 40+

MAP 1.1. Average Annual Precipitation West of the 100th Meridian. (Adapted from *Atlas of the New West,* ed. William E. Riebsame and James Robb. New York: W. W. Norton & Company, 1997.)

Ongoing concerns over the chronic drought seem to forget this basic fact of physical geography. The history of the region's settlement and development, however, makes it clear that the West is a "hydraulic society," dependent on a vast network of dams, reservoirs, and canals to move water from its source to where it is most needed—for mining and agriculture, and increasingly for urban centers and instream environmental values.[2] In the West, conflicts arise over water in part because so many different users rely on common waterworks.

While the lack of water (and generally poor soils) in the West has determined mining, ranching, and agricultural practices and shaped urban growth patterns, it is the region's landscape that most impresses and captivates people. From high plains to rugged mountains, from deserts to rain forests, the West is defined by its wide-open spaces, abundant wildlife, and

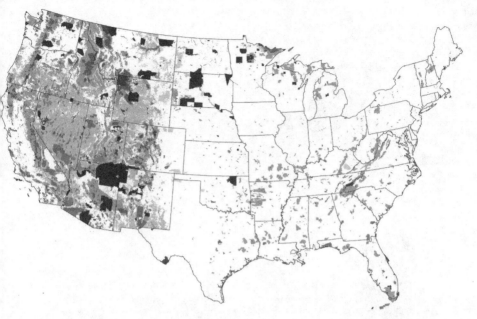

MAP 1.2. Federal Government Lands in the United States. (Courtesy of the University of Montana, Center for the Rocky Mountain West.) *Source:* U.S. Geological Survey.

unparalleled scenery. The landscape has shaped history, inspired myths, and attracted people from all walks of life. It is also the focus of many public policy debates, largely because so much of the West is common ground.

More than 90 percent of all federal land is found in the eleven westernmost states and Alaska. The U.S. Forest Service and the Bureau of Land Management administer about 34 percent of the western landscape, including 83 percent of Nevada, more than 60 percent of Idaho and Utah, and more than 45 percent in four other western states (Arizona, California, Oregon, and Wyoming). The region also holds most of the nation's tribal lands, constituting about one-fifth of the landscape in the eleven westernmost states. Finally, these western states also hold about 45 million acres of "school trust" lands—federal land grants given upon statehood to help fund education. Taken together, these public and tribal lands dominate not only the physical geography of the region but also its politics.

Since the 1990s, the West has also been the country's fastest-growing region. The five fastest-growing states of that decade were Nevada, Arizona, Colorado, Utah, and Idaho. Between 1990 and 1998, the region's cities grew

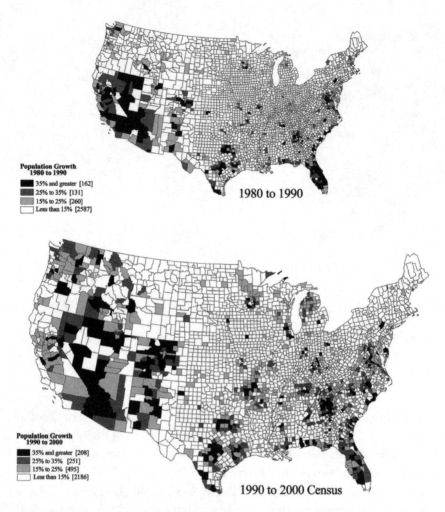

MAP 1.3. Areas of Population Growth in the United States. (Courtesy of the University of Montana, Center for the Rocky Mountain West.) *Source:* Bureau of Census, U.S. Department of Commerce.

by 25 percent and its rural areas by 18 percent, both significantly higher rates than elsewhere in the United States. According to the 2000 U.S. Census, Americans on the move are turning once-quiet suburbs in Arizona, Nevada, and California into the fastest-growing cities in the country.[3] Some of the people moving to these suburbs left larger nearby cities, but much of the growth comes from the continued migration of people from other regions. The West is also one of the most urbanized regions of the country, with

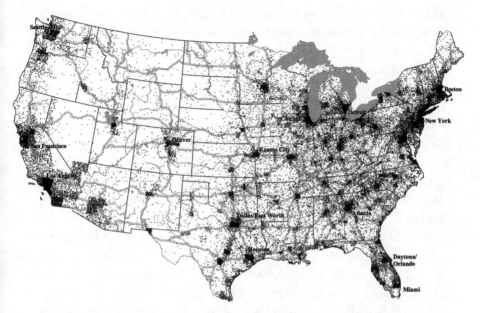

MAP 1.4. Population Density of the Contiguous United States by County, 2000. Each dot represents 3,000 people. (Courtesy of the University of Montana, Center for the Rocky Mountain West.)

most people living in cities and with rural areas averaging fewer than ten people per square mile.

Historically, disputes over natural resources in the West have changed along with the demographics of the region. The first conflicts were between settlers and natives over land ownership. Once this issue was more or less established, conflicts emerged among settlers wanting to use the same resource—minerals, grazing lands, and water—for the same purpose. As people started moving into the West in the 1960s, more and more disputes arose over the use of common resources for different purposes. Debates over consumptive versus nonconsumptive uses of the land, commodity versus noncommodity uses, the economy versus the environment, and visions of the "Old West" versus the "New West" have been driven in large part by the changing demographics of the region.

Some of the West's fastest-growing cities are not job centers but residential, large-scale communities, revealing that not everyone who moves to the West is looking for work. That said, some of the region's growth is due to "footloose entrepreneurs," people whose work (computers and software,

biotechnology, telecommunications, and so on) allows them to locate any-
where. Such people are increasingly attracted to both urban and rural places
in the West.[4] This shift in demographics, along with changes in the global
economy, means that the region has slowly moved from a resource-based
economy to a knowledge-based economy. Many western politicians continue to promote the myth that the economy revolves around the extraction
of natural resources, but there is an emerging consensus among economists
of all stripes that the region's future will revolve around a knowledge-based
economy, not the traditional industries of farming, ranching, mining, and
logging. Today, the West's natural assets—open space, forests, rivers, and
vistas—add more economic value by attracting footloose entrepreneurs
than can be gleaned by developing the raw materials.

As the demographics and economies of the West diversify, the region's
political geography appears to be seeking its own gyroscopic balance. After
the 2002 elections, the West's 117 congressional districts were split: 59 Republican, 58 Democrat.[5] Similarly, of the eleven governorships, five were Republican (Colorado, Idaho, Montana, Nevada, and Utah) and six were in
Democrat hands (Arizona, California, New Mexico, Oregon, Washington,
and Wyoming).[6] The 2003 recall of Democrat Gray Davis in California, and
the subsequent election of Republican Arnold Schwarzenegger, though
widely seen as a contest of charisma rather than partisanship, shifted that
ratio to six Republican, five Democrat. During this same period, Democrats
controlled only two of the eleven western state legislatures (California and
New Mexico). Republicans controlled both the house and senate in seven
states (Arizona, Colorado, Idaho, Montana, Oregon, Utah, and Wyoming),
and the parties split the chambers in Nevada and Washington (Republicans
controlled the senate and Democrats the house in both states).[7]

The West's aridity and landscape, demographic and economic trends, and
political geography help define the region's identity and set it apart from the
rest of the country. They also provide a foundation for understanding the
nature of disputes over natural resources in the West.

Nature of Western Resource Disputes

Box 1.1 provides a simple but comprehensive list of characteristics common
to most western resource disputes. This framework provides one way to analyze western resource disputes, identify the source of disagreements, and
understand the behavior of the disputing parties. It helps explain both the

---

BOX 1.1   Common Characteristics of Western Resource Disputes

Multiple Parties

- Clash of values
- Competing interests
- Complicated relationships
- Varying types and levels of power

Complex Information

- Lack of information
- Misinformation
- Different views on what information is relevant
- Different procedures to collect and assess data
- Different interpretation of data
- Different levels of comfort with risk and uncertainty

A Briar Patch of Policies and Institutions

- Multiple jurisdictions
- Competing missions and mandates
- Lack of meaningful public participation
- Multiple opportunities for appeal
- A fundamental question of who should decide

---

chronic nature and the durability of disputes and suggests what needs to change in order to arrive at more sustainable solutions.

Multiple Parties

The first and most obvious characteristic of western resource disputes is that they involve multiple parties—farmers and ranchers; conservationists and environmental advocates; old-timers and newcomers; local, state, federal, and tribal governments; business and industry; community leaders and private citizens. Given these multiple parties, disputes emerge and are difficult to resolve for a number of reasons.

Many disputes arise because of a *clash of values*. Environmental philosophers have helped us understand that natural resources provide a plethora of values, including biological, economic, recreational, aesthetic, scientific, historical, cultural, religious, and intrinsic values.[8] While many of these natural values are compatible with one another, there is an inherent tension between economic value, which is often consumptive, and other natural values, which are frequently nonconsumptive and difficult to quantify. Such disputes are often framed as a choice between livable communities and vibrant economies or a healthy landscape. The disagreement over the use of water for agricultural purposes or the protection of endangered fish in the Klamath River basin is a case in point.

Natural values other than economic may also conflict with one another, such as the tension over managing national parks for recreation as well as for biological, scientific, historical, cultural, and aesthetic values (or the tension over providing water to one endangered fish to the detriment of another, as in the Klamath). People who care about the West also hold strong ideological beliefs, such as the nonnegotiable and often conflicting principles of private property and the public trust. In the Klamath situation, for example, conservationists argue that maintaining stream flows and protecting endangered fish produces a greater public benefit than using that water to irrigate a relatively small amount (in the national scope of agricultural production) of cropland. Irrigators counter that reducing or eliminating their water allocation not only ignores the legal right they hold to that water but also unduly restricts how they can use their land, amounting to a "taking" of their private property rights.

Conflict among values is often framed as an issue of rights. In the Klamath Basin, the basic value conflict between people who believe that the best use of the water is irrigating crops and others who believe that fish and wildlife deserve priority is being played out, at least in part, in terms of the legal rights to use water. Because values and rights are almost always a factor in western resource disputes, it often helps to set aside—but not ignore—these differences and refocus on what the parties need to satisfy their interests.[9] If the issues cannot be reframed to focus on the needs or interests of the parties, it may be difficult, if not impossible, to constructively resolve the dispute and prevent recurrences. In the Klamath Basin water crisis, key players continue to characterize the central dispute as "fish versus farmers," which limits the field of apparent options for resolving the problem and splits the disputants into two hostile camps rather than helping them work together to solve the common problem of insufficient water at critical times.

Sometimes disputes over western resources are based on *competing interests*. In the Klamath situation, for example, the U.S. Fish and Wildlife Service represents two interests (protecting species listed under the Endangered Species Act and fulfilling the broader priorities of the basin's wildlife refuges) competing for the same limited resource. Interest-based conflicts occur over substantive issues (such as the allocation of water), procedural issues (whether citizens and tribal people, for example, have meaningful opportunities to participate in the process of decision making and dispute resolution in the Klamath), and psychological issues (perceptions of trust, fairness, and respect). To effectively resolve interest-based disputes, all affected parties must have their interests meaningfully satisfied in each of these three areas. In the Klamath case, few of the parties have seen their interests satisfied in any one of these areas (and all are competing for the same limited resource—water)—and so the conflict continues.

Many western resource disputes are also intensified because of *complicated relationships* among the multiple parties. Historic tension, lack of trust, and misperceptions often prevent the affected parties from focusing on the substantive issues and their real interests because they see the opposition as inherently suspect. Impaired relationships erode any sense of community and prevent people from developing a common sense of place or purpose. Coalitions often form among groups with similar interests, and communication outside the coalition becomes increasingly difficult. New players frequently emerge as issues are reframed and new solutions are proposed. Parties may vary in the degree to which they want to maintain and improve their relationship with other stakeholders.

Given the multitude of players that are commonly involved in western resource disputes, it is not surprising that the parties possess *varying types and levels of power.* In the Klamath situation, each party has its own perspective on the history of the problem and the legitimacy of the other parties' concerns, and chooses from a smorgasbord of strategies for advancing its interests over the competing interests of other parties. Each party may also prefer or insist on one decision-making forum over others, hoping for a more favorable outcome from the courts, say, than from an agency's internal planning process. Some parties will have more access to money or decision makers or have more scientific and technical resources than others.

Complex Information

Another common characteristic of western resource disputes, and another source of such disputes, is complex information. As illustrated by the Klamath Basin situation, many disputes are characterized by a lack of information, rampant misinformation, different views on what types of information are relevant, different procedures for collecting and assessing data, and different interpretations of data. In the Klamath Basin, the parties are trying to come to grips with interrelated and highly complex water and biological systems, further complicated by the overlay of dams, ditches, water rights, and a multiplicity of laws and regulations. It's no surprise, then, that the federal agencies responsible for managing most of the resources in the basin have so far been unable to agree on what constitutes the "best available science." Information-related problems are magnified when long-term impacts are uncertain or appear to be irreversible, and when people differ in their willingness to accept risk.

The complexity of information also influences the way different parties "frame"—or interpret and understand—a situation. How an issue is framed influences the degree to which people perceive it as intractable. The debate over federal lands and resources, for example, is frequently framed as a competition of local versus national interests. But what do we mean by "local" or "national"? How do we define such terms, much less bring them together for meaningful discussions?

A Briar Patch of Policies and Institutions

In response to the physical geography of the western landscape, unique policies and institutions have grown up organically from the land and the people who inhabit it. Historian Walter Prescott Webb argued that there is an "institutional fault" running along the 100th meridian.[10] West of the 100th meridian, where most areas receive fewer than 20 inches of precipitation annually and irrigation is necessary to grow most crops, society has created a number of distinctive institutions adapted to demands of the landscape. Two of the region's most influential and durable laws emerged in the mid- to late nineteenth century: the prior appropriation doctrine in water law and the Hardrock Mining Law of 1872. These and other policies, which are examined more closely in chapters 2 and 3, promoted the laissez-faire attitude of the time, providing free and open access to public resources governed by an unrefined rule of capture. This 150-year-old body of laws and policies still pervades western resource policy and favors commodity interests. The laws are joined with numerous other laws and policies (notably the National Environmental Policy Act) that apply disproportionately to western resources, such as timber in the national forests, grazing on public lands, endangered species, and wilderness.[11]

Each piece of the framework governing western resources, taken by itself, can be seen as good public policy, developed in response to the concerns and needs of the time in which it was enacted. Each substantive goal and procedural requirement is, for the most part, well intended. Taken together, however, the policies and institutions create a briar patch of often overlapping and contradictory efforts to manage resources and resolve disputes. As illustrated by the Klamath River basin situation, issues may cross many different jurisdictions, and responsibilities are often fragmented or overlapping. The fractured political geography of the region means that any given dispute may involve several federal agencies, tribal governments, governors, state and congressional legislators, counties, and cities. The convoluted mix of laws, policies, institutions, and jurisdictions means that a clash in priorities is inevitable. Should tribal water rights take precedence over irrigation water rights? Are endangered species more valuable than the local economy based on irrigated agriculture? Should one endangered fish be protected to the detriment of another endangered fish?

This institutional briar patch was planted during the West's earliest days and continues to grow and branch out as social structures—and decision-making fashions—change. In itself, the briar patch is often a barrier to solving the West's problems, as each side rallies around the particular law, policy, or decision-making strategy that best supports its interest. The more insistently people cite their supporting law or policy, the more entangled each side becomes, caught on the thorns of the other's preferred laws and policies.

The challenge of preventing, managing, and resolving disputes over western resources is further complicated by a widely perceived lack of opportunity for meaningful public participation. Recent studies of public participation in environmental decision making reveal strong broad-based support for the idea of public involvement, but serious problems with how that idea is put into practice by government agencies. In some jurisdictions, decision makers may talk about public participation but do little to encourage it.[12] In other areas, citizens agree that agencies seek public input and advice but feel that they don't always listen to what is said. Most public participation processes are limited because only certain people choose to or are able to participate, and there are very few ways to accurately capture the feelings and insights of unaffiliated, rank-and-file citizens.

When public participation processes are not transparent and credible, people withdraw, feeling angry, disenfranchised, and determined to undercut whatever outcome is reached. The quality of outcomes suffers, and the seemingly endless process of winners and losers erodes a sense of community, reducing society to little more than a loose collection of interest groups.[13] During the past thirty years, dissatisfied citizens have also seen an increase in opportunities to appeal government actions, thanks to judicial decisions and legislation allowing citizen suits. It's no surprise that the number of appeals has increased. For example, the number of appeals filed against U.S. Forest Service decisions under the Administrative Procedures Act, the National Environmental Policy Act, the National Forest Management Act, and the Endangered Species Act now averages about 630 a year.[14] Although appeals offer an important safeguard against misguided management, and frequently prompt better planning and implementation, they also delay on-the-ground action (sometimes for many years) and increase costs.[15] The solution, according to some, is to minimize or eliminate opportunities for public and environmental review, including appeals.

Some people say that the irritations created by the briar patch of policies and institutions are more than skin deep. Speaking about federal lands, Daniel Kemmis, former mayor and state legislator from Montana, argues that "the national public lands system is broken, and there's no prospect of doing anything but limping along unless we do something to fix it."[16] Kemmis raises fundamental questions about where the legitimate seat of western decision making resides—Washington, D.C., or the West— and concludes that, "if the national government continues to lose ground in terms of its ability to manage so much of the West, and if westerners continue to gain ground in terms of their ability to work together across interest[s] and ideological lines on public lands issues, it will make more and more sense to begin thinking about realigning sovereignty to give westerners more control over the public lands."[17] As long as this tug of war between western and national interests remains unresolved, Kemmis reasons, westerners will continue to face gridlock on many issues, and decisions—when they are made—will continue to be second-guessed and challenged in the courts, state capitals, and town meeting halls. The fundamental questions of who should decide how western resources are used, and how disputes should be resolved, are not limited to federal lands. This undercurrent also defines debates over water use, growth management, and tribal resources in the West.

Alternative Approaches to Resolving
Western Resource Disputes

The basic elements of any natural resource dispute in the West—or any public policy dispute, for that matter—are power, rights, and interests.[18] In the Klamath Basin situation, the affected parties have different interests at stake. In addition, certain standards or rights exist that will influence the shape of the outcome, such as the water rights of irrigators and the tribes, and the policy to protect endangered species. Finally, a certain balance of power exists among the stakeholders. Some, for example, have more effective access to relevant decision makers, while others use tradition and symbolism to advance their interests. In resolving a natural resource dispute, the stakeholders may choose to focus on one or more of these basic factors. They may seek to integrate their interests, determine who is right, or determine who is more powerful.

In many cases, the disputants set out to determine who is more powerful. Power in this sense is more than the ability to force others to do something they don't want to do. In natural resource and other public policy disputes, power also includes the capacity to impose costs, invoke authority, or reward someone for certain behavior. Relationships with the right people, knowledge about a particular subject, and financial resources create other types of power. The ability to enforce an official precedent, or develop a viable alternative, also creates power. Given the various sources of power, it is often difficult to determine who is more powerful and how long that power can be sustained in a politically and economically dynamic system.

Natural resource politics in the West and elsewhere are replete with examples of the use of power. Throughout the latter part of the nineteenth century and for much of the twentieth century, the corporate power of the Anaconda Company set the course for the state of Montana. The copper company owned many of the state's newspapers and, through campaign support and bribes, also owned not a few of its elected officials. Using a less direct form of power, environmentalists periodically engage in civil disobedience by sitting in trees to protest logging, thereby at least delaying the harvest of some trees, imposing unanticipated costs, and raising public awareness about forest management. Elections, majority rules, strikes, civil disobedience, and ballot initiatives are all examples of ways in which people try to solve problems, keep bad things from happening, or promote policy objectives through the use of power. A great deal of legislation and regulation is characterized as "command-and-control," meaning that it imposes decisions and actions (and associated costs) on others.

The history of the West also includes a number of infamous examples of less subtle uses of power to shape land ownership and use. Skirmishes were common between cattle and sheep ranchers, and vigilantes made their decisions with guns and stout rope. In one famous case at the end of the nineteenth century, the cattle barons of the Wyoming Stockgrowers Association (WSGA) brought in a trainload of twenty-two hired guns from Texas to eliminate independent cattle ranchers operating in Johnson County.[19] While the marauders were burning a house and shooting the occupants, a neighbor escaped to warn others and returned with superior numbers. The governor, an ally of the cattle barons, sent for the U.S. Cavalry to quell the "insurrection" in Johnson County. Instead, the federal troops rounded up the hired guns, who were later released on bail (paid by the WSGA) and sent back to Texas.

A second approach to resolving disputes is to determine who is right. In this context, the parties rely on some independent, legitimate, and fair standard to determine rights or rightness. Some rights are formalized into law or contract. Others are generally accepted standards of behavior, such as reciprocity, precedent, equality, or seniority. The problem of instream flow protection—how to keep water in rivers and streams to protect fish, water quality, and riparian areas—is a good example of how a rights-based procedure works. Under western water law, farmers and ranchers have senior water rights that allow them to divert water out of a stream, which can hurt fish populations. While conservationists and others may complain about dewatering, they have historically had few if any rights to keep water in the stream. Decisions on the legal allocation of water often involve a third party, such as a court or an administrative agency, with the power to hand down a binding decision.

Power- and rights-based procedures are adversarial in nature. They tend to result in winners, losers, and poor working relationships among the competing parties. In both cases, decisions are made, but the underlying problems are rarely resolved and the losers do not go away.

A third approach is to integrate interests. This is where collaboration and consensus building come in. The essence of collaborative decision making is to integrate the interests of affected parties, sometimes referred to as stakeholders. Interests are needs, desires, concerns, and fears—the things that underlie people's positions (the items they want). Integrating interests is not easy. It involves probing and understanding competing interests and then creating solutions that integrate the needs and interests of as many people as possible. The most common procedure for doing this is negotiation, the act of back-and-forth communication with the intent of seeking agreement. In some situations, the parties may rely on an impartial third party to facilitate communication and package agreements.

As mentioned above, some disputes over natural resources in the West are value based; they revolve around the divergent beliefs and values people have about natural resources. Core values motivate people and shape their interests and behavior. Conflict occurs when one person, organization, or community attempts to impose its values on others. Such conflicts are highly resistant to being truly resolved, even through power-, rights-, or interest-based strategies. In many cases, the most effective way to address value-based disputes is to reframe the issues and identify specific areas of disagreement that may be open for discussion.[20] (For example, disputes over western water are frequently framed as "farmers versus fish," but farmers, anglers, and fisheries advocates are more likely to work together toward a solution if the issue is reframed as "drought management.") Reframing may not resolve the underlying value conflict, but it can help disputants focus on a common problem, which in turn fosters better working relationships and greater trust.

Given that the West was settled in an institutional vacuum where the rules governing the use of land, water, and other resources had to be created, it is not surprising that the context for resolving natural resource disputes is defined by a mix of interests, rights, and power. And, as illustrated by the Klamath Basin situation, the ability to integrate interests is influenced by people's rights, which in turn is determined by the relative balance of power. To date, mediation has not succeeded in the Klamath Basin, in part because water rights are uncertain until adjudication is complete and because other rights—those of the tribes, agricultural landowners, and endangered species—are in direct competition for the same resources. In turn, those conflicts are shaped by the ongoing debate over scientific information and knowledge. Finally, the distribution of power within the basin was thrown off balance when the White House used its power to impose temporary solutions.

Using this simple framework of alternative principles for resolving disputes—interests, rights, and power—figure 1.1 presents the historical emergence of the major decision-making and dispute resolution strategies

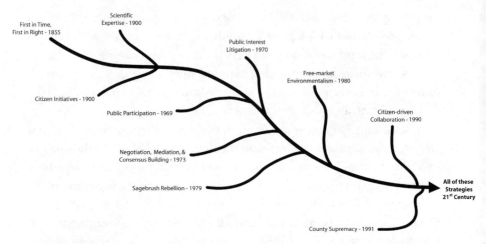

FIGURE 1.1. The Evolution of Strategies to Resolve Western Resource Disputes.

available today. This illustration—which is designed as a kind of compass to orient people in a vast legal and institutional landscape—suggests that, during the past 150 years, four dominant ideas or models have emerged to resolve western resource disputes: (1) privatize natural resources and allow the market to resolve disputes over competing uses; (2) delegate decisions to scientific and technical experts; (3) provide multiple opportunities for citizens to participate in decisions and resolve disputes; and (4) devolve the authority for decision making and dispute resolution from one level to another. In most cases, more than one strategy has emerged within each model.

Each of these models and strategies is embedded, some more firmly than others, within the legal, institutional, and cultural fabric of natural resource decision making in the West. In most western resource disputes, the parties involved find themselves caught in the crosscurrents at the confluence of these strategies. The question raised by the Klamath Basin situation and countless other examples throughout the West is, "Which strategy is most likely to promote the mix of values that people who care about the West can agree on—viable communities, vibrant economies, and healthy landscapes?"

While natural resource disputes in the West share many common characteristics, they are too complex and variable for any one model or strategy to be appropriate in all circumstances. In fact, different strategies are likely to be appropriate and effective in different situations. To determine which approach might be most effective in any given situation, it helps to consider the following four criteria.[21]

1. How satisfied are the stakeholders likely to be with the outcome of a particular process?
2. What is the chance that the issue will be resolved—and not recur—through one process or another? How sustainable is the outcome likely to be?
3. What are the likely costs—time, money, and emotional energy— of relying on one process rather than another?
4. How will the use of one process over another impact the relationships among stakeholders?

These four criteria are interrelated. Dissatisfaction with outcomes may lead to the recurrence of disputes, which increases transaction costs and strains relationships. Because these four different costs typically increase and decrease together, they can be referred to collectively as "the costs of disputing." As you read through the following chapters, we encourage you to apply these criteria to each decision-making and dispute resolution strategy to determine whether it is "high-cost" or "low-cost." Since it is difficult to assess which approach might be best, independent of the options available in any given situation, we begin by examining the merits of the different strategies chapter by chapter. We also offer some tools for integrating the principles of interest-based negotiation into natural resource decision making and governance. Then, in chapter 9, we compare the relative merits of the various dispute resolution strategies against one another and provide a framework for determining which strategy or strategies are most appropriate for a given situation.

NOTES

1. Wallace Stegner, *The Sound of Mountain Water* (Garden City, NY: Doubleday, 1969), 33.
2. Donald Worster, *Rivers of Empire: Water, Aridity and the Growth of the American West* (New York: Pantheon Books, 1985).
3. "Western Suburbs Lead Nation for Fastest Growth," *Helena Independent Record,* July 10, 2003, 2A.
4. Ray Rasker, "Your Next Job Will Be in Services: Should You Be Worried?" in *Across the Great Divide: Explorations in Collaborative Conservation and the*

American West, ed. Philip Brick, Donald Snow, and Sarah Van de Wetering, 52–57 (Washington, DC: Island Press, 2001).

5. U.S. Congress, http://www.senate.gov and http://www.house.gov.

6. Western Governors' Association, http://www.westgov.org.

7. Project Vote Smart, http://www.vote-smart.org.

8. Holmes Rolston III, *Environmental Ethics: Duties to and Values in the Natural World* (Philadelphia: Temple University Press, 1988).

9. Larry Susskind and Patrick Field, *Dealing with an Angry Public: The Mutual Gains Approach to Resolving Disputes* (New York: Free Press, 1996), 152–97.

10. Walter Prescott Webb, *The Great Plains* (Boston: Ginn, 1931).

11. Charles F. Wilkinson, *Crossing the Next Meridian: Land, Water, and the Future of the West* (Washington, DC: Island Press, 1992).

12. Susan Casey-Lefkowitz, "Global Trends in Public Participation" (undated background paper, Environmental Law Institute, Washington, DC).

13. Marcus E. Ethridge, "Procedures for Citizen Involvement in Environmental Policy: An Assessment of Policy Effects," in *Citizen Participation in Public Decision Making*, Contributions in Political Science, no. 158, ed. Jack DeSario and Stuart Langton, 115–31 (New York: Greenwood, 1987).

14. Hanna J. Cortner, Grethcne M. R. Teich, and Jacqueline Vaughn, "Analyzing USDA Forest Service Appeals: Phase I, the Database" (Ecological Restoration Institute, March 2003).

15. USDA Forest Service, *The Process Predicament: How Statutory, Regulatory, and Administrative Factors Affect National Forest Management* (June 2002).

16. *State Planning Directors in the West* (Portland, OR: Western Consensus Council and Lincoln Institute of Land Policy, October 15–16, 2002).

17. Daniel Kemmis, *This Sovereign Land: A New Vision for Governing the West* (Washington, DC: Island Press, 2001).

18. This section draws heavily on the work of William L. Ury, Jeanne M. Brett, and Stephen B. Goldberg, *Getting Disputes Resolved: Designing Systems to Cut the Costs of Conflict* (San Francisco: Jossey-Bass, 1989).

19. This illustration is based on the story as told by Gary Wills, *A Necessary Evil: A History of American Distrust of Government* (New York: Simon & Schuster, 1999).

20. Roy J. Lewicki, Barbara Gray, and Michael Elliott, *Making Sense of Intractable Environmental Conflicts* (Washington, DC: Island Press, 2003).

21. This section draws heavily on the work of Ury, Brett, and Goldberg, *Getting Disputes Resolved*.

2 —

First in Time, First in Right

The story of resolving natural resource disputes in the American West takes place in an expansive landscape of more than 1.6 million square miles—in area, about 44 percent of the fifty-state total.[1] The United States acquired title to this land through conquest, treaty, exchanges, and purchase, but the West did not truly join the nation until settlers arrived and occupied the far corners. Settlement, and all of the commercial activity it entails, was in large part a process of claiming *public* land, water, and other resources for *private* use. Competition for and privatization of these resources drove many of the earliest disputes in the West. Today, these forces continue to provoke debate and generate potential strategies for resolving conflicts over western resources.

The itch to move west and stake a claim has been afflicting Americans since the close of the Revolutionary War, and so the debate over private right to public land and resources is at least as old.[2] In the 1780s and 1790s, thousands of pioneers surged out of the original colonies toward the Ohio Territory. To ease treaty negotiations with tribes that still held title to these lands, Congress sent troops under Colonel Josiah Harmar to evict the squatters as far west as the Ohio River. Despite Harmar's apparent enthusiasm for the job, settlers continued to arrive faster than he could run them off. In 1807, Congress passed an act "to prevent settlements being made on lands ceded to the United States, until authorized by law." Violators risked steep fines and up to six months in jail, but much of the westward settlement occurred beyond the reach of law. Ironically, while the United States was trying to put the brakes on the land rush, Spain induced prospective settlers to cross the Mississippi with offers of free land, exemption from taxes, and even "provisions and the implements of husbandry." Nevertheless, U.S. territories to the north were more popular, and unauthorized settlement continued unabated.

As early as 1791, Congress entertained the notion—albeit only in specific cases—of giving settlers a "preference" to purchase land for which there was no previous title. The idea resurfaced periodically over the next forty years, sometimes in the form of petitions by settlers asking for a "preemptive" right to purchase the land they lived on. The settlers hoped for some protection against land speculators who might buy their homesteads out from under them. Opponents to preemption argued that there was a more immediate need to put money in federal coffers and that condoning the squatters' actions would lead to an invasion of the public domain by a "lawless horde." But by 1828, the congressional Public Lands Committee saw that it was "impossible to prevent settlements on the public lands." In its report to the House, the committee argued that "it is right and proper that the first settlers . . . should be allowed a privilege greater than the other purchasers . . . he who renders a benefit to the public, who by his enterprise and industry has created . . . a home in the wilderness, should be entitled to his reward." Despite congressional misgivings at the time, these notions of primacy—being first to stake a claim—and beneficial use were to become the linchpins of western resource doctrine for decades to come.

In 1830 and again in 1841, after spirited debate, Congress enacted statutes granting settlers a "preemptive" or first right to purchase the land they occupied. This was no doubt good news to the estimated 30,000 people living in what is now Iowa, where no land had yet been offered for sale. In effect, Congress had finally endorsed what it could not prevent—the tide of settlers staking claims, often well ahead of the survey crews, simply by occupying and improving the land before the next person behind them.

Prior Appropriation—The Other "Golden" Rule

By the 1830s, American pioneers had reached California's Central Valley, intent on ranching, farming, and other commercial enterprises. Thomas Larkin arrived from Massachusetts in 1832 and quickly became a successful merchant and land speculator. He also served as U.S. consul to Mexican California and fell into favor with the governor, Manuel Micheltorena. To win local support for his administration, Micheltorena awarded numerous land grants totaling more than 600,000 acres in the Sacramento Valley—and several went to Thomas Larkin. Larkin hired John Bidwell, leader of the first overland wagon train to reach California, to survey the upper Sacramento Valley and select a "rancho" to be granted by the governor to Larkin's children. Bidwell had been working for a Swiss immigrant, Captain John Sutter, scouting out lands in the Sacramento Valley, and he knew the area well. He chose a 44,364-acre parcel for Larkin and also surveyed and mapped other ranchos in the valley for other prominent pioneers. Bidwell made a copy of the map for Governor Micheltorena, and one for Larkin as well.

Mexican control of the region soon began to unravel, however, and the U.S. Army occupied California in 1846. Two years later, on February 2, 1848, Mexico ceded California to the United States. Just nine days earlier, on January 24, 1848, John Sutter and James Marshall had found gold in the mill race of the sawmill they were building on the American River, about forty miles east of present-day Sacramento. More gold was soon discovered nearby, and the rush was on. Within three years, the population of California mushroomed from two or three thousand people to two or three hundred thousand people. Although most of the diggings were on public land, prospectors wanted access to the entire region, and they contested the legitimacy of Micheltorena's land grants. Congress sent land commissioners out to California to settle the titles to the grants, and Bidwell's map detailing the location of each rancho and pre-1848 grant dates proved crucial in the successful defense of Larkin's and other landowners' claims.

This situation highlighted the first of two serious problems facing the flood of prospectors—their sheer numbers overran the available sites for prospecting. Scarcely one person in a thousand could find room to stake a claim.[3] Those who did manage to secure a patch of dirt quickly discovered the second problem—many of the gold strikes were placer deposits (in gravel beds on or close to the surface) located a considerable distance from the nearest stream or river. Miners had little choice but to build dams, ditches, and elaborate flumes to divert water and deliver it to the claims.

Just as there was not enough ground for all the prospectors, there was not enough water to work all of the claims. Gold fever encouraged a degree of lawless chaos, and disputes over water were common—and sometimes set-tled at the barrel end of a gun. But most prospectors hailed from civilized, well-regulated communities back east, and they sorely felt the absence of local institutions, such as courts (which soon followed), for resolving dis-putes. In response, these new westerners created their own rules to govern the use of minerals, water, and other resources.

They realized that the "riparian" water rights system in use on the East Coast, which allocated water based on the ownership of land adjacent to streams, was not suited to meet their needs in the arid, unsettled West.[4] To begin with, no one actually held undisputed title to any of the land, nor would they until the federal government opened the way to legal private ac-quisition through the 1862 Homestead Act and subsequent mining laws. Riparian law also would not help miners whose claims were located far from existing streams. So, to maintain their economic self-interests and resolve disputes over water, the miners applied a not-unfamiliar strategy—preemption, or "first in time, first in right." In short, the first person to put water to use gained an exclusive, preemptive right to that water. The oldest rights would be absolutely superior to more junior rights, and senior users were not required to share the resource. Echoing the language of the Public Lands Committee from twenty years earlier, the miners agreed that the prin-ciple of first in time, first in right would hinge in part on the promise that the person holding the right would put the resource to "beneficial" use. From the earliest days of western settlement, water uses deemed beneficial included mining, agriculture, grazing, timber, and manufacturing.

The principles of prior appropriation and beneficial use were reinforced during the mid-nineteenth century through a series of laws and policies to further privatize western public resources. Reports of the West's bountiful land and resources had begun circulating in earnest after Lewis and Clark's return to St. Louis in 1806. Thomas Jefferson had anticipated the theoretical challenges that lay ahead, but it took the better part of the nineteenth cen-tury to unriddle them: How to foster the settlement and development of the West? How to support agriculture in the arid West, given that any such in-dustry would require irrigation? And how to best use the West to contribute to the national economy?

In actual practice, pioneers and entrepreneurs pressing westward ahead of the surveyors, sheriffs, courts, and policy makers of the day first provided the answers. Congress, state legislatures, and other decision makers then followed, eventually crafting a body of laws and policies that reflected the reality of western exploration, settlement, and development, and the philosophy of free enterprise.[5] Ushering in what is often referred to as the "era of disposal," these policies provided free and open access to the West's public resources.[6] They allowed and encouraged people to secure private property rights to water, minerals, and range resources.

The idea of providing free and open access is based on the notion that private, self-interested action leads to the public good. This laissez-faire philosophy, first articulated by John Locke and later elaborated upon by Adam Smith, contends that society progresses on the strength of private initiative, the use of well-defined property rights, contracts, and the orderly rules of legal commerce.[7] The role of government is to enable—not regulate—private initiative, and thus the best government is the least government, intervening only to keep the peace and to maintain property rights. In the context of western lands and resources, this suggested that government should not retain ownership of the public domain but should dispose of it. Through various laws and policies, the federal government granted western land and resources to states, settlers, miners, and railroads, as well as for reclamation and timber.[8]

As people took advantage of the policies of free and open access, inevitable disputes arose over water, land, and other resources. Realizing that the ideas and institutions used to govern resources in the East were not appropriate in the Great Plains and the arid West, frontier entrepreneurs developed their own customs and institutions to resolve disputes over the use and ownership of natural resources. The local custom of first in time, first in right was a simple principle, easy to understand and enforce. Prior appropriation became not only a way to claim private property rights to public resources but also a way to resolve disputes among competing claims.

The principle of first in time, first in right was first integrated into western water law by California's general assembly in 1851. Shortly thereafter, in 1855, the Supreme Court of California agreed with a lower court that riparian law did not apply in the mining districts because the miners did not own the land that held their claims. In its place, the court affirmed the local custom of first in time, first in right—the common sense of the time—to settle disputes over water use. Conflicts, Justice Heydenfeldt wrote, "must be decided by the fact of priority . . . *qui prior est in tempore, potior est in jure* [who is first in time, is first in right]."[9] Other western states soon followed suit, recognizing that prior appropriation encouraged free enterprise and development, which increased taxable revenues and diminished federal control. The Colorado legislature endorsed the idea in 1861, and the Oregon legislature followed in 1864. States and territories embraced prior appropriation as a way to reward, and provide certainty and stability to, water development for economic purposes. (Interestingly, in their constitutions, all of the same western states declared water to be a *public* resource, even while insisting that its private use was to be encouraged. This paradox continues to muddy water policies to this day.)

The federal government, still legal owner of the public domain, remained silent on prior appropriation until Congress endorsed private property rights to mineral and water resources, as defined by the western mining districts, in the Mining Law of 1866.[10] Section 1 of the act declared mineral resources on the public lands to be "free and open to exploration and occupation by all citizens of the United States . . . subject to such regulation as may be prescribed by law, and subject also to the local customs or rules of miners in the several mining districts." The statute went on to expressly affirm the principle of first in time, first in right: "Whenever, by priority of possession, rights to the use of water for mining, agricultural, manufacturing, or other purposes, have vested and accrued, and the same are recognized and acknowledged by local customs, laws, and decisions of courts, the possessors and owners of such vested rights shall be maintained and protected in the same."[11]

Congress further endorsed the prior appropriation doctrine when it passed the Desert Land Act of 1877, stating "that the right to the use of water . . . on or to any tract of desert land of six hundred and forty acres shall depend upon *bona fide* prior appropriation."[12] The principle of first in time, first in right continued to shape governance of western resources into the twentieth century. After years of alleged rangeland abuses by livestock growers, Congress passed the Taylor Grazing Act of 1934.[13] The stated purpose of the act is to "stop injury to the public grazing lands by preventing overgrazing" and to "stabilize the livestock industry dependent upon the public range."[14] But the act also articulates a method to allocate grazing privileges or "range rights." According to the statute: "Preference shall be given in the issuance of grazing permits to those within or near a district who are landowners engaged in the livestock business . . . or owners of water or water rights."[15] This clause clearly suggests that people with existing land and water rights had a superior right to the range resource compared to people who might come later.

The first director of what is now the U.S. Bureau of Land Management (BLM), after consulting with farmers and ranchers, further refined the system of allocating range rights and resolving disputes over the range resource by instituting a modified "squatter's right." Under this system, the allocation of range rights among people with existing land and water rights was based on past use, once again relying on the western custom of first in time, first in right. Since it was difficult, if not impossible, to determine who was "first in time" on the range, a "priority period" was established as the five years immediately prior to the passage of the act (1934). A farmer or rancher who used the public range (in connection with his private property) for any two consecutive years or any three years during this priority period had priority "rights."

To allocate range rights, it was first necessary to determine the grazing capacity of a particular piece of land—that is, the maximum number of livestock that could be grazed without harming the range. Advisory boards composed exclusively of farmers and ranchers initially determined the carrying capacity of the range. This early effort to involve stakeholders in the decision-making process was articulated in section 9 of the Taylor Grazing Act, which envisioned "cooperation with local associations of stockmen." The composition of these advisory boards is a far cry from the much more inclusive community-based groups that are commonplace today, and some observers view the boards as evidence that federal range management policy was effectively "captured" by a single interest—stockmen. Nevertheless, the policy recognized the value of local knowledge of the resource and provided a means to incorporate it into the formal decision-making process.

Opportunities Lost and Found

As the idea of prior appropriation spread westward on the shoulders of farmers and other pioneers, the policies and institutions that incorporated this principle of governance did not emerge in a vacuum. Other cultural traditions, for example, that of the Hokoham (see box 2.1), relied on alternative allocation and dispute resolution strategies, some very different from those introduced by the new pioneers but largely lost during the mid-nineteenth century. Even different groups of settlers instituted alternative approaches.

BOX 2.1 Native American Approaches to Dispute Resolution

Before Europeans arrived in the New World, native communities had highly evolved systems for allocating resources and resolving conflicts of all kinds. Well before the first Spaniards arrived, the Hokoham, for example, developed the first large irrigated agriculture community in Arizona's Valley of the Sun.[1] Segments of their 125-mile canal system are still used today by Phoenix-area irrigators.[2] No one knows for certain how the Hokoham organized workers to build their canals, allocated water and cropland, or resolved related disputes. Clearly, though, this sophisticated water distribution system required significant planning, organization, and a collective sense of purpose.

Many tribal communities shared similarities in their approaches to resolving internal disputes over property, food sources, and other resources. Disputants typically received advice or admonishment from other tribal members who acted as neutral third parties for the good of the whole community.[3] Traditional sanctions emphasized restitution and what is known today as restorative justice, although banishment and formalized vengeance were also common.[4] In contrast to the adversarial American court system, typical Native American strategies relied on a "circle of justice," which connected everyone involved with a conflict and compelled them to cooperate to resolve the central problem.[5] Cohesiveness of the tribe could mean the difference between survival and disaster. Most western tribes, then, subscribed to the notion of community property, rather than personal or private property, particularly in regard to land, water, and other natural resources. In some cases, this extended to intertribal cooperation over resources, as in the upper Klamath River basin, where three distinct tribes shared fishing and hunting grounds until settlement forced them onto ever smaller reservations.[6]

In an attempt to assimilate tribes into non-Native society and wean them away from community or tribal ownership, Congress passed the General Allotment ("Dawes") Act of 1887, authorizing the U.S. president to allot portions of reservation land to individual tribal members.[7] It was hoped this would instill in tribal members the "virtues" of private property and personal ambition to "improve" one's life through acquiring personal wealth. Due to the unfortunate racial blinders of the times, it would have been seen as preposterous to suggest that the Native communitarian approach might have merits. In the end, the Dawes Act undermined the basic relationship of tribes to their lands and offered little to replace it. As the new western society took shape around the reservations, the Native approach to natural resource use was largely ignored.

1. Emil W. Haury, *The Hokoham* (Tucson: University of Arizona Press, 1976).
2. Michael C. Meyer, *Water in the Hispanic Southwest: A Social and Legal History 1550–1850* (Tucson: University of Arizona Press, 1984), 12.
3. John A. Folk-Williams and Cheryl D. Fairbanks, "Native American Resources" (paper submitted to the Western Consensus Council, October 27, 2001).
4. J. Myers and E. Coochise, "Development of Tribal Courts: Past, Present, and Future," *Judicature* 79, no. 3 (November/December 1995): 147.
5. A. P. Melton, "Indigenous Justice Systems and Tribal Society," *Judicature* 79, no. 3 (November/December 1995).
6. "Klamath Tribes History," http://www.klamathtribes.org.
7. See 25 *U.S.C.A.* 331 et seq. (1887).

In settling the Salt Lake Valley, for example, Brigham Young and his advisers realized that efficient, fair use of water and significant cooperation would be indispensable to their communities' success. Soon after arriving in Utah in 1847, Mormon leaders platted an entire city with wide boulevards, homesteads with gardens, and farming and grazing fields on the perimeter of the settled area. Each parcel had access to water, and church officials oversaw the distribution of water and resolved any disputes. Residents worked together to capture and deliver this water and developed many of the technologies and social institutions that were later employed in the national reclamation movement. In this culture, water was a community resource, managed and distributed to meet the community's needs (themes echoed in John Wesley Powell's powerful conception of the Watershed Commonwealth; see box 2.2). Only in 1880 did this communitarian approach give way in Utah to the doctrine of preemption and the notion of water as a private property right.[16]

A few other agrarian communities in the West shied away from the resources-as-private-property approach. In such experimental utopias as the

BOX 2.2 Watershed Commonwealths

After exploring the land and resources of the American West, John Wesley Powell, a Civil War veteran and scientist, argued in 1890 that the most appropriate institutions for governing western resources are commonwealths defined by watersheds.[1] He reasoned that "there is a body of interdependent and unified interests and values, all collected in [a] hydrographic basin, and all segregated by well-defined boundary lines from the rest of the world. The people in such a district have common interests, common rights, and common duties, and must necessarily work together for common purposes." Powell went on to conclude that such people should be allowed to organize, "under national and state laws, a great irrigation district, including an entire hydrographic basin, and . . . make their own laws for the division of waters, for the protection and use of the forests, for the protection of the pasturage on the hills, and for the use of the powers [created by the flow of water]."

His basic proposition was that the arid region of the country should be organized into hydrographic commonwealths, or watershed democracies. Each commonwealth would be self-governing and assume responsibility for "controlling and using the great values" that are found in the land, water, and other resources of the West. Each commonwealth would establish courts to adjudicate rights in compliance with laws and priorities established by the local community as well as by state and federal jurisdictions. Residents would select their own "resource managers," while the role of the state would be limited to adjudicating disputes among watershed jurisdictions—a very early recognition of the transboundary nature of certain natural resources and impacts.

Powell was ahead of his time. He understood that the natural systems within a watershed—water, soils, flora, and fauna—are interrelated and that management of one affects the others. He argued, in the spirit of Thomas Jefferson, that if the forests and other resources are to be appropriately managed, the people directly interested should perform the task. In other words, he argued for a face-to-face style of democracy in which the people most interested in land, water, and resource issues would sit down and develop solutions to their common problems.

While Powell's vision was ignored during the nineteenth century and most of the twentieth century, his "plan to establish local self-government by hydrographic basins" seems to be emerging organically throughout the West in the twenty-first century. In chapter 7, we examine the implications of the countless number of citizen-initiated, place-based forums that are emerging to address land, water, wildlife, and other natural resource and environmental issues.

Anticipating the nature of bureaucracies, and the next major strategy for dispute resolution that emerges in this story (in chapter 3), Powell also observed that "an army of aliens set to watch the forests would need another army of aliens to watch them, and a forestry organization under the hands of the general government would become a hotbed of corruption . . . because ill-defined values in great quantities are involved."

1. John Wesley Powell, "Institutions for Arid Lands," *Century Magazine*, May/June 1890, 111–16.

Anaheim colony in California or the Greeley colony in Colorado, unspoiled land and water provided opportunities to create new social orders built on irrigated agriculture and premised on cooperation and sharing in many aspects of life, including water distribution.[17] In other areas, such as along Idaho's Snake River, eastern capitalists funded private irrigation companies that acquired large land holdings and real and speculative water rights. The land was subdivided and sold to settlers, along with a promise of irrigation water. Some of these companies succeed, while others failed because they lacked capital to build dams and canals. Still others failed because they were simply fraudulent enterprises.[18]

Some traditions of resource governance, while largely lost today, had an indirect influence on the doctrine of prior appropriation as it was emerging in the West, and even as it is applied today. For example, Spanish people developed very similar approaches to resolving disputes over water and mineral resources and thus reinforced the principle of first in time, first in right.

When the Spanish began colonizing the Southwest in 1520, they brought water law doctrines influenced by Roman law and other sources.[19] The Spanish also brought water management experience from their semi-arid homeland.[20] One of the most prominent freedoms granted to conquered nations was the right for miners to claim common land as personal property.[21] In virtually all statutes governing mining claims in northern Europe, Spain, Mexico, and South America, individuals acquired rights to mining claims, and the state validated those claims by recognizing a description of the exact location of the mine. Almost without exception, these laws are based on what was then called the "Doctrine of Priority," or the principle of first in time, first in right. Even with this body of law, the Spanish faced the considerable challenge of managing a vast New World empire from a distance of over 5,000 miles, with the fastest mode of two-way communication being a lengthy round-trip sailing voyage. Local policy, therefore, tended to develop more efficiently under local custom and in response to immediate needs. In some places, as among the Indian Pueblos along the Rio Grande where existing ditches were used by natives and newcomers alike, the Spanish influence was assimilated into the cultural practices of the Indians.

By 1650, almost 400,000 royal pronouncements had been issued by Spain to govern the New World. But lacking an integrated organizational scheme, these rules were of little use to colonial officials. The Spanish were forced to develop new approaches to govern from such a distance. Spanish law had been codified in 1260 by King Alfonso X as *Las siete partidas,* a version of which was adopted for use in the New World in 1681. This *Recopilación de leyes de los reynos de las Indias* (Summary of the Laws of the Indies) decentralized Spanish authority and distributed it among local officials in the colonies. These laws provided the basis for rules and practices of mine surveying and the continuance of ownership through investment in mining infrastructure.[22] The Laws of the Indies provided powerful guidance for distribution of land and ownership of mines throughout California and New Mexico prior to 1848, as well as a foundation for California's district mining laws in most areas of the state.[23]

The Laws of the Indies also set forth principles and pragmatic, equitable procedures for resolving disagreements over water in the colonies. Legal title and prior use were honored, but—significantly—they did not defeat the claims of especially needy people, the changing needs of the Crown, important third-party rights, or the common good.[24] In weighing multiple, often competing factors and avoiding a "winner-take-all" solution, Spanish law offers useful insights for resolving natural resource disputes in the twenty-first-century West.

At least one important local water management organization inspired by the Spanish survives to this day. The *acequia* (literally, the "canal") is a community ditch organization found along rivers and streams in northern New Mexico. Members cooperate seasonally to clean the ditches. A *mayordomo* supervises distribution and resolves disputes, frequently using the passed-down principles of Spanish law.[25] In nearly all other respects, Spanish influence over western resources declined with Mexican independence in 1821 and the treaty of Guadalupe Hidalgo, which ceded California, Nevada, Arizona, Utah, and parts of New Mexico, Colorado, and Wyoming from Mexico to the United States in 1848. Rapid American settlement following the 1849 California Gold Rush overwhelmed most remaining vestiges of Spanish and Mexican rule.

While these alternative systems of governance were largely displaced by the principle of first in time, first in right, some of these ideas are resurfacing today, as we'll see in later chapters. Because water has always been one of the scarcest and most valuable resources in the West, it is not surprising that many of the strategies center on water issues.

Then and Now

The idea of first in time, first in right emerged into the dominant strategy for resolving disputes over scarce mineral, water, and range resources in the mid-nineteenth century because it was a relatively low-cost method to resolve disputes. It provided a simple, easy-to-understand system of rights to use public resources. These private property rights could be separated from the land and transferred to other beneficial uses through an administrative process that protects third parties. The system is therefore both predictable and flexible, an important feature of any method for resolving disputes. And given its durability over more than 150 years, the system of prior appropriation apparently provides relatively stable, satisfactory outcomes at a minimum cost. It also appears to foster and sustain working relationships, at least among people who have established rights. In the context of mining camps and communities in the nineteenth-century West, the idea of prior appropriation efficiently and effectively resolved disputes among people who were interested in using limited natural resources for similar purposes.

The principle of prior appropriation has proved an enormously durable method to govern some of the West's most valuable resources, particularly water. Although changes have been made in western water law and policy to accommodate instream uses and other environmental values, a group of noted scholars conclude that "water allocation is . . . still heavily influenced by deeply entrenched state laws that have distributed most western water on a first-come, first-serve basis to users who have actually diverted water from a watercourse and applied it to a specified beneficial use."[26]

The durability of prior appropriation is due in part to its simplicity and the fact that it is based on private property rights, which appear to be more sacrosanct in the West than in any other region of the country. The idea is deeply embedded within the legal and institutional framework governing western resources, and people with senior rights—whether to water, minerals, or rangelands—have a strong economic interest in maintaining the doctrine. The doctrine is also consistent with the persistent ideology of privatizing public resources and seeking to devolve authority over western lands and resources, a separate dispute resolution strategy that is discussed in chapter 6.

Christopher Klyza, in *Who Controls Public Lands?*, suggests that once an idea like this principle becomes institutionalized, it is very difficult to dislodge or even reform the idea despite challenges from interest groups and agencies. These "privileged ideas," as Klyza refers to them, not only dictate the design of policies, institutions, and norms of practice but also assume the status of innocent until proven guilty in the marketplace of ideas.[27] Phil Foss, in *Politics and Grass: The Administration of Grazing on the Public Domain*, reinforces this perspective by observing that the long and consistent use of the principle of first in time, first in right does not establish the justice or efficacy of the principle, but it does create a presumption of equity and justice. He goes on to say that "the burden of proof then falls on those who would question the established precedent."[28]

Although it may be an efficient system to resolve disputes among people who have established rights, the effectiveness of prior appropriation in the twenty-first century is limited as new values and interests assert themselves—interests that do not have established rights in the system. As the embattled interests in the Klamath Basin illustrate, this method of making decisions based on chance chronology incurs intolerably high social, economic, and environmental costs. The crux of the dispute is how to balance the century-old water rights of farmers and ranchers to irrigate land with the more recent social values of protecting tribal claims and endangered species. Which value or interest takes precedence when there is not enough water to meet all of the needs? While strict adherence to the prior appropriation doctrine would provide a clear answer, it offers no guidance for resolving the heart of the dispute: how to integrate the underlying values. Assuming that the principle of first in time, first in right will continue to guide the resolution of some western resource disputes, one of the most compelling challenges is to incrementally reform the system of prior appropriation in a way that respects existing rights and integrates the new values and interests associated with the West's natural resources.

Potential Tools—Market-based Mechanisms and the Public Trust Doctrine

The assumption built into the principle of prior appropriation—that the first use of a public resource is by definition the best use—is no longer a sufficient strategy for resolving disputes over western resources. Recognizing this limitation, and the reality that the system of first in time, first in right is not likely to be tossed aside, people who care about the West have offered two tools during the past twenty-five years to improve the efficacy of this foundational strategy for resolving western resource disputes—market-based mechanisms and the public trust doctrine. Surprisingly, perhaps, these tools embrace at least some of the underlying values of our prescriptive framework. They provide for a more inclusive and sometimes more informed and deliberative approach to applying the principle of first in time, first in right. These tools are not cure-alls and may not be appropriate in every situation; think of them as options to consider when faced with the limitations of first in time, first in right.

Market-based Mechanisms

In the early 1980s, the Political Economy Research Center (PERC), among others, began promoting the use of markets to encourage conservation, reallocate natural resources to higher-valued uses, and thereby help resolve otherwise intractable environmental disputes. The basic contention of market-based approaches is that a system of well-defined property rights, along with the ability to transfer those rights, creates an opportunity to replace confrontation with cooperation. Given the potential for economic gain by leasing or selling property rights, people will have an incentive to wisely manage their resources to increase the amount other people are willing to pay.[29]

Market-oriented strategies to resolve natural resource disputes are based on some of the same tenets as the prescriptive framework of this book:

- Individuals and groups are inherently self-interested. To effectively resolve disputes, it is imperative to create the appropriate incentives and social institutions that allow people to satisfy their interests.
- The information required to make good decisions and resolve disputes varies considerably from time to time and place to place. The process of making decisions and resolving disputes should allow the best available information and knowledge to be considered, regardless of the source.
- Self-interested individuals with diffuse knowledge have the capacity to generate many creative options to solve their common problems and to assess the trade-offs associated with alternative courses of action. In this respect, market-oriented solutions, like negotiation and consensus building, are focused more on the process of decision making and less on the specific outcomes associated with particular issues.
- Individuals engage in voluntary agreements that promote cooperation. These agreements are based on a certain degree of accountability to the interests of the individual or group.

Since market-based mechanisms are built on a system of well-defined property rights, they can be seen as an extension or evolution of prior appropriation. Many economists argue that property rights evolve over time, developing largely in response to increased value.[30] The origin and evolution of the principle of first in time, first in right suggests that property rights typically evolve when there is a net benefit to defining and defending them. As water, land, open space, and other western resources become more highly valued in the twenty-first century, it makes sense that there would be an increased effort to define and enforce property rights as one way to allocate resources and resolve disputes among competing interests.

Markets are increasingly proposed as solutions to problems related to water, mining, agriculture, federal lands, fish and wildlife, state parks, and a number of other western resource issues. To a limited degree, the idea has taken hold. In 1991, after several years of drought, California instituted a water bank to allow temporary water transfers from farms to thirsty cities. Idaho and several other western states have likewise created water banks. In 1995, Montana passed legislation allowing anyone to lease water rights to maintain instream flows for fish populations.[31] Arizona and several tribal governments are looking for ways to market their unused shares of Colorado River water to California and Nevada.[32]

Farmers and ranchers in Arizona, New Mexico, and North Dakota are experimenting with grass banking, which allows them to rest overgrazed ranges and public allotments by moving cattle to a "grass bank" owned by a not-for-profit organization, in return for conveyance of conservation easements on a ranchers' land. Similarly, Congress is considering pilot legislation to buy out ranchers' permits for grazing on public lands and set aside the land for wildlife habitat and forage.[33] Two bills propose a $100 million pilot effort to determine whether ranchers are interested. Participation in the buyouts would be voluntary, offering willing ranchers a safety net, a way out of what some people see as an industry in decline. According to newspaper reports, 60 to 70 percent of ranchers in Arizona and Utah support the proposal. Some would likely use their windfall to buy private grazing land. Conservationists say the program would ultimately save money because subsidies for federal grazing permits and damages to the range, they say, cost taxpayers about $500 million a year. Opponents worry, however, about the impacts on rural economies and small communities, long dependent on ranching. Tourism and other New West industries, they say have yet to prove themselves as reliable.

The arena where market-based mechanisms have been most aggressively developed and used is the reallocation of water. According to a recent report published by PERC: "If water rights were clarified, water banking is a market approach that could facilitate transfers of water to higher valued uses. The primary role of a water bank is to obtain water from willing sellers and market it to water users."[34]

In the Klamath Basin, for example, two entrepreneurial ranchers have created the Klamath Basin Rangeland Trust, a not-for-profit organization.[35] While it's a tough sell in a community that has historically defined itself by farming and cattle ranching, the intent of the trust is to convince longtime residents that there's potentially more money in a government-sponsored water bank that pays them to leave the water in the creeks to benefit endangered fish and farmers downstream. Realizing that there is not enough water for both irrigation and endangered salmon and suckers, the two ranchers are buying irrigated pasture leases, warning, "Either something like this is going to happen voluntarily, or there will be some kind of adversarial chaos in this valley."

The U.S. Bureau of Reclamation also views water banking as a central part of its strategy to meet its combined obligations to Indian tribes, endangered species, and farmers in the basin. The goal of the bank would be to generate an additional 100,000 acre-feet of water by reducing irrigation demand (by compensating farmers for water left instream for a single irrigation season), developing offstream water storage, and using groundwater to supplement and replace surface water.

Farmers and ranchers in the Klamath have been slow to embrace such water markets—only one ranch signed up with the trust in 2002, although several ranches apparently expressed interest in 2003. There are legal and institutional barriers to water transfers in the Klamath, but given the will, there are ways to overcome these hurdles.[36] At a deeper level, the limited use of markets to resolve natural resource conflicts may be influenced by a reluctance to articulate social goals by determining who is willing to pay.[37] This system of dispute resolution favors economic values and assumes that intangible environmental values—such as endangered species—can be reduced to some economic calculus.

At first blush, the use of markets to solve land use, natural resource, and environmental problems seems like an oxymoron. The history of the West is replete with examples of overreliance on market mechanisms to set natural resource and environmental policy, leading to "market failures" and depleted and degraded public resources.[38] Proponents of market-based mechanisms point out, however, that some of the West's worst environmental damage has come at the hand of government.[39] It was the federal government, not private business, they assert, that built the many dams throughout the West, laying waste to native fisheries and wetlands. And it is the federal government, market advocates say, that has encouraged timber harvesting on federal lands, compromising wilderness and wildlife habitat values. In truth, government and the private sector market should each shoulder some of the blame for the degradation of the West's landscapes and ecosystems.

While most people are willing to use markets as an efficient means to achieve a certain public policy goal, there is considerable resistance to relying on markets to determine the "ends" of natural resource policy. As Mark Sagoff, a philosopher of public policy, cautions: "Knowing that markets transfer resources to those who pay the most for them, environmentalists worry that the highest bidder too often coincides with the lowest denomina-tor."[40] In contrast to the political process, where the resolution of disputes is determined through a process of deliberation on the merits of competing interests, the market presumes that the most effective resolution of a dispute is determined by who is willing to pay the most or by what is most effi-cient.[41] Economic efficiency, however, may not be the most desirable goal for a given resource management situation.

In addition to confusing means and ends, the system of property rights needed to implement market-based approaches suggests that some third parties will undoubtedly be powerless to participate in decisions that will af-fect them. If only a limited number of people are allowed to fish or hunt in order to sustain the resources, and these opportunities are allocated through a system of private property rights and willingness to pay, this solution clearly cuts against notions of public access to western resources. The conse-quences of such market-based strategies run counter to growing demands for increased community participation in environmental decision making.

Economist Thomas Michael Power argues that market-oriented instru-ments "can solve certain types of environmental conflicts to the mutual sat-isfaction of all involved—a rare and attractive option in an otherwise contentious struggle."[42] Like other strategies to resolve western resource dis-putes, however, market-based approaches are not a panacea. They may be appropriate once society has determined the relative balance among social, economic, and environmental values through an open, democratic process. Markets can then help determine the least costly way to achieve the desired outcome.

Public Trust Doctrine

One way to clarify the appropriate role of the market in resolving western resource disputes is to apply the public trust doctrine. This doctrine has an-cient roots in Roman and English law and was first applied by the U.S. Supreme Court in 1892 to prohibit the State of Illinois from granting sub-merged land along Chicago's waterfront to the Illinois Central Railroad Company.[43] The doctrine's underlying precept is that certain natural re-sources and environmental values are held in trust by the State and cannot be privatized or eroded by either government or market forces.[44] In other words, the public is presumed to be entitled to the benefits of natural sys-tems. Historically, the doctrine was applied only to navigable or tidal waters, but its scope has expanded during the past two decades.[45]

In 1983, the California Supreme Court applied the doctrine to the Mono Lake case, concluding that the State of California has a duty of continued supervision over the exercise of private water rights and must ensure protection of larger public interests, including the natural environment. Specifically in this case, the city of Los Angeles could be enjoined from diverting the streams feeding Mono Lake if the long-term impact diminishes the natural values of the lake.[46] Joseph Sax, a professor of law at the University of California, Berkeley, says that this important judicial decision amounts to a "general manifesto," directing public and private stakeholders to reconcile the traditional commodity uses of natural resources with the maintenance of natural values. The decision, according to Sax, acknowledges the legitimate value of different, often conflicting interests. Equally important, it creates an expectation that affected parties should move beyond the old winner-take-all model of resolving western resource disputes and search for mutual gain solutions.[47] The case strongly suggests that even water rights acquired through prior appropriation are subject to adjustment in order to maintain and restore natural ecosystem values. In short, the government's role goes beyond sorting out competing interests and allocating rights to a responsibility to continually evaluate and adjust those rights in light of changing information and values.

To illustrate the public trust doctrine's potential role in resolving natural resource disputes in the West, consider the general framework for water management in Hawaii. Hawaii's state constitution stipulates that "all public natural resources are held in trust by the State for the benefit of the people," and that "the State has an obligation to protect, control, and regulate the use of Hawaii's water resources for the benefit of its people." The constitution directs the state's water resources agency to "establish criteria for water use priorities while assuring appurtenant rights and existing correlative and riparian uses."[48] Interpreting these constitutional provisions, the Hawaii State Water Code clarifies that the state has both the authority and the duty to preserve the rights of present and future generations in the waters of the state, and that the state has a duty to take the public trust into account in the planning and allocation of water resources.

Hawaii's public trust doctrine is not uncommon; most western states have similar language in their constitutions. Hawaii appears to be unique, however, in the degree to which it allocates water on the basis of the public trust doctrine. The state's water code declares that water should be allocated not only to domestic, agricultural, commercial, and industrial uses but also to protect traditional and customary Hawaiian rights, maintain ecological balance and scenic beauty, provide for fish and wildlife, and offer opportunities for public recreation. To achieve these purposes, the Commission on Water Resource Management is responsible for developing a water plan that allocates water on the basis of "reasonable beneficial use," and for regulating water development and use.[49]

In 1997, the commission issued water use permits for agricultural and other out-of-stream uses on the Waiahole Ditch water system. The decision was appealed to the Hawaii Supreme Court, which overturned the commission decision and ruled that the public trust doctrine and the state's water code provide that, at least in this case, instream public uses of water receive special consideration over off-stream private uses. This and similar applications of the public trust doctrine suggest that it is possible for appropriate jurisdictions to establish priorities for water use and then allow the market to reallocate water rights from one use to another consistent with the priorities established by law and the political process.

As an experienced observer of the politics and policy surrounding western natural resources, Professor Sax concludes that the public trust doctrine will be difficult to apply in the particularly contentious issues of mining, timber harvesting, grazing, wildlife protection, irrigation, and use of federal lands. The goal, he says, "should not be simply to declare winners and losers, but to produce 'physical solutions,' where multiple goals are simultaneously achieved."[50]

These principles of accommodation and mutual gain not only are consistent with the prescriptive framework of this book but also implicitly acknowledge another critical ingredient in the prescriptive framework: the value of information and knowledge. To discover "physical solutions" that accommodate all legitimate competing interests, stakeholders must work together to gather information that clarifies the consequences of alternative courses of action. To emphasize this point, Professor Sax implies that the most common and contentious disputes over natural resources in the twenty-first-century West will not revolve around the setting of environmental limits on resource use or on the protection of undisturbed natural places. Rather, he says, "the places where resource-environment controversies are focused are . . . highly manipulated places which, if any natural processes or natural features are to be maintained or restored, call for sophisticated ecological knowledge."[51]

The public trust doctrine with its implicit principles of dispute resolution—accommodation and mutual gain, and information and knowledge—provides one way to modernize the system of prior appropriation and improve the resolution of natural resource disputes. It strongly suggests that even amorphous public property rights to natural values need to be integrated along with more clearly defined private property rights. The doctrine implies that, while there is a legitimate role for markets, not all interests can be reduced to an economic value, and thus the resolution of disputes necessarily goes beyond the simple calculus of who is willing to pay. It also implies limits on the "privateness" of rights such as water rights. The public trust doctrine emphasizes the continued public interest in the underlying resource for which private use rights are allowed.

The idea of first in time, first in right provides the foundation for resolving disputes over many of the West's most precious natural resources. Although it emerged more than 150 years ago in response to the need for an efficient system to allocate resources and resolve disputes, it continues to be the defining (and in some places, cherished) principle governing water, mining, and—to some degree—rangelands in the West. Markets and the public trust doctrine acknowledge the role of prior appropriation and private property rights in allocating resources and resolving disputes, and they provide different strategies to improve the effectiveness of this doctrine by integrating interests and values that are not otherwise represented.

NOTES

1. *World Almanac and Book of Facts* (Mahwah, NJ: World Almanac Books, Primedia Reference, 2000).
2. This summary of settlement policy from 1780 to 1841 is based heavily on Benjamin Horace Hibbard, *A History of the Public Land Policies* (Madison: University of Wisconsin Press, 1965), 144–70. The other standard text on this topic is Paul Gates, *A History of Public Land Law Development* (Washington, DC: Gaunt, 1987).
3. John D. McGowen, "The Development of Political Institutions on the Public Domain," *Wyoming Law Journal* 2, no. 1 (Fall 1956): 1–15.
4. Robert G. Dunbar, *Forging New Rights in Western Waters* (Lincoln: University of Nebraska Press, 1983). Dunbar and others have noted that the riparian system was established on the premise that water belonged to the owner of the land adjacent to the stream and that while each land owner had a right to use the

water still he was still obligated to return it to the stream undiminished in quality and quantity.

5. Christopher McGrory Klyza, *Who Controls Public Lands? Mining, Forestry, and Grazing Policies, 1870–1990* (Chapel Hill: University of North Carolina Press, 1996).

6. For a detailed examination of the history and disposition of the public domain, see George Cameron Coggins, Charles F. Wilkinson, and John D. Leshy, *Federal Public Land and Resources Law*, 4th ed. (New York: Foundation Press, 2001).

7. John Locke, "On Property," in *The Second Treatise on Government* (1690); Adam Smith, *Inquiry into the Nature and Causes of the Wealth of Nations* (1776).

8. Coggins, Wilkinson, and Leshy, *Federal Public Land and Resources Law*.

9. *Irwin v. Phillips*, 5 Cal. 140 (S. Ct. Calif. 1855), p. 18.

10. John Leshy, *The Mining Law: A Study in Perpetual Motion* (Washington, DC: Resources for the Future, 1987).

11. *Mining Law of 1866*, 30 *U.S. Code* 51; *Mining Law of 1872*, 30 *U.S. Code* 22.

12. *Desert Land Act of 1877*, 43 *U.S. Code* 321.

13. This discussion is based on Phillip O. Foss, *Politics and Grass: The Administration of Grazing on the Public Domain* (Seattle: University of Washington Press, 1960). Another excellent resource on western rangeland policy is Karl Hess Jr., *Visions upon the Land: Man and Nature on the Western Range* (Washington, DC: Island Press, 1992).

14. *Taylor Grazing Act of 1934*, 43 *U.S. Code* 315.

15. *Taylor Grazing Act of 1934*.

16. Dunbar, *Forging New Rights in Western Waters*, 9–17.

17. Dunbar, *Forging New Rights in Western Waters*, 20–23.

18. Dunbar, *Forging New Rights in Western Waters*, 23–28.

19. *Corpus Juris Civilis*. Roman law distinguished between more important, perennial streams and lesser, intermittent streams. The former were considered to be public or common property. Likewise, the Spanish considered water to be *res communis*—that is, public property not susceptible to private ownership. The Romans encouraged development of minerals by allowing miners in conquered nations the right to mine. German rulers in the Middle Ages imitated the Romans by encouraging existing mines and leasing land for new initiatives. Like the Romans, the Germans provided miners unprecedented freedom and property rights to encourage new development. These Germanic land laws set the historic institutional framework for the property law and public decision making to validate mining claims.

20. Michael C. Meyer, *Water in the Hispanic Southwest: A Social and Legal History 1550–1850* (Tucson: University of Arizona Press, 1984), 20–21.

21. William E. Colby, "The Freedom of the Miner and Its Influence on Water Law,"

in *Legal Essays in Tribute to Orrin Kip McMurray*, ed. Max Radin and A. M. Kidd (Berkeley: University of California Press, 1935), 67–84.

22. John A. Rockwell (John Arnold), *A Compilation of Spanish and Mexican Law, in Relation to Mines, and Titles to Real Estate, in Force in California, Texas, and New Mexico; and in the Territories Acquired under the Louisiana and Florida Treaties, When Annexed to the United States*, vol. 1 (New York: John S. Voorhies, 1851), 20. This work also contains a translation of the mining ordinances of New Spain (the Gamboas mining ordinances), which were the laws in relation to mines of gold, silver, and quicksilver, contained in the "Novisima recopilacion"; and the laws and decrees of Mexico, on the subject of mines, colonization, and the right of foreigners to hold real estate.

23. Wilson I. Snyder, *Mines and Mining: A Commentary on the Law of Mines and Mining Rights, Both Common Law and Statutory*, vol. 1 (Chicago: T. H. Flood, 1902).

24. Meyer, *Water in the Hispanic Southwest*, 147–64.

25. Stanley Crawford, *Mayordomo: Chronicle of an Acequia in Northern New Mexico* (Albuquerque: University of New Mexico Press, 1988).

26. See Coggins, Wilkinson, and Leshy, *Federal Public Land and Resources Law*, 378.

27. Klyza, *Who Controls Public Lands?*

28. Foss, *Politics and Grass*, 70.

29. See http://www.perc.org for background information and current applications of free market environmentalism.

30. See Terry L. Anderson and P. J. Hill, "The Evolution of Property Rights: A Study of the American West," *Journal of Law and Economics* 18 (1975): 163–79; and Donald J. Pisani, "Enterprise and Equity: A Critique of Western Water Law in the Nineteenth Century," *Western Historical Quarterly* (January 1987): 15–37.

31. Matthew J. McKinney, "Instream Flow Policy in Montana: A History and Blueprint for the Future," *Public Land and Resources Law Review* 11 (1990): 81–133. See also Clay J. Landry, *Saving Our Streams through Water Markets: A Practical Guide* (Bozeman, MT: Political Economy Research Center, 1998); and Lawrence J. MacDonnell et al., *Water Banks in the West* (Boulder, CO: Natural Resources Law Center, 1994).

32. Shaun McKinnon, "California, Nevada Ask Arizona for Water," *Arizona Republic*, March 10, 2003.

33. Brent Israelsen, "Grazing Buyout Bills Are Floated," *Salt Lake Tribune*, October 21, 2003; Dale Rodebaugh, "Ranchers Cool to Proposed Western Grazing Law," *Durango Herald*, October 27, 2003; Crosby Allen, "Economics Don't Pan Out for Grazing Buyout," *Headwaters News*, October 29, 2003.

34. Roger E. Meiners and Lea-Rachel Kosnik, *Restoring Harmony in the Klamath*

Basin, Policy Series 27 (Bozeman, MT: Political Economy Research Center, 2003), 22.

35. This story is based on Jeff Barnard, "Banking on Water," *Missoulian*, February 17, 2003, B1.

36. Meiners and Kosnik, *Restoring Harmony in the Klamath Basin*, 16–25.

37. Mark Sagoff, "Free Market Versus Libertarian Environmentalism," *Critical Review* 6 (Spring/Summer 1992): 221–30.

38. See Samuel P. Hays, *Conservation and the Gospel of Efficiency: The Progressive Conservation Movement, 1890–1920* (Cambridge: Harvard University Press, 1959); and Patricia Nelson Limerick, *The Legacy of Conquest: The Unbroken Past of the American West* (New York: Norton, 1987).

39. See Terry L. Anderson and Donald R, Leal, *Free Market Environmentalism Today* (New York: Palgrave, 2001); and Karl Hess Jr., "John Wesley Powell and the Unmaking of the West," in *The Next West: Public Lands, Community, and Economy in the American West*, ed. John A. Baden and Donald Snow (Washington, DC: Island Press, 1997): 151–80.

40. Sagoff, "Free Market Versus Libertarian Environmentalism," *Critical Review*, 211–12.

41. For a particularly provocative proposal that seeks to integrate the political process with a market-based mechanism, see Lawrence D. Spears and Karen Paige Hunt, "Protecting Rural Lands: A Market-Based, Efficient, and Culturally Appropriate Strategy Using Rights of First Refusal and the Nonprofit Sector," *Hastings-West Northwest Journal of Environmental Law and Policy* 8, no. 2 (2002): 235–57.

42. Thomas Michael Power, "The Price of Everything," *Sierra*, November/December 1993, 87–96.

43. *Illinois Central Railroad Co. v. Illinois*, 146 U.S. 387 (1892).

44. For excellent reviews of the history and arguments for and against the public trust doctrine, see Coggins, Wilkinson, and Leshy, *Federal Public Land and Resources Law*, 382–89; and Charles F. Wilkinson, "The Headwaters of the Public Trust: Some Thoughts on the Source and Scope of the Traditional Doctrine," *Environmental Law* 19, no. 425 (1989).

45. Joseph L. Sax, "Bringing an Ecological Perspective to Natural Resources Law: Fulfilling the Promise of the Public Trust," in *Natural Resources Policy and Law: Trends and Directions*, ed. Lawrence J. MacDonnell and Sarah F. Bates (Washington, DC: Island Press, 1993), 148–61.

46. See *National Audubon Society v. Superior Court*, 33 Cal. 3d 419, 658 P.2d 709, 189 Cal. Rptr. 346, *cert. denied*, 464 U.S. 977 (1983).

47. Sax, "Bringing an Ecological Perspective to Natural Resources Law," 148–61.

48. "Constitution of the State of Hawaii, as Amended and in Force January 1, 2000," http://www.hawaii.gov/lrb/con/.
49. S.A.K. Derrickson et al., "Watershed Management and Policy in Hawaii: Coming Full Circle," *American Water Resources Association* 38, no. 2 (2002).
50. Sax, "Bringing an Ecological Perspective to Natural Resources Law."
51. Sax, "Bringing an Ecological Perspective to Natural Resources Law," 159.

---   3   ---

The Promise
of Scientific Expertise

A s the western frontier collided with the twentieth century, Congress and
other leaders worried that the policies of free and open access, governed by the principle of prior appropriation, were encouraging fraud,
waste, abuse, and lawlessness.[1] Under the homestead laws, many settlers acquired public lands only to use them for nonagricultural purposes. Land
speculators were more interested in turning a profit than in developing the
land's potential over the long term. Lumber companies harvested only the
very best trees, leaving usable timber and increasing the risk of wildfire and
disease. The same companies commonly failed to reseed and restore the harvested hillsides, leading to erosion and downstream flooding. Range resources were likewise abused. Free grazing on the public domain led to a
"tragedy of the commons," a severe overgrazing of the range by cattle and
sheep.[2] While some cattlemen attempted to prevent overgrazing by fencing
off parcels of range for their own use, competing stockmen often tore the
fences down. Finally, many of the West's best mineral, timber, range, and
agricultural resources were rapidly being acquired by private interests, and
the federal government would soon be left with "the lands nobody wanted."[3]

While many people clamored for the continued disposal and development of the West's lands and resources, another mind-set was quickly taking hold, one that recognized and appreciated the aesthetic values of the untamed western landscape. In part, this was a carryover from the artistic and literary romanticism of the eighteenth century, which continued to influence writers and popular culture well into the mid-1800s. Reading the invigorating accounts of adventurers such as John C. Fremont, Edwin Bryant, Francis Parkman, and John Wesley Powell, and the romantic fiction of James Fenimore Cooper, residents of crowded eastern cities could imagine the West as a place of austere beauty, expansive horizons, and natural restorative power.[4] Henry David Thoreau grounded that vision in the uniquely American philosophy that civilization needed a balance of wilderness to survive. "In wildness is the preservation of the world," Thoreau asserted in 1851, and the West's wild lands offered ample sanctuary to the growing urban masses.[5]

Others saw the social value in wilderness as well, and in 1872, Congress designated Yellowstone the world's first national park, setting a precedent for preserving natural—and particularly western—resources by retaining them in public ownership. Yosemite, Sequoia, and Kings Canyon national parks followed in 1890, the Grand Canyon in 1893, and Mount Rainier in 1899. (It's nearly impossible to overstate the allure of the western landscape to an increasingly urbanized nation then clustered along the eastern seaboard. Even today, of the seventy U.S. national parks and preserves with a natural—rather than historical or military—emphasis, fifty-four are west of the 100th meridian, and these fifty-four make up fully 94 percent of the national park and preserve land base. Of the sixteen nature-oriented national parks and preserves in the East, only one—Acadia, in Maine—was created before 1920.)[6]

The nascent national park system represented the hopes of many within the conservation movement—the preservation of nature in its wilder state. John Muir was one of the more vocal and compelling advocates for preservation, rallying support for Yosemite, Kings Canyon, the Grand Canyon, and the Sierra Club. Even as preservationists lobbied to protect large tracts of the West, other conservationists were more influenced by the philosophy of utilitarianism. Professional foresters, such as Yale-educated Gifford Pinchot, favored the "wise use" of resources for "the greatest good for the greatest number of people," based on long-term public interests and the maximum sustained yield.

As policy, conservation was supported in the General Revision Act of

1891, which revised several of the land and resource disposal policies and provided for the president to set aside federal "forest reserves." Initially, the purpose of the forest reserves was unclear; Muir hoped it was to preserve areas from resource extraction, but Pinchot and others expected to manage them for their commodities. In 1897, Congress passed the Forest Management Act, the first legislative mandate to "manage" western public resources. The act cleared the way for the "wise uses" of the reserve's resources through professional forestry management. Shortly thereafter, the reserves were designated as national forests and provided the land base in 1905 for the U.S. Forest Service (with Pinchot as chief forester), the first major federal land management agency.

During this same time, historian Frederick Jackson Turner caught the public's ear with an essay in *Atlantic Monthly* in which he argued that the expanse of free land and the pioneers' "wilderness experience" fostered a uniquely American brand of individualism, independence, and self-government.[7] But just seven years later, in 1903, Turner lamented that the settlement and development of the West was complete. The 1890 census, he said, showed no remaining vast tracts of land for American conquest and so marked the first decade in American history without a frontier. Turner worried that "the great supply of free lands which year after year has served to reinforce the democratic influences in the United States is exhausted."[8] Many historians question the merits of Turner's "frontier thesis," but it was widely circulated at the time and so helps explain the shift in focus from settlement and development to management and stewardship.[9] As these new ways of thinking took hold, they helped usher in a fundamentally different model for making decisions and resolving disputes over western resources.

Proposals for change came from a variety of sources, but most forcefully from a growing number of conservationists, preservationists, and urban planners. As the West was declared "settled," city dwellers in the East were struggling with rapid growth and their own epidemic of fraud, waste, and corruption. Answers to these problems were found in the progressive era theory of scientific management, wherein experts trained in various sciences would conduct rational planning and informed decision making; reduce fraud, waste, abuse, and political corruption; and increase the efficient use of land and other resources. This theory supported and informed both the conservationist's goal of wise and efficient use of western resources and the aspirations of the emerging profession of city planning.[10]

At the turn of the century, the progressive "gospel of efficiency" was spreading with a religious zeal throughout all areas of American life. In the natural resources arena, this meant that the management of land, water, and other resources should be turned over to professional foresters, rangeland specialists, wildlife biologists, and other scientific experts. The idea of scientific management took root for three reasons.[11] First, people recognized that fraud and abuse of resources in the public domain were widespread and that there were no effective controls in place. Second, professional conservationists and planners presented a rational and influential solution to the problem. They backed their proposal with scientific documentation, and they had the ear of President Teddy Roosevelt, an enthusiastic supporter of conservation efforts. Third, the political and social climate welcomed efficiency and professionalism at work and even in family life. It was reasonable to extend this approach to government management of natural resources.

The New Model: Scientific Management

The basic premise behind the original conception of scientific management was that natural resource issues were essentially technical matters, better addressed by experts than by politicians, judges, or even the resource users themselves. Through rational planning, scientific investigation, and objective analysis, the theory went, professional resource specialists would manage resources most efficiently, meet society's needs, uphold laws, and derive the most economic benefit with the least cost.[12] This concept was promoted by Gifford Pinchot and his colleagues in the "wise use" camp of conservationists. They also argued that the professional specialists should be housed within federal agencies, providing a centralized authority to combat the forces of politics and corporate greed. In the absence of centralized control, Pinchot believed, western entrepreneurs, each trying to beat the others to market, would destroy the resource base.[13]

The promise of scientific management found its home in the U.S. Forest Service (founded in 1905), the U.S. Bureau of Reclamation (1907), the National Park Service (1916), the U.S. Fish and Wildlife Service (1940), and the Bureau of Land Management (1946)—in effect, every federal agency with jurisdiction over western resources. This philosophy also underpins the legislative authority expressed in such statutes as the Wild and Scenic Rivers Act of 1968, the National Environmental Policy Act of 1969, the Endangered Species Act of 1973, the National Forest Management Act of 1974, the Federal Land Policy and Management Act of 1976, and many other laws that govern the use and protection of western resources—all of which presume the need for scientific and technical experts to make decisions. Centralized control has not stopped at the federal level, however. State, tribal, and even local governments typically have agencies and technical staff who specialize in managing natural resources. At each of these levels, the scientific paradigm defines who should make decisions and how those decisions should be made. It delegates authority or power to scientific and technical experts who assert command and control over nature, the definition of the public interest, and the decision-making process.

Scientific management won adherents because it offered two basic advantages over the free market and political processes of the time. First, resource management decisions would be based on the best available scientific and technical information—gathered and analyzed by expert professionals. Taking such decisions out of the hands of politicians and the public—people who typically lacked resource expertise—was Progress with a capital P. Second, science promised to mitigate the negative consequences of the nineteenth-century policies of free and open access; scientific and technical expertise would lead to more efficient, effective resource use and management, for the greatest public benefit.

Delegating decisions to agencies of experts initially helped curb some of the fraud and abuse of the public's natural resources, at least until special interests learned to influence the agencies. Over the long term, many of the West's public resources have no doubt benefited from the skilled and knowledgeable stewardship afforded by scientific specialists. They have deepened our understanding of the West's ecology, geology, and hydrology. Through scientific management, we have gained or honed the useful concepts of carrying capacity, sustained yield, biodiversity, and ecosystem management, among others. But the model also has its downside.

Limitations of Scientific Management

From the outset, the progressive agenda of "science for the good of all" was based more on rhetoric and the politics of Gifford Pinchot's "moral crusade" than on pure science.[14] In effect, scientists were trusted with political or value-based decisions under the guise of science. By the 1940s, citizens and officials began to realize that scientists were no more suited to make such decisions than most politicians were to deduce scientific conclusions. More to the point, science and politics had not been cleanly separated, nor—when it came to setting resource policy—could they be. Public distrust of scientific expertise grew through the second half of the twentieth century, and today citizens and officials are taking a long, hard look at the efficacy of this model of governance. As we move into the twenty-first century, many people agree that the process of making decisions, resolving disputes, and governing western resources can and should be improved. They cite a number of problems associated with scientific management (as shown in box 3.1).

Each of the problems listed in box 3.1 can lead to significant difficulties in resolving real-world disputes over natural resource decisions. But perhaps the most serious difficulties stem from three central shortcomings of the scientific model: (1) a lack of opportunities for meaningful citizen participation, (2) a fragmented political and jurisdictional system as well as fragmented disciplines and areas of expertise, and (3) chronic disputes over scientific and technical information. Let's examine each of these in more detail.

BOX 3.1 Problems with Scientific Management

- Fundamental tension with nineteenth-century policy and practice
  - Disposition/privatization
  - First in time, first in right
- Competing, conflicting uses and interests
  - National versus local
  - Economic versus other values
  - Inefficient allocation of resources
- Framing—those who frame the problem also frame the decision or solution space
- Fragmented jurisdictions and responsibilities
  - Briarpatch of laws, policies, and institutions
  - Inefficient management
- Disputes over scientific and technical information
- Lack of meaningful citizen participation
- Multiple opportunities for appeal
- A fundamental question of governance: who should decide?

Lack of Meaningful Citizen Participation

Perhaps the most immediate and obvious limitation of delegating authority to scientific and technical experts is that it rests on a flawed assumption about the relationship between science and politics. As practiced, scientific management often fails because it mixes scientific "facts" and social "values" without acknowledging the critical distinction between the two. Professional resource managers are taught that a scientific understanding of a situation will lead them to the "best" solution, but the affected public interests are all too rarely satisfied and have their own sense of what is best and how things ought to be. In short, a valid technical solution is not necessarily a socially acceptable one. Instead, it's often seen as meeting only the agency's needs and interests. When managers make this critical error, they also reap public skepticism about the honesty, objectivity, and neutrality of their expertise.

The model of scientific management assumes that society would set clear goals in the political process and then expert managers would pursue those goals through a separate and efficient administrative process.[15] Problems arise, however, when society does not clearly agree on values or insists on competing values, or when the means (management actions) to an end (value) cannot be separated. The mission of the National Park Service, for example, is "to conserve the scenery and the natural and historic objects and the wildlife . . . and to provide for the enjoyment of the same in such manner and by such means as will leave them unimpaired for the enjoyment of future generations."[16] The dilemma park managers find in this mandate is in providing public access and enjoyment while ensuring that resources remain unimpaired. How much visitor use is too much? What exactly does "unimpaired" mean? At what point should use be curtailed to protect resources? Or, conversely, to what extent should resources be "hardened" (using boardwalks in a geyser basin, for example, or paving campground roads and parking lots) to accommodate increased use and "enjoyment"?

Mark Rey, the undersecretary of agriculture (which oversees the U.S. Forest Service) in the George W. Bush administration, says that "a myth . . . has grown up in the midst of natural resource decision making . . . that good science can, by itself, somehow make difficult natural resource decisions for us and relieve us of the necessity to engage in the hard work of democratic deliberations that must finally shoulder the weight of those decisions."[17] In the 1960s, Charles Lindblom argued that public decisions are made through a process of "muddling through."[18] Unlike the rational model of decision making promoted by scientific managers, in practice natural resource planning and decision making tends to be a fluid—sometimes messy—process of defining the desired outcomes (a value-laden exercise) while simultaneously exploring different ways to get there (within the limits of available science and technology). This suggests that science cannot operate independent of value judgments in making public decisions and resolving disputes over western resources. Science and values must somehow work together.

This fundamental flaw in the model of scientific management becomes all the more apparent when public officials and resource managers attempt to balance the instrumental values of western resources with more intrinsic values. After World War II, the West grew rapidly, and hunters, anglers, skiers, and preservationists came into conflict with miners, loggers, grazers, farmers, and developers. As citizens throughout the country became more supportive of wilderness areas, wild and scenic rivers, endangered species, and other environmental values in the 1960s and 1970s, Congress responded by passing a plethora of laws acknowledging these preservation-oriented values. The new mandates, however, did not tell the agencies what to do; they did not prioritize resource values or the interests of different users. Rather, the new laws told the agencies to consult citizens throughout the decision-making process.

Julia Wondolleck, a longtime observer of the U.S. Forest Service, explains that "rather than bounding the decisions to be made, these mandates only increased the number of objectives to be satisfied by land managers with no clear direction given as to how the inevitable conflict between objectives should be resolved. . . . How would the conflict generated between different groups competing for use of the same lands be resolved so that decisions will be harmonious? Congress apparently thought that the answers to these questions would come from involving the public in decisions and from making the decision-making process a rational one."[19]

Congress's intent was laudable, but the practice has fallen far short of the promise. A case in point is the ongoing debate over snowmobiling in Yellowstone National Park.[20] In a 1997 lawsuit, the Fund for Animals claimed that snowmobiling in the park was disturbing wildlife, enabling bison to wander on groomed trails toward hunters outside the park, degrading air quality in the park, and impairing the experience of other winter visitors. In response, the National Park Service undertook a four-year study to evaluate and possibly modify the 1990 winter use plan, which allowed snowmobile use. The

Park Service held two dozen public hearings and received 46,500 written public comments, about half of which favored a ban on snowmobiles while half opposed it. Based on its environmental impact analysis and public comment, the Park Service issued a decision to phase out all snowmobile use in the park by the winter of 2002–2003. But opponents lobbied regional congressional representatives, and the International Snowmobile Manufacturers Association filed a lawsuit to stop the phaseout. In response, the Park Service agreed to postpone action and reevaluate the impacts of snowmobile use in the park.

Another two years (and $2.4 million) of further study and public debate pushed the number of comments received to a record 360,000. Interpreting the results apparently led to more disagreement—some said the comments remained split fifty-fifty over allowing snowmobiles in the park, while others said 80 percent were in favor of banning the machines outright. In March 2003, the Park Service issued a final decision, setting daily limits for snowmobile use in the park, requiring guided access to minimize wildlife disturbance, requiring machines with the latest (cleaner and quieter) technology, and developing a new fleet of mass-transit snow coaches. This set off another round of public outcry, and as of this writing, the "final" decision faces continued challenges. In late 2003, environmental groups filed and won a lawsuit in U.S. District Court in Washington, D.C., to restore the phased-out, total ban of snowmobiles in the park. In January 2004, motorized-use advocates countered with an appeal and a simultaneous suit in a U.S. District Court in Wyoming to re-instate the March 2003 plan allowing limited use of cleaner machines. Members of Congress have entered the fray, drafting proposed legislation favoring both sides of the debate.[21]

Clearly, scientific management, in and of itself, cannot effectively resolve the conflicts among multiple interests in western resources. As we will see in more detail in the next chapter, most attempts to integrate facts and values—through the standard "notice and comment" approach to public participation—have merely reinforced the culture of scientific management within agencies and left the needs and interests of citizens unsatisfied.[22] Policy analyst Robert Nelson argues that the "not in my backyard" (or NIMBY) sentiment is symptomatic of this system of decision making, a statement of popular opinion that "the professional experts do not know best, that the federal government or another central authority should not direct the lives of the citizenry."[23]

Fragmented Systems

According to historian Samuel P. Hays, "the crux of the gospel of efficiency lay in a rational and scientific method of making . . . decisions through a single, central authority."[24] That authority would coordinate the management of western resources.[25] After setting aside more than 16 million acres (mostly in the Pacific Northwest) under the watch of the U.S. Forest Service, Teddy Roosevelt called this overarching philosophy the "New Nationalism," balancing the power and reach of interstate corporations with the countervailing force of federal government. Roosevelt's intent was to protect public resources by placing them in the hands of experts (embodied at the time in the person of Gifford Pinchot) and also to create a sense of national citizenship, bonding Americans together in a common, coast-to-coast purpose.[26]

Robert Nelson argues that the West, more than any other region of the country, is a product of this progressive ideology.[27] The progressives abandoned the nineteenth-century policies of free and open access and reserved nearly half of the contiguous West as federal lands. The federal government built the large dams and irrigation projects that made the West habitable; it also supported and subsidized—as it still does—historic commodity uses of the West (mining, grazing, and timber harvesting) as well as managing wilderness areas, endangered species, and clean air and water. In the absence of anyone else assuming responsibility for conservation and preservation of the Western landscape, we can be thankful that the progressives—through their system of centralized authority—were willing to step up to the plate.

The benefits achieved by centralization, professionalization, and bureacratization have not been without costs, however. In the first instance, by centralizing the authority to make decisions and govern the use of western resources at the national level, this strategy virtually eliminates the possibilities for citizens to assume responsibility for their communities and landscapes, to become active stewards in shaping their future. In *Visions upon the Land*, Karl Hess asks: "How could people muster the desire and energy to be active and concerned stewards [of the land] when distant bureaucracies assumed their roles and when laws and policies effectively isolated them from meaningful contact with the land and its life?" The legal and institutional framework for making decisions and resolving disputes steadily displaced families, neighborhoods, churches, and voluntary associations.[28]

The second consequence of this strategy, and one of the biggest challenges facing citizens and officials throughout the West, is the multitude of federal, state, and local agencies that play some role in shaping policy and resolving disputes. Describing the political landscape in 1900, Gifford Pinchot points to the existence of "twenty-odd Government organizations in Washington which had to do with natural resources."[29] Today, the number of federal agencies and offices that have some type of jurisdiction over federal lands in the western United States totals more than seventy.[30] There are also more than a dozen congressional committees that oversee these agencies, and countless laws these committees are responsible for implementing. When he was chief of the U.S. Forest Service, Jack Ward Thomas warned that "the management of these lands is approaching 'gridlock.' . . . The primary cause is the crazy quilt of laws passed by the different Congresses over a century with no discernible consideration for the interaction of those laws. The total of the applicable law contains mixed mandates, and produces mixed and confusing results. This is compounded by myriad court decisions that sometimes confuse more than clarify."[31] In addition to the federal agencies and laws, western states and many tribal governments each have their own agencies and legislatures with jurisdiction over various aspects of natural resource policy.

Add to this list the agencies and commissions of counties, municipalities, and other local governments, and the upshot is a fragmented system of decision making that rarely corresponds to the nature of land use, natural resource, and environmental problems. More often than not, these agencies obey competing missions and mandates and often find it difficult, if not impossible, to coordinate their activities around transboundary resources, such as air, water, and wildlife. This inability to share the responsibility for solving problems—not to mention the authority to make decisions—not only wastes limited resources but also frustrates citizens.

The case of the Klamath River basin provides a good example of how an issue can transcend agency boundaries and responsibilities and of how fragmented jurisdictions can lead to gridlock. Within the Klamath Basin, more than nineteen federal, tribal, state, and local agencies claim some authority over the Klamath's water. Their mandates and legal constraints often clash. After the 2001 drought, the National Marine Fisheries Service pressed for more water in the lower Klamath Basin to protect threatened coho salmon, but the U.S. Fish and Wildlife Service wanted to hold water in the upper basin for endangered populations of shortnose and Lost River suckers. Also, within the same department (Interior), two agencies—the Bureau of Reclamation and the U.S. Fish and Wildlife Service—are mandated to manage the same water supply for uses that are often in direct competition (irrigation and wildlife, respectively). Even a single agency can be stymied by fragmentation of its duties. The U.S. Fish and Wildlife Service includes an arm that manages the wildlife refuge system and another one responsible for administering the Endangered Species Act. During the Klamath drought, refuge managers were concerned that decisions favoring endangered species were putting other wildlife at risk, yet one refuge staff person reported, "We rarely cross paths with the team who works on endangered species."[32]

The situation is much the same in the context of federal land management. In southwest Montana, for example, nearly three-quarters of the land base of Beaverhead, Madison, and Silver Bow counties is managed by the U.S. Bureau of Land Management (BLM) and the U.S. Forest Service (USFS). In this corner of the state, the BLM oversees about 1 million acres, and the Forest Service manages another 3.32 million acres, in the Beaverhead-Deerlodge National Forest. In the summer of 2001, the BLM began work to revise its resource management plan, the basic document governing land management under BLM jurisdiction. The Forest Service, meanwhile, was preparing to revise its forest plan, a similar governing document. The BLM hired the Montana Consensus Council (MCC), an independent nonprofit organization, to help design a process that would maximize citizen participation while being consistent with the Federal Land Policy and Management Act and the National Environmental Policy Act. MCC surveyed and interviewed more than 100 stakeholders—citizens and organizations representing a diversity of viewpoints, including local as well as national interests—to identify their issues and concerns and to determine how they would like to be involved in the planning process. Many of the stakeholders pleaded with the BLM and the USFS to work together on a joint management plan for federal lands in southwest Montana. From a citizen perspective, the jurisdictional boundaries separating BLM from USFS ground are arbitrary barriers, particularly when both agencies deal with the same issues—sage grouse, allocating motorized and nonmotorized use of public lands, grazing, and so on. Despite public pressure, the two agencies continued preparing separate planning documents. Not to be outdone, a local county commission, historically a conservative group that promotes commodity uses of public lands, is preparing its own resource management plan, arguing that federal law requires BLM and USFS land management to be consistent with county-level plans.[33]

A similar jurisdictional struggle surrounds the development of oil and gas in the Rocky Mountains. The federal government owns a patchwork of oil and gas rights on private property across the West, leaving the regulatory role to the states. In Colorado and Montana, industry-friendly state oil and gas boards oversee permitting and development, typically with little opportunity for public involvement. At the urging of local residents, counties, cities, and towns are fighting industry and state agencies over who should make decisions regarding oil and gas development.[34] Local jurisdictions assert their powers over land use, as spelled out in statute. But the courts say that these local powers conflict with state laws that call for oil and gas resources to be put to "beneficial use," much the same way that water is supposed to be put to beneficial use. As the coal bed methane industry booms in Colorado, at least eleven counties and fifteen cities have adopted laws to protect public health, safety, the environment, and orderly land use.[35] Such a strong local response suggests that state regulations are not stringent enough, and that national and state policy to promote energy development is not well accepted, particularly where the drill rig meets the ground. When industry successfully challenges local ordinances in court, the drill rigs roll in, sometimes—as in the case of Greeley, Colorado (which has eighty oil and gas wells within city limits)—right into town.[36]

This fragmented system of management authorities flows, at least in part, from the philosophy of scientific management. Each use of western resources—minerals, water, range, timber, fish and wildlife, outdoor recreation, and preservation—creates specialized problems that are best resolved (at least in theory) by people with relevant expertise. Thus, we need a distinct agency to manage fish and wildlife, another agency for water, another for timber, and so on. Most natural resource managers start their careers by receiving training in a specialized discipline, such as forestry, range management, outdoor recreation, or watershed management. After three and one-half years of training in their field of choice, students typically participate in some type of "capstone" course, where they work together on a common problem. This is their only exposure to working across disciplines. While the curriculum in many natural resource schools has slowly changed, this basic approach is still intact.

In sum, the fragmented system of jurisdictional responsibilities and professional training defies ecological insights established by John Wesley Powell, Aldo Leopold, and other champions of integrated thinking.

POTENTIAL TOOL—REGIONAL COLLABORATION

As mentioned in chapter 2, John Wesley Powell argued in 1890 that the most appropriate institutions for governing western resources are common-wealths defined by watersheds. His prescription to organize around watersheds was largely ignored in the formative years of natural resource policy in the West.[37] However, his vision of watershed democracies is part of a larger story of how American citizens and communities have attempted to govern public affairs on the basis of regions.

A *region*, according to *Webster's*, is "a broad geographic area containing a population whose members possess sufficient historical, cultural, economic, or social homogeneity to distinguish them from others."[38] While there have been various attempts over the years to foster regional, transboundary approaches to managing natural resources and environmental problems, the history of such efforts is characterized by a mix of successes and failures. Short of reforming existing institutions, which may be desirable but would require a great deal of time and effort, the best approach to overcoming problems associated with the fragmentation of political, jurisdictional, and disciplinary systems is to engage in collaborative processes defined by the natural territory of the problems—or what is sometimes referred to as the "problem-shed." Such problem-sheds often correspond to watersheds, ecosystems, bioregions, and other organic regions. Regional efforts not only focus on specific places and issues, regardless of political and jurisdictional boundaries, but also foster an interdisciplinary approach to problem solving. While they may start by focusing on a specific issue, most eventually touch on a mix of social, economic, and environmental issues because such issues are typically intertwined.

Regardless of their scale or objective, regional initiatives share a common set of values and beliefs—the need to think and act regionally. Regional practitioners or regional stewards are "boundary crossers," a term coined by nationally syndicated columnist Neal Pierce.[39] They are people and organizations who work across multiple political jurisdictions and disciplines, as well as the public and private sectors, to build collaborative solutions to public problems that transcend traditional boundaries.

At the beginning of the twenty-first century, there is renewed interest throughout North America in addressing land use, natural resource, and environmental problems on the basis of regions. There seem to be at least five primary forces driving the proliferation of regional initiatives. First, regionalism is a response to the *failure of existing institutions* to effectively solve a pressing problem, crisis, or threat that transcends political and jurisdictional boundaries. People are increasingly frustrated by the rigidity and inaction of existing institutions and are looking for better ways to resolve transboundary issues, such as transportation planning in the Portland Metropolitan Area, air quality on the Colorado Plateau, wildlife management in the Greater Yellowstone Ecosystem, and land use and recreation in the Columbia River Gorge.

Second, people with diverse viewpoints recognize a *common fate,* a sense that "our" future is linked to "their" future, and that cooperation is the best path to sustain the social, economic, and environmental values of a place they share in common. Given the alternatives, people and communities feel compelled to pool resources and work together to solve common problems. Regional initiatives are thus catalyzed not only by the failure of existing institutions to respond but also by the visions and goals shared by people inhabiting a common landscape, by a sense of responsibility or self-interest in a particular place, or by an opportunity that emerges from exchanging information and ideas through conferences, training workshops, and publications.

Third, Congress and other governmental bodies are promoting decentralized, regional approaches through *laws, executive orders, and policies.*[40] The restoration of endangered species is more and more frequently pursued through habitat conservation plans, which are defined by the bioregional needs of fish and wildlife.[41] In 1998, the Western Water Policy Review Commission concluded that the best approach to manage water in the West is to "change the function and approach of the federal agencies to a 'nested' governance structure [that] reflects the hydrologic, social, legal, and political realities of the watershed."[42] Also, the Committee of Scientists, assembled to review the efficacy of planning and management for national forests, urged the U.S. Forest Service to prepare and periodically update bioregional assessments of the social, economic, and environmental assets of bioregions and watersheds.[43]

A fourth reason for the emergence of regional thinking and action is that *advances in information, communication, and transportation technologies* allow people to work together at different regional scales, from global to continental to watersheds. Local economies are increasingly connected to global trends, which forces people to think and act across boundaries to remain competitive.

Finally, regionalism is based on *what people care about*—the social, economic, and environmental values of a particular place. Thinking and acting on the basis of regions simply makes sense to people. In sum, people who care about the communities and landscapes of the West are in the process of developing what Professor Charles Wilkinson refers to as an "ethic of place"—a code of behavior and thought shaped by the challenges and opportunities (and landscape, climate, and demographics) unique to the region.[44]

In 2000, the Western Consensus Council, a not-for-profit organization, joined forces with the John F. Kennedy School of Government at Harvard University to document, evaluate, and promote regional approaches to land use, natural resource, and environmental policy in North America, particularly the American West.[45] Students at the University of Montana surveyed more than seventy regional initiatives in the West, creating a profile for each initiative that explains why it was started, what is has accomplished, key ingredients to success, and the obstacles and challenges it faces. Based on this preliminary inventory and assessment, we can see at least five primary functions of regional initiatives in the West (see box 3.2). These various func-

---

BOX 3.2 Objectives of Regional Initiatives

- Build knowledge and understanding
    - Conduct research
    - Acquire information
- Build community
    - Inform and educate citizens and leaders
    - Promote mutual understanding
    - Shape public values
    - Stimulate conversation
    - Foster a common sense of place
- Share resources and information
- Solve specific problems
    - Provide input and advice
    - Advocate for a particular interest or outcome
    - Resolve disputes
- Govern
    - Make and enforce decisions

tions reinforce one another and scribe a natural progression from knowledge and community building to advocacy and governance.

The first, *build knowledge and understanding*, seems to be a common initial purpose of many regional efforts, and perhaps it is a necessary precursor to other missions an initiative might later adopt. Some regional organizations use knowledge building to promote a deeper sense of the social, economic, and ecological characteristics of a region, while others hope to develop the capacity of citizens and officials within a region to work together on issues of common concern. Regional initiatives that move on to *community building* begin to use their refined knowledge of the region to inform and educate citizens and leaders, promote mutual understanding, shape public values, stimulate conversation, and foster a common sense of place.

In response to concerns over rapid growth and declining quality of life in Utah, for example, business leaders teamed up with local and state policy makers to help guide the development of a broadly and publicly supported Quality Growth Strategy—a vision to protect Utah's environment, economic strength, and quality of life. This public/private partnership, Envision Utah, has been highly effective in tying growth management planning—unwelcomed by many westerners—to the more widely accepted values of economic development and quality of life. Since its inception in 1997, Envision Utah has developed strategies to preserve critical lands, promote water conservation and clean air, improve the state's regionwide transportation system, and improve the range of available housing options. It also provides financial and technical assistance for demonstration projects and coordinated design workshops in eight communities along the Wasatch Front, Utah's fastest-growing region.

Another function of many regional initiatives is *sharing resources and information*. This enables improved coordination of services and programs among agencies and organizations within the region. The Outside Las Vegas Foundation, for example, helps to coordinate federal land management on 7 million acres surrounding the fastest-growing community in the country. The foundation encourages community stewardship of these lands, leverages public and private funding to support public use of the lands, and fosters collaboration among the U.S. Forest Service, National Park Service, Bureau of Land Management, and U.S. Fish and Wildlife Service.

Some regional initiatives emerge to *solve specific problems*. Participants may sit on advisory councils and provide input and advice to decision makers within the region. In more limited situations, regional bodies are created to *govern*—that is, to make and enforce policy within the region. There are precious few examples of regional institutions that have the authority to govern, either in the West or in North America. Such institutions do not fit well within the established system of local, state, and federal governments, reaching well outside of the box of traditional decision-making models.[46] During the 1960s, a few large metropolitan areas in the East consolidated city and county governments in an effort to reduce costs and increase efficiency. Since then, many metropolitan and rural areas in the West and throughout the United States have spawned regional councils of government, voluntary associations of local governments that share information and resources. Most of these lack the authority to implement regional actions, however, so their governance role is limited primarily to implementing the federal transportation program, which requires regional planning as a condition for funding.

The San Diego and Portland metro areas conduct land use and urban planning through regional agencies or councils with significant decision-making authority. In other cities, private-public partnerships have sprung up to address specific regional issues, such as housing, human services, transportation, land use, and economic and community development. In a few cases, state legislatures or city councils have recognized the value and credibility of these regional initiatives and granted them funding and decision-making authority.

Two other western examples of regional governance are more focused on environmental issues. The Tahoe Regional Planning Agency was created by compact and statute in 1969. Its mission is to preserve, restore, and enhance the unique natural and human environment of the Lake Tahoe region, which includes both California and Nevada. The agency adopts and enforces environmental standards and regulates land use, density and rate of growth, and scenic impacts.

The Columbia River Gorge Commission was authorized by the 1986 Columbia River Gorge National Scenic Area Act and was created through a compact between Oregon and Washington in 1987. It was established to develop and enforce policies and programs that protect and enhance the scenic, natural, cultural, and recreational resources of the Gorge, while encouraging compatible growth within existing urban areas of the Gorge and allowing economic development outside urban areas consistent with resource protection. The commission includes representatives from the states of Oregon and Washington; the U.S. Forest Service; four treaty tribes (Nez Perce, Umatilla, Warm Springs, and Yakima); Clark, Klickitat, and Skamania counties in Washington; and Hood River, Multnomah, and Wasco counties in Oregon.

Some regional initiatives are designed to *advocate for a distinct agenda.* Such advocacy may target a solution to a particular problem, or it may be more programmatic or policy oriented. Some of the more widely known examples in the West include the Greater Yellowstone Ecosystem management effort, the Grand Canyon Trust, and the Pacific Northwest Economic Region organization.

The cumulative body of experience with regional initiatives in the West suggests that most place-based efforts work within the existing legal and institutional framework. They are designed to build more effective relationships, establish ongoing networks, and solve problems through the use of collaborative processes. Regional initiatives emerge at different geographic scales and use different institutional arrangements. This ad hoc approach offers an effective way to supplement the existing processes for public decision making and dispute resolution.[47]

The growing interest and experience with regional approaches suggests that there may be value in creating new institutions or consolidating existing ones into regional bodies that have the ability to govern. The process of reforming our systems of governance—including procedures for citizen participation, public decision making, and dispute resolution—will certainly be politically difficult and will take time. Acknowledging this, Daniel Kemmis argues in *This Sovereign Land* that, at least with respect to federal lands in the West, we should create sufficient space within the existing legal and institutional framework to encourage a set of experiments in governance—an idea that we examine in chapter 8.[48]

Although there is no single model for regional initiatives, practitioners and researchers have identified seven key principles (listed in box 3.3). Each of these can be adapted to the unique circumstances of each place or region.

As some people consider the merits and possibilities of regional forms of governance, others are helping build the capacity of citizens, leaders, and future resource managers to think and act regionally. The Lincoln Institute of Land Policy, for example, has initiated a series of courses, clinics, and publications to promote and support regional collaboration; the Alliance for Regional Stewardship provides a network for regional stewards and practitioners; and the School of Natural Resources at Utah State University

BOX 3.3 Principles for Regional Collaboration

1—Make the Case

Working across boundaries is tough. There is tremendous inertia in existing political arrangements. The reasons for working regionally must be clear and compelling. There must be clear evidence that engaging in a regional effort is both warranted and defensible and for asserting the very existence of the region in question. Regional partnerships are typically initiated when a core group of leaders recognizes a crisis, threat, or opportunity that is not likely to be adequately addressed through existing institutional arrangements.

2—Mobilize and Engage Key Participants across Issues and Territories

To be effective, regional initiatives must engage the right people. If your objective is to advocate for a particular interest or outcome, that will require a different group of people than if you are trying to resolve a multiparty dispute or address a multijurisdictional issue. In the latter case, you should seek to be as inclusive as possible—include people who are interested in and affected by the issue; those needed to implement any potential recommendation (i.e., those with authority); and those who might undermine the process or the outcome if not included. Regional activities that engage only organizations and people with a regional focus or mission tend to lack diversity in the strategies they develop. This in turn leads to a lack of buy-in and participation by a broad range of agencies and leaders.

3—Define the Region Based on Peoples' Interests

How people define a region naturally flows from their interests and concerns. Regions are most often defined on the basis of sense of place (history, culture, landscapes, and watersheds) and function (infrastructure, economy, and institutional arrangements). However defined, the region must engage the hearts and minds of people and appeal to shared interests. The precise boundaries of a region are often less important than clarifying the core area of interest. Boundaries can be soft and flexible, adaptable to changing needs and interests.

4—Foster Mutual Learning

Regional efforts often begin by providing opportunities to learn about the region and the need to think and act across boundaries. Building this common understanding fosters a sense of regional identity and often the will to act. Many regional partnerships enable participants to jointly develop and rely on the best available information, regardless of the source, thereby creating a greater sense of ownership in the region's story. Regional efforts should consider a variety of scenarios and options to shape the future of the region. All participants should have an equal opportunity to share views and information.

5—Form Partnerships through Collaborative Decision Making

Since most regional initiatives do not have legal or governing authority, they must create power. One of the best ways to create power (or, in this context, the ability to foster social change and shape public policy) is through collaborative decision making. Collaboration is a social learning process where people share knowledge, ideas, and experiences through cooperative, face-to-face interaction. The premise of collaboration is that if you bring together the right people in constructive ways with good information, they will produce effective, sustainable solutions for the challenges and opportunities they face. Genuine collaboration occurs when people listen to each other, consider the rationales or interests behind competing viewpoints, and seek solutions that integrate as many interests as possible. Collaborative decision making may or may not result in consensus or unanimous agreement, but it allows participants to create effective coalitions to get things done.

Beyond building effective coalitions, some regions may want to create regional bodies of governance. Today, the only elected regional government in the United States is the Portland Metropolitan Council in Oregon. While such bodies may be valuable and effective in certain circumstances, it is just as important to realize that government alone cannot deal effectively with most regional problems. Governance—how people come together to address common problems—is more than government. At the regional level, citizens, business, labor, nonprofits, educators, and government must work together to set directions, solve problems, and take action.

6—Take Strategic Action

The objectives of a regional partnership should determine what the partnership does. Experience suggests that early successes help build momentum and trust. Develop the capacity to (1) communicate your message; make it relevant and compelling, and use multiple strategies to inform, educate, and mobilize people (e.g., media, public events, publications, Web sites); (2) link your effort to established decision-making systems; seek access to power, rather than power itself; and (3) monitor, evaluate, and adapt; develop indicators of performance; and clarify who will do what, when, and how.

Being "strategic" and deciding what to do requires an understanding of how regional action supplements efforts at the local level. The desired outcomes for a region are often contingent upon many seemingly disconnected local decisions. Regional strategies need to recognize these contingencies up front and create opportunities to build bridges, coordinate actions, and do things that would not otherwise get done.

7—Sustain Regional Action and Institutionalize Regional Efforts

Assuming there is a need to sustain a regional partnership, the key challenge is to keep stakeholders engaged and to recruit more leaders. Since the region is no one's community, building a sense of regional identity, responding to the needs and interests of partners, and capturing and sharing accomplishments are critical to sustain any regional effort.

To be effective, regional initiatives should be both idealistic and opportunistic. People's attention will naturally devolve to more established, usually local institutions, if the mission of regional efforts is not consistently and continuously reviewed, revised, renewed, and adapted to new information and opportunities.

Finally, regional stewards should also assess the value of integrating regional efforts into existing institutions, and/or designing new institutions. Partners need to identify and develop the capacities to sustain the regional initiative—people, resources (e.g., money and information), and organizational structure.

has created what may be one of the first programs for bioregional planning in the West, if not the country.[49]

The challenge of working across boundaries—political, jurisdictional, and disciplinary—can best be addressed through multiple short- and long-term strategies. As some people work within the existing legal and institutional framework to collaborate regionally, others need to teach future leaders in the art of regional thinking and envision regional forms of governance.

Of course, regional efforts are not without their shortcomings. Their track record is at best mixed, particularly in the experience of regional councils of government. Critics say that regional efforts are usually time intensive, which can drive up costs and lead to participant burnout. Agencies and decision makers within the region may resist sharing responsibility and authority. Some skeptics point out that identifying a region creates new and possibly undesirable boundaries.

Disputes over Scientific and Technical Information

Given the underlying philosophy of scientific management to make decisions and resolve disputes on the basis of "sound science" or "good science," it is ironic that so many disputes arise over scientific and technical information. But if "good" information is scarce, *credible* information is rarer still. Too often, information (or how it is presented) is skewed to support one point of view, or the source is not trusted by all the disputants.

In the Klamath Basin situation, even the basic facts of water quantity and availability are up for dispute, in part because the basin's water system—which includes miles of ditches, canals, and even tunnels; innumerable dams and diversions; and natural lakes, river channels, and tributaries—is numbingly complex, minutely managed for many different uses, and largely dependent on long-term, unpredictable weather cycles. Layered onto this complex physical environment are the multidisciplinary scientists of at least half a dozen federal agencies, their often competing statutory mandates, and tribal and local interests and knowledge.

In another example, Steve Stringham, a grizzly bear expert in Alaska, asserted in January 2003 that "recovery of grizzlies depends on sound scientific research."[50] The problem, however, is that even the experts cannot seem to agree on what constitutes "sound" scientific information. Louisa Willcox, a grizzly bear expert with the Natural Resources Defense Council, claims that federal agencies are using incomplete data to show that bear populations are recovering. She believes that the use of "bad" science is designed to push the huge carnivores off the endangered species list and thereby open up more western land to energy development.[51] Chris Servheen, who has coordinated grizzly bear recovery for the federal government for the past twenty-two years, says that he is not under any political pressure to delist the bears. Rather, he states: "Our objective is to get them to the point where they don't need to be protected under the act." Grizzly bears were listed as threatened in the lower forty-eight states in 1975. While most experts agree that the population is doing better today than it was twenty-nine years ago, Stringham says that critical information is either not gathered or not made public and "thus it is unclear if bears are actually recovering."[52]

The dispute over snowmobiles in Yellowstone National Park is an example of how value differences and politics can sway people's perceptions of ostensibly "scientific" decisions. For six years, Park Service scientists studied snowmobile emissions and noise and their effects on various wildlife species. Yet snowmobile fans and foes alike accused the Park Service of playing politics rather than relying on science to arrive at a sound decision. The first study was initiated under the environmentally friendly Clinton administration. When the initial plan to phase out snowmobiles was announced, a spokesperson for the BlueRibbon Coalition, a motorized-use advocacy group, said that the Park Service abandoned science for "thinly grounded allegations attack[ing] attributes of the machines, like sound and emissions, that can easily be mitigated. They created the perception of problems that barely exist, manufactured an anti-snowmobile feeding frenzy, and then seized on a total ban as the only solution. This is not management. This is pure politics." Decision makers, she continued, "must have taken a crystal ball, some tea leaf readings, and a very sharp pencil to get from the information presented in the EIS [environmental impact statement] to that ban recommendation."[53]

But when the ban was overturned during the Bush presidency, people on the other side of the table used the same argument to make their case. "The Bush administration ignored its own scientific studies on the environmental and health risks of snowmobiles," said Chuck Clusen of the Natural Resources Defense Council. "Its decision violates everything our national parks stand for." Bob Seibert, a park ranger, apparently agrees. "They took a logical planning process and turned it into a political stage," he says. Overturning the ban and implementing new regulations has not had the promised effect, Seibert says: "If we've made any progress in air quality, we can't see it. The staff have expressed the same complaints as before—runny eyes, sore throats and headaches." Meanwhile, the Montana Department of Environmental Quality says pollution at the west entrance to the park has exceeded national standards for carbon monoxide and hydrocarbons on some calm winter days, but it's impossible for the state's air-monitoring equipment at the west entrance to measure any change in air quality since the new rules were enacted because it's too short a time span.[54]

Most land use, natural resource, and environmental issues in the West are science intensive, meaning that they involve the use of complex, often incomplete scientific and technical information. Why is there so much disagreement over the one element—information—that scientific management is ostensibly best suited to address? As the vignettes presented above suggest, disputes over scientific and technical information may emerge for a number of reasons:

- Lack of data or gaps in information, knowledge, and understanding
- Scientific uncertainty—and an unrealistic belief in certainty
- Disagreement over the nature of the problem
- Different approaches to collecting and analyzing data
- Competing interpretations of what the data mean—"dueling" experts
- The emergence of new or updated information

Each team of scientists—indeed, each individual scientist—unavoidably brings unseen assumptions and judgments to his or her work. As one forestry researcher says, "Data are not just data. Information is always accompanied by interpretation."[55] To understand this in broad terms within the Klamath Basin situation, for example, the Bureau of Reclamation premises its environmental analysis on providing water for irrigators, while the U.S. Fish and Wildlife Service interprets data in the context of refuge management and threatened and endangered species. The National Marine Fisheries Service enters the fray with its focus on anadromous fish, including the regionally endangered coho salmon. Within each agency, individual biologists, hydrologists, and other scientists have their own "preferences," at least some of which find their way into the work, even when simply gathering or analyzing baseline or "descriptive" data. Also, natural systems such as the Klamath River basin are so complex and ever changing that science cannot yet understand and explain them, and any shortcomings are magnified as the size of the system or study time frame increases.

In a report released in June 2002, the U.S. Forest Service asserts that it is facing a "process predicament."[56] According to the report, the cumulative effect of multiple requirements for interagency coordination, environmental analysis, and public participation often results in "analysis paralysis." Decision makers and experts often overanalyze an issue in an attempt to build an "air tight" and "legally defensible" decision. Or, conversely, continuing appeals and litigation lead to open-ended analysis and review. In some cases, experts invest huge amounts of time analyzing the potential consequences of the alternatives, yet those future scenarios remain fuzzy and unpredictable.

The ultimate consequence of analysis paralysis and disputes over scientific and technical information is an inability to make decisions and, according to the Forest Service, take action "to sustain the health, diversity, and productivity of the nation's forests and grasslands."[57] In one example, a severe storm in 1995 blew down and damaged trees over a 35,000-acre tract of California's Six Rivers National Forest.[58] Managers proposed a timber salvage project to reduce the wildfire risk posed by the sudden abundance of fuels, but they struggled with shifting goals in forest plan revisions, inflexible regulations, and confusing statutory requirements. At least twice, Forest Service decisions were appealed, further delaying the salvage project. Then, in the fall of 1999, wildfires burned 125,000 acres in the region, fueled in part by the downed timber. Environmental conditions were drastically changed, so forest managers spent another half year preparing a new watershed analysis, which then led to the preparation of an environmental impact statement (EIS). In 2002, a federal judge sided with conservation groups in declaring the EIS inadequate, and the salvage project was tabled once again. Seven years had passed since the blowdown, and management was no closer to implementing any on-the-ground restoration.

As explained earlier, the scientific model optimistically assumes that facts and values can be easily distinguished and managed. Resource managers try to accommodate conflicting interests—from multiple-use, consumptive values to preservation values—by basing their decisions on professional expertise. But disputes over scientific and technical information almost always indicate deeper disagreements over social, economic, and environmental priorities and values. Too often, people are lulled into endlessly debating the data instead of meaningfully integrating their underlying interests in a deliberative and more cooperative process.

The scientific model also assumes that all relevant social, economic, and environmental information is available to the decision maker. In the real world, however, significant information gaps are commonplace. When confronted with decision makers' "wish lists" of data gathering and analysis, agencies often say they don't have the staff or funding to do the requested work. In other cases, the desired information is beyond the reach of the best available science. Given the adversarial nature of the decision-making process, citizens and advocacy groups are forced to hire their own scientific and technical experts to conduct analyses, forecasts, and impact assessments.

Finally, attempts to scientifically analyze and resolve a problem can be stymied when the decision makers presume to frame the problem before sufficiently understanding it and assigning someone else to find an agreeable solution. In Montana, for example, a state commission appointed two citizen advisory councils to address recreational crowding and conflicts between commercial users (fishing outfitters), out-of-state visitors, and in-state residents on the Big Hole and Beaverhead rivers. Unfortunately, the commission did not define what it meant by "crowding," nor had anyone yet determined the recreational carrying capacity of either river. In short, members of the advisory councils were not sure—and could not readily agree— whether crowding was a legitimate problem on the rivers. The commission also said it would not consider any proposals that set outfitter use levels based on past use, unduly limiting options to resolve the issue—before talks even began—without first consulting with the affected parties.

POTENTIAL TOOLS—JOINT FACT FINDING AND
ADAPTIVE MANAGEMENT

Clearly, scientific information and technical experts must play a critical role in managing natural resources. Scientists can and should help frame issues, generate options, analyze consequences, and generate policy-relevant knowledge. However, when they disagree—as Daniel Kemmis notes—"the resulting image of science for sale creates deep public cynicism about scientists . . . [and] corrodes confidence in the decision-making process itself. How can lay people, either citizens or officials, possibly hope to know what is right for their ecosystems when scientists cannot even agree?"[59] The challenge is to produce data that is seen as scientifically credible, legitimate in the eyes of all stakeholders, and relevant, thereby creating a common understanding of the issues in dispute, regardless of the diversity of interests and viewpoints.

Joint fact finding. One practical strategy to achieve this type of common understanding is joint fact finding, in which "stakeholders with differing viewpoints and interests work together to develop information, analyze facts and forecasts, develop common assumptions and informed opinion, and, finally, use the information they have developed to reach decisions together."[60] The idea here is not to mold citizens into scientific and technical experts. The objective is to allow stakeholders to work side by side with technical experts to seek agreement on what they know; what they don't know; what they want or need to know; the most appropriate methods of gathering information; and the limitations of alternative analytical methods.

Joint fact finding is based on a collaborative approach to decision making, rather than an adversarial approach. It provides a number of benefits over the adversarial use of science. First, it allows nontechnical people to learn more about the technical aspects of the issues in question. Second, it allows stakeholders to be part of the process of generating information that will be used in shaping policy, making decisions, and resolving disputes. This not only reduces the suspicion that stakeholders may have regarding the credibility of information but also allows "indigenous" knowledge to be integrated with "expert" knowledge.[61] People live and work in particular places, and they know those places in a variety of ways. This ingrained knowledge and understanding is a valuable source of information that complements the data gathered by technical experts through well-established scientific methods. A variation on this approach, known as collaborative learning, encourages agencies and technical experts to lead the learning process while remaining open to ideas from all stakeholders and new information as it comes to light.[62]

Third, joint fact finding can lead to more creative decisions. When diverse stakeholders work together to gather, analyze, and interpret information, they draw on one another's expertise, knowledge, and intuition. The exchange of ideas typically results in options that no single individual could have generated alone. Fourth, the process of learning together makes it explicit to all participants that decisions are almost always made in an atmosphere of uncertainty. Joint fact finding allows people to acknowledge this uncertainty up front and to mitigate the impulse to claim "we need more information before acting." As the following examples demonstrate, it allows participants to focus on the more compelling questions of what people need to know in order to make well-informed decisions.

In 1998, CONCUR, a mediation group specializing in environmental disputes, convened an independent panel to conduct joint fact finding on agricultural water use efficiency in the Sacramento–San Joaquin river delta east of San Francisco. The panel included five nationally recognized scientists, who offered their expertise in on-farm and district conservation practices, delta hydrology, and aquatic ecology. In-state technical advisers and various stakeholders also participated in the discussions. CONCUR prepared for the joint fact-finding work by drafting initial terms of reference or ground rules, briefing stakeholders, and coordinating with key policy makers to ensure that the panel's work would be timely and presented in a useful format. The panel challenged the delta's water managers to work through a rigorous process to calculate the types and amounts of agricultural water loss. Based on the resulting analysis, panelists recommended replacing the traditional reliance on best management practices with an objective-driven, incentive-based approach to conserving water. The panel also identified several information gaps where further research was needed. CONCUR then drafted a single text report summarizing the panel's work and ten recommendations, which was in turn used by a steering committee to develop an innovative water use efficiency program for agriculture in the delta. Water users and other stakeholders in the delta support the program because they were included in the fact-finding process and because the program itself is supported by well-documented data and rigorous, rational analysis.

In contrast, in the Klamath River basin dispute, the parties have disagreed over whose data to rely on, what additional data might be needed, and how to interpret the data. Federal agencies dispute one another's data and conclusions, and citizens either champion the studies that support their position or distrust any and all information, whether or not it favors their cause. No doubt the administration thought it had a good idea when it asked the National Research Council (NRC) to consider the facts of the case and issue an "independent" report. But the NRC report merely provided yet another

BOX 3.4 Best Practices for Joint Fact Finding

Start-up and Preparation

- Agree on what you know, what you don't know, and what you need or want to know.
  - Individuals can do this separately and then combine their responses.
  - Participants might do this all together.
  - A subgroup could complete this task and then report to other participants.
- Determine the objectives of joint fact finding.
  - Package available information in a useful format.
  - Clarify technical uncertainty.
  - Develop management options.
  - Seek agreement.
- Agree on what level of uncertainty is acceptable.
- Ensure that time and funding are adequate for a thorough process.
- Define the process for gathering information.
  - What questions will be asked?
  - What methods will be used?
  - What are the confidentiality needs?
  - Who will do what and when?
- Define the limitations of the methodology.
  - Acknowledge that it is difficult to quantify certain costs and benefits.
  - The response rate for surveys may be limited or biased (or both).
  - Generalizing from case studies may lead to inaccurate conclusions.
- Select an appropriate, credible "fact finder."
  - The participants themselves? They might need technical help.
  - Independent fact finders or experts? They should be credible to all stakeholders, with a breadth and depth of expertise suitable for the task at hand.

> - A panel of experts? They should represent a range of opinions and backgrounds.
> - Clarify expectations for reporting; use a single text.
>
> *Conduct the Fact Finding*
>
> - Develop criteria to select fact finders.
>   - Type of experience.
>   - Level of expertise.
>   - Reputation.
> - Recruit independent scientific experts.
> - Create opportunities to integrate "indigenous knowledge."
> - Synthesize findings, conclusions, and uncertainties.
>
> *Link Outcomes to Objectives*
>
> - Discuss how the information will be used or interpreted.
>
> *Develop a Monitoring and Evaluation Strategy*
>
> - Adapt management plans as appropriate.

mound of information for people to argue about. The situation is ripe for joint fact finding, which could help to develop more credible information as well as build areas of common understanding and precursors to agreement. Box 3.4 presents a set of best practices for joint fact finding.

It is important to recognize up front that joint fact finding can be difficult when the participants have different levels of expertise. Participants may not initially agree on how to frame specific questions, on the selection of an expert, and on how to interpret the information. Moreover, participants may be reluctant to learn something that is counter to their interests. The results of a joint fact-finding initiative may also be inconclusive.

Adaptive management. In light of these concerns, another important strategy to bear in mind for resolving scientific and technical disputes is adaptive management. According to Kai Lee, adaptive management means making decisions using the best information available, monitoring the results, learning from experience, and adapting future management prescriptions appropriately.[63] Adaptive management is based on the premise that uncertainty is a given—social, economic, and environmental values change, landscapes evolve, and unanticipated impacts occur. This does not mean that decisions should be postponed until we have better, more complete information. As the Megram case study illustrates, there are serious consequences for waiting. It means that we should learn by doing and should create an expectation of learning as we go.

Unfortunately, it is often difficult to embrace adaptive management in practice. In *The Process Predicament,* the Forest Service suggests that rules for public participation, decision making, and administrative appeals are "linear and inflexible." Such strict rules (or rigid interpretation of them) discourage adaptive management, which requires a more flexible decision-making environment.

Even when monitoring and evaluation plans are incorporated into negotiated agreements, the participants often experience burnout or simply have other priorities, and it is hard to keep people focused on the learning and adapting aspect of the process. In 1994, farmers, ranchers, recreationists, and conservationists in Montana successfully negotiated a historic agreement that allows private parties to lease water rights to leave water in-stream to protect fishery resources. As part of the agreement, the participants agreed to periodically meet to evaluate the performance of the program and its impact on existing water rights holders. The participants have met only once or twice since the agreement was signed, and there is apparently no ongoing, systematic effort to monitor and evaluate the program.

Other cases of joint fact finding and collaborative problem solving have experienced similar results. In 2002, the Consensus Building Institute and the Western Consensus Council evaluated the performance of fifty cases of community-based collaboration on federal land and resources in the eight states that compose the Rocky Mountain West.[64] To learn something about the implementation of community-based negotiated agreements, the researchers set out to include cases that had been in operation for less than two years, for two to five years, and for six or more years. Surprisingly, it was nearly impossible to find people who had participated in community-based groups six or more years ago. The groups had either disbanded or were no longer meeting on a regular basis.

While joint fact finding and adaptive management pose their own set of challenges, they offer a promising way to move beyond the gridlock and analysis paralysis created by disputes over scientific and technical information. As more citizens, officials, and experts experiment with these approaches, we are likely to refine the "best practices" to make them work.

Scientific management emerged, at least in part, in response to perceived waste, fraud, and abuse associated with the nineteenth-century policies of free and open access. In contrast to the disjointed process of allowing individuals to make decisions, privatize resources, and resolve disputes through the principle of first in time, first in right, scientific management imposed a sense of order over who should make decisions about western resources and how those decisions should be made.

Ironically, perhaps, scientific management has not significantly reformed or reduced the influence of privatization and the historic principle of prior appropriation. For much of the twentieth century, the framework for making decisions and resolving disputes over western resources was dominated by these two strategies. The principle of first in time, first in right allows private individuals to make decisions and resolve disputes on the basis of rights. By contrast, the paradigm of scientific management delegates authority (or power) to make decisions and resolve disputes to scientific and technical experts.

As we enter the twenty-first century, these two strategies continue to dominate the legal and institutional framework that governs how decisions are made and how disputes are resolved. Taken together, these strategies endure largely on the basis of inertia. They are so deeply embedded within laws, policies, and institutions that they in large part define the culture of decision making and dispute resolution. Any attempts to improve the process of decision making and dispute resolution must acknowledge the fundamental challenge of changing this culture, which is at best a long-term proposition.

The next five chapters explain different attempts to reform this dominant pair of strategies. Public participation and public interest litigation represent attempts to improve the process from the inside out, providing more opportunities for citizen engagement within the established framework. Citizen initiatives and calls for the devolution of authority question the very foundation of the established framework, raising the fundamental question of who should decide. Why should professional resource management agencies, staffed by scientific and technical experts, rather than the parties themselves resolve conflicts? Finally, negotiation and consensus building have emerged as a practical way to supplement and improve all of these other strategies.

NOTES

1. Samuel Trask Dana and Sally K. Fairfax, *Forest and Range Policy: Its Development in the United States*, 2nd ed. (New York: McGraw-Hill, 1980).

2. Karl Hess, *Visions upon the Land: Man and Nature on the Western Range* (Washington, DC: Island Press, 1992).

3. www.blm.gov/education/tl/pages/page02.html.

4. Roderick Nash, *Wilderness and the American Mind*, 3rd ed. (New Haven, CT: Yale University Press, 1982).

5. Nash, *Wilderness and the American Mind*. Chapter 5 (p. 84) of Nash's book begins with an account of Thoreau's lecture at the Concord Lyceum, likely the first time he articulated this sentiment so clearly.

6. National Park Service, U.S. Department of the Interior, data on national park designation dates and land area reprinted in *The World Almanac and Book of Facts* (2000).

7. Frederick Jackson Turner, "The Problem of the West," *Atlantic Monthly*, September 1896, http://www.theatlantic.com/issues/95sep/ets/turn.htm. See Nash, *Wilderness and the American Mind*, p. 146, for a discussion of Turner's essay.

8. Frederick Jackson Turner, *The Frontier in American History* (New York: Holt, Rinehart & Winston, 1962). Turner's paper was presented at the meeting of the American Historical Association in Chicago on July 12, 1893.

9. See, for example, Patricia Limerick, *The Legacy of Conquest: The Unbroken Past of the American West* (New York: Norton, 1987).

10. John W. Reps, *The Making of Urban America: A History of City Planning in the United States* (Princeton, NJ: Princeton University Press, 1991).

11. Julia M. Wondolleck, *Public Lands Conflict and Resolution: Managing National Forest Disputes* (New York: Plenum, 1988).

12. Samuel P. Hays, *Conservation and the Gospel of Efficiency: The Progressive Conservation Movement, 1890–1920* (Cambridge, MA: Harvard University Press, 1959), 2, 28.

13. Gifford Pinchot, *Breaking New Ground* (New York: Harcourt, Brace, 1947).

14. Robert H. Nelson, *Public Lands and Private Rights: The Failure of Scientific Management* (Lanham, MD: Rowman & Littlefield, 1995).

15. Nelson, *Public Lands and Private Rights*.

16. *National Park Service Organic Act*, 16 *U.S. Code* 1 (August 25, 1916) (39 Stat. 535), as excerpted at http://www.nps.gov/legacy/mission.html.

17. Quoted in Daniel Kemmis, "Science's Role in Natural Resource Decisions," *Issues in Science and Technology* (Summer 2002): 31–34.

18. Charles E. Lindblom, "The Science of Muddling Through," in *Public Policy: The Essential Readings*, ed. Stella Z. Theodoulou and Matthew A. Cahn (Englewood Cliffs, NJ: Prentice Hall, 1955), 113–127.

19. Wondolleck, *Public Lands Conflict and Resolution*, 136.

20. This description of the public debate over snowmobiles in Yellowstone National Park is based on press releases from the National Park Service (http://www.nps.gov/yell), the BlueRibbon Coalition (http://www.sharetrails.org), and the Natural Resources Defense Council (http://www.nrdc.org), and the following news stories: Becky Bohrer (Associated Press), "Park Service to Phase Out Snowmobiles over Three Years," *Arizona Daily Sun*, November 24, 2000; Katharine Q. Seelye, "Yellowstone Snowmobile Ban May Be Lifted," New York Times News Service, June 25, 2001; John Keahey, "New Lawsuit Seeks to Restore Yellowstone Snowmobile Ban," *Salt Lake Tribune*, December 4, 2002; Brett French, "Yellowstone Snowmobile Ban Stirs Community's Fears," *Billings Gazette*, January 23, 2002; Brett French, "New Rules: Park Service Test Drives Regulations at West Entrance," *Billings Gazette*, January 24, 2002.

21. "Judge Revives Yellowstone Snowmobile Case," AP News Service, *Aberdeen News*, January 6, 2004; Rebecca Huntington, "Yellowstone Sleds Set Judges in Legal Dual," (sic), *Jackson Hole News and Guide*, January 28, 2004.

22. The new laws largely reinforced the presumption that experts should make the necessary tradeoffs and decisions as they seek to accommodate multiple conflicting interests within the professional expertise model of decision making. The scientific management paradigm is oriented toward production and use—not preservation.

23. Robert H. Nelson, "Is Libertarian Environmentalist an Oxymoron? The Crisis of Progressive Faith and the Environmental and Libertarian Search for a New Guiding Vision," in *The Next West: Public Lands, Community, and Economy in the American West*, ed. John A. Baden and Donald Snow (Washington, DC: Island Press, 1997).

24. Hays, *Conservation and the Gospel of Efficiency*, 28.

25. Daniel Kemmis, *This Sovereign Land: A New Vision for Governing the West* (Washington, DC: Island Press, 2001).

26. Kemmis, *This Sovereign Land*.

27. Nelson, "Is Libertarian Environmentalist an Oxymoron?" 1.

28. Hess, *Visions upon the Land*, 245.

29. Gifford Pinchot, *The Fight for Conservation* (Seattle: University of Washington Press, 1967), 319.

30. The Federal Web Locator (http://www.infoctr.edu/fwl/index.htm#fedweb.top) lists all federal government agencies in the United States. The site is owned and operated by the Center for Information Law and Policy.

31. *Breaking the Gridlock: Federal Land Pilot Projects in Idaho* (report to the Idaho State Board of Land Commissioners by the Federal Lands Task Force Working Group, December 2000).

32. Personal conversation with staff at Upper Klamath National Wildlife Refuge, January 15, 2003.

33. "Beaverhead County Resource Use Plan Amendment" (July 2001), http://www.beaverheadriver.com/bcruc.

34. Ray Ring, "Local Governments Tack an In-Your-Face Rush on Coalbed Methane," *High Country News*, September 2, 2002.

35. Ray Ring, "Backlash: Local Governments Tackle an In-Your-Face Rush on Coalbed Methane," *High Country News*, September 2, 2002.

36. Ring, "Backlash."

37. The standard biography of Powell and his ideas is Wallace Stegner, *Beyond the Hundredth Meridian: John Wesley Powell and the Second Opening of the West* (Boston: Houghton Mifflin, 1954; Lincoln: University of Nebraska Press, 1982).

38. Philip Babcock Gove, *Webster's Third New International Dictionary of the English Language*, unabridged (Springfield, MA: Merriam-Webster, 1971), 1912.

39. Cited in Doug Henton et al., *Regional Stewardship: A Commitment to Place*, monograph no. 1 (Denver, CO: Alliance for Regional Stewardship, 2000).

40. See Robert B. Keiter et. al., "Legal Perspectives on Ecosystem Management: Legitimizing a New Federal Land Management Policy," in *Ecological Stewardship: A Common Reference for Ecosystem Management*, ed. N. C. Johnson et al. (Kidlington, Oxford: Elsevier Science, 1999).

41. Craig W. Thomas, "Habitat Conservation Planning," in *Deepening Democracy: Institutional Innovations in Empowered Participatory Governance*, ed. Archon Fung and Erik Olin Wright (New York: Verso, forthcoming).

42. Western Water Policy Review Advisory Commission, *Water in the West: The Challenge for the Next Century* (Denver: Western Water Policy Review Advisory Commission, June 1998), xvi.

43. Committee of Scientists, U.S. Department of Agriculture, *Sustaining the People's Lands: Recommendations for Stewardship of the National Forests and Grasslands into the Next Century* (Washington, DC: Committee of Scientists, 1999).

44. Charles F. Wilkinson, *The Eagle Bird: Mapping a New West* (New York: Pantheon, 1992), 137.

45. For a published summary of this research project, see Matthew McKinney et al., "Regionalism in the West: An Inventory and Assessment," *Public Land and Resources Law Review* (Missoula: University of Montana, 2002), 101–91.

46. See Martha Derthick, *Between Nation and State: Regional Organizations of the United States* (Washington, DC: Brookings Institution, 1974).

47. Douglas R. Porter and Allan D. Wallis, *Exploring Ad Hoc Regionalism* (Cambridge, MA: Lincoln Institute of Land Policy, 2002).

48. Kemmis, *This Sovereign Land.*

49. See Lincoln Institute of Land Policy, http://www.lincolninst.edu; Alliance for

Regional Stewardship, http://www.regionalstewardship.org; and "Master of Science in Bioregional Planning" (State Board of Regents Program Approval), http://ww.usu/fsenate/Agenda/Senate/Apr01/Bioreg.html.

50. Nicholas K. Geranios, "Grizzly Experts Want Better Science on Bears," *Helena Independent Record* January 4, 2003, 5A.

51. Geranios, "Grizzly Experts Want Better Science on Bears."

52. Geranios, "Grizzly Experts Want Better Science on Bears."

53. Blue Ribbon Coalition, "NPS Decision in Yellowstone Locks Out Snowmobiles," www.sharetrails.org, media release, November 28, 2003.

54. Brett French, "New Rules: Park Service Test Drives New Regulation at West Entrance," *Billings Gazzette,* January 24, 2002; John Keahey, "New Lawsuit Seeks to Restore Yellowstone Snowmobile Ban," *Salt Lake Tribune,* December 4, 2002.

55. Jim Burchfield, "Finding Science's Voice in the Forest," in *Across the Great Divide: Explorations in Collaborative Conservation and the American West,* ed. Philip Brick, Donald Snow, and Sarah Van de Wetering (Washington, DC: Island Press, 2001), 236–43.

56. U.S. Forest Service, *The Process Predicament: How Statutory, Regulatory, and Administrative Factors Affect National Forest Management* (U.S. Forest Service, June 2002).

57. U.S. Forest Service, *The Process Predicament.*

58. U.S. Forest Service, *The Process Predicament.* This example is a synopsis of the Megram Fire Recovery Plan case study presented in appendix C, pp. C-21 through C-28.

59. Daniel Kemmis, "Science's Role in Natural Resource Decisions," 33.

60. John R. Ehrmann and Barbara L. Stinson, "Joint Fact-finding and the Use of Technical Experts," in *The Consensus Building Handbook: A Comprehensive Guide to Reaching Agreement,* ed. Lawrence Susskind, Sarah McKearnan, and Jennifer Thomas-Larmer (Thousand Oaks, CA: Sage, 1999), 376.

61. Frank Fischer, *Citizens, Experts, and the Environment: The Politics of Local Knowledge* (Durham, NC: Duke University Press, 2000).

62. Steven E. Daniels and Gregg B. Walker, *Working through Environmental Conflict: The Collaborative Learning Approach* (Westport, CT: Praeger, 2001).

63. Kai N. Lee, *Compass and Gyroscope: Integrating Science and Politics for the Environment* (Washington, DC: Island Press, 1993).

64. Matthew McKinney et al., *Community-based Collaboration on Federal Lands and Resources: An Evaluation of Participant Satisfaction* (Helena and Cambridge: Western Consensus Council and Consensus Building Institute, October 2003). Report available from www.umtpri.org.

---   4   ———

Integrating Science
and Citizens

By the late 1950s and on through the early 1970s, it became increasingly
clear that resource management agencies needed additional direction
on how to resolve the growing number of disputes among resource users.
During this period, decision makers began to recognize that natural resource decisions involved not just technical facts but also values. The public's growing concern about the impacts of natural resource use, combined
with an increasing awareness of the values of preservation and environmental quality, suggested that it is essential to involve not only scientific
and technical experts in the decision-making process but also citizens.
How should the best use of resources be determined? How should the inevitable disputes be resolved among competing natural resource uses and
values?

Theodore Lowi captures the essence of the political philosophy that
emerged from this era in *The End of Liberalism: Ideology, Policy, and the Crisis of Public Authority*. He argues that this new philosophy, referred to as "in-
terest-group liberalism," compels us to allow and encourage widespread
participation of affected interest groups throughout the decision-making

process.[1] Despite the obvious tension with the progressive-era model of scientific management and expert decision making, this idea of citizen participation has significantly influenced the framework for governing western resources. In the space of a few years, Congress passed the National Environmental Policy Act (NEPA) in 1969, the Forest and Rangeland Renewable Resources Planning Act in 1974, the National Forest Management Act in 1976, and the Federal Land Policy and Management Act in 1976—all of which contained provisions that require federal land management agencies to notify the public of proposed actions and give them an opportunity to review and comment.

With these new requirements, Congress hoped to create a process in which scientific and technical expertise could be integrated with social and political values, thereby producing fair, effective, and efficient decisions. Although government officials provide numerous opportunities under these laws for citizen participation, a sense of dissatisfaction with the process and its outcomes often remains. As David Mathews argues, something is missing in our framework for making public decisions.[2] While these laws provide more opportunities for citizens to participate in decision making, they indirectly reinforce the scientific management paradigm by embedding the requirements of public participation into the long-established administrative framework of expert decision making.

Philosophical Roots: The Rationale for Citizen Participation

Theodore Lowi may have captured the essence of an emerging social demand during the 1960s for citizen participation in public decisions, but the idea of citizens participating in public life is one of the oldest concepts in political theory. In *Politics*, Aristotle argues that citizens should be directly and actively involved in the affairs of government to fulfill their human potential. He asserts that the responsibilities of citizenship broaden one's perspective and deepen one's social identity, placing individual needs and interests in a larger context. By participating in public life, citizens develop the social and political skills necessary to maintain a democracy—they learn how to cooperate and manage conflict. Jean-Jacques Rousseau, in *The Social Contract*, likewise argued for the direct participation of citizens in public affairs. He believed that through the process of participation in public decisions, citizens would learn how their interests are related to the interests of others, and that this understanding, in turn, would generate a sense of a "general will" to serve the "general interest."[3]

In contrast to the views of Aristotle and Rousseau, which emphasize the role of citizenship and the communitarian values of citizen participation, Jeremy Bentham, in *An Introduction to the Principles of Morals and Legislation,* argues that the role of citizens in public life should be limited to electing legislators to represent their interests. Bentham rejects the presumption that people have a natural right to participate in government and believes that a community is nothing more than the sum of its parts—individual interests. If there is no community interest above and beyond the interests of individuals, then it stands to reason that a body of elected officials—legislators—is the most efficient way to maximize the interests of individuals. In what is supposed to be a responsive, adaptive decision-making system, citizens participate in the process and ensure that their interests are being met by holding elected officials accountable during elections.[4]

John Stuart Mill, in *Considerations on Representative Government,* returns to the propositions of Aristotle and Rousseau, arguing first and foremost that the role of government is "to promote the virtue and intelligence of the people themselves."[5] This is best accomplished, according to Mill, through active participation in the political process, where individuals are compelled to consider and weigh their private interests in the context of public interests.

While Mill seems passionate about the educational value of active citizen involvement in governance, he just as quickly shifts gears and asserts that the only practical way to organize the state is through a system of representative government, similar to the proposal of Bentham and Mill's father, James Mill. John Stuart Mill goes even further in designing a representative system of government by arguing that only the well educated are qualified to govern in a responsible fashion.[6] This presumption of elitist rule flies in the face of Mill's early contention about the significant role of direct citizen participation in the process of governance, a tension that Mill never fully resolves in his writing.

In formulating an American process, Thomas Jefferson agreed with Aristotle and Rousseau that citizens have not only a duty but a right to be involved in public affairs and governance. According to Jefferson, this civic "republican" form of government requires a high degree of interaction among citizens to facilitate face-to-face, hands-on problem solving.[7] This "politics of engagement," as characterized by Daniel Kemmis in *Community and the Politics of Place*, is based on the premise that people can rise above their individual interests to pursue a common good.[8]

James Madison and Alexander Hamilton apparently agreed with Jefferson's premise but argued that it would be difficult or impossible to apply at a national level. They articulated a much different role for citizen participation in *The Federalist Papers*. The Federalists started with the assumption that people naturally focus on their private interests, and that conflict among different groups of interests was inevitable. They believed that Jefferson's republican form of engagement would result in the "tyranny of the majority," so they argued for a political system that would balance or integrate the private interests of individuals in such a way that the highest good would emerge. Much like the invisible hand of Adam Smith's free market, the Federalists assumed that the highest good would emerge when individuals, acting alone, each pursued their private interest, not some indefinable common good.[9]

In the twentieth century, political theorists largely extended and refined the debate between Jefferson and Madison. Beginning with Walter Lippman's *Public Opinion* (1922) and reflected in most writing on political theory through Robert Dahl's *A Preface to Democratic Theory* (1956), pundits tended to focus on the impediments to direct citizen participation in the face of rapidly advancing urbanization and industrialization, followed by bigger government and organized interest groups. In most cases, the conclusions of these writers is that citizen participation must and should be limited to electing public officials and participating in interest groups to influence the political process. As Terry Cooper observes, the normative views of these authors seem to be based more on the way the world is, rather than on what it ought to be.[10]

By contrast, more recent work in political theory has emphasized the need for and the value of direct citizen participation in public decision making. In a little-known article titled "A Critique of the Elitist Theory of Democracy," Jack Walker argues that the work of earlier twentieth-century political theorists abandons the democratic ideal of popular sovereignty and direct citizen participation in shaping public policy. Building on the insights of Walker and others, a new theory of deliberative democracy has emerged during the past few years that addresses the inadequacies of current public processes.[11] In sum, deliberation provides an opportunity for citizens to be intimately engaged in public dialogue, determining the legitimacy of public policy options. People with diverse views are expected to articulate their claims in terms that the public as a whole can understand, if not accept. One critical ingredient of deliberation is that people must be able to reflect on competing arguments, realizing that preferences and positions are likely to evolve as different ideas and facts emerge during a dialogue.

Based on this brief overview of the philosophical roots of citizen participation, five basic reasons to involve citizens in public decisions can be seen. The first, ably argued by Aristotle, Rousseau, and Jefferson, is that citizen participation is a natural right as a member of a democratic polity. To the degree that citizens are not involved in shaping and influencing their government, it becomes something other than a democracy.

Second, citizen participation provides an ongoing sense of accountability to make sure that public decisions fulfill the will of citizens. Citizen input and advice allow public officials to be more responsive and adaptive, to build political support for a policy or program, and to facilitate ownership and improve the process of implementation. Without such opportunities, citizens may feel compelled to protest decisions or even overthrow a particular regime.

Third, citizens can help create better policies and programs and improve the quality of the final decision and outcome. This rationale presumes that citizens have information and ideas to contribute to the process of making public decisions. Such decisions involve choices among competing needs and interests, and it is imperative to gather information from the people who espouse them. It is also important to acknowledge the value of "local" or "indigenous" knowledge as a way to complement and supplement the information of experts.[12] Many people are not scientists, but they are familiar with the social, economic, and environmental dynamics of a particular place and have knowledge that is useful in solving public problems.

Fourth, as argued by Aristotle and Rousseau, citizen participation is essential for complete human fulfillment. People do not fully realize their talents and abilities apart from the experience of sharing in governing. Personal fulfillment is often touted as the primary reward of the community service movement and recent proposals for civic engagement, volunteerism, and renewed citizenship.

The fifth and final reason to encourage citizen participation is arguably the most common and least satisfying—to fulfill legal requirements.

Legal Framework for Public Participation

Public participation emerged in the mid-twentieth century in response to the progressive-era model of delegating authority to experts to implement and, in some cases, shape public policy.[13] Beginning in the late nineteenth century, as discussed in chapter 3, the resolution of disputes over western resources became dominated by the scientific management model of public administration. The need for scientific and technical expertise to effectively manage natural resources, along with an ever-expanding governmental bureaucracy, increasingly came into conflict with two core values of democracy—transparency (or accountability) and participation.

During the New Deal era, as the federal government expanded its role in the nation's economy, Congress first responded to this need for greater accountability by passing the Federal Register Act of 1936. This act allowed public access to official documents related to agency rulemaking, proposed rulemaking, and other formal actions. While this was a small step by today's standards, it represents the first formal acknowledgment of the value of citizen participation in public decision making.

Ten years later, in 1946, Congress passed the Administrative Procedures Act (APA), significantly expanding the role of citizen participation. The APA established a systematic, consistent process that federal agencies must use when making law through administrative rulemaking. Rather than simply providing public access to government records, the APA requires federal agencies to be more proactive by providing public notice about proposed rules, information on which the rules are based, and an opportunity to review and comment on the proposed rules. It also allows for judicial review of the rulemaking process. The federal APA has been adapted and adopted by most state and local jurisdictions and continues to be the cornerstone for citizen participation in all public policy arenas, including western resources.

From the late 1940s through the early 1960s, most government agencies focused on providing information and education to the public.[14] These early efforts focused more on maintaining the authority and discretion of public administrators and less on providing opportunities for meaningful citizen participation. They emphasized the one-way flow of information—from agency to public. Beginning in the 1960s, however, in response to the growing belief that government "experts" were making decisions that did not reflect the will of the public, citizens demanded an opportunity to be consulted and heard on decisions that affected their lives.[15] This shift in the public suggested a new model for public decision making, one based on pluralism, which asserts that scientific and technical experts cannot independently arrive at what is in the "public interest." Rather, government administrators should arbitrate among different interests within the public. In contrast to seeking the "greatest good for the greatest number" through a process that involved only scientific and technical experts (the mantra of Gifford Pinchot and other champions of scientific management), pluralism suggests that the public good can be defined only through a process of dialogue among competing interests, including citizens and scientific experts. This model would need a two-way flow of information, allowing the public to inform agency decisions.

Building on this premise, Lowi concludes that it is imperative to allow and encourage the widespread participation of affected interest groups throughout the decision-making process.[16] Sherry Arnstein, in one of the classic articles on citizen participation, captured this emerging sentiment by articulating a "ladder of citizen participation." Arnstein explicitly states that her practical typology was "designed to be provocative" by focusing on the redistribution of power as an essential element of meaningful citizen participation.[17]

This new theory of public decision making and dispute resolution, and the critical role of citizens, catalyzed a string of new legislation that greatly expanded citizen access to government information and decision making. From 1966 to 1976, Congress passed the Freedom of Information Act (1966), the Federal Advisory Committee Act (1972), the Privacy Act (1974), and the Government in the Sunshine Act (1976), creating a basic framework for citizen participation throughout the federal government. Congress passed a similar set of laws that gave citizens more access to the process of making decisions and resolving disputes over the use of western resources. The National Environmental Policy Act (1969), the National Forest Management Act (1974), and the Federal Land Policy and Management Act (1976) govern the processes for citizen participation and decision making on federal lands and resources. Other laws, such as the Endangered Species Act (1973), while grounded in the scientific management approach, provide additional opportunities for citizen participation. These laws require natural resource management agencies to weigh social, economic, and environmental factors but do not set priorities among competing policy objectives. In lieu of telling the agencies what to do, Congress told them to "consult the public" at every stage of the decision-making process. State and local jurisdictions throughout the West have integrated similar expectations for public participation in land use, natural resource, and environmental decisions.[18]

In the context of western resources, these new laws and requirements for public participation emerged for three reasons. First, many more people became recreational users of western lands and thus had a stake in how the land was managed. Until the 1960s, the primary stakeholders of federal lands were farmers, ranchers, loggers, miners, and other commodity interests. Second, the ideology of environmental quality and preservation, which had been around since at least the turn of the century, gained a new urgency when Rachel Carson struck a public nerve with her best-selling *Silent Spring* (1962), warning of widespread ecological degradation. Consequently, during the 1960s and 1970s, the "public" in public participation was almost synonymous with conservation and environmental interests.[19] And finally, the "public" was better educated and more sophisticated politically than it was during the first five decades of the twentieth century. Consequently, people were less inhibited about speaking out and challenging the analysis and conclusions of public officials and scientific experts.

During the past thirty years, scholars and practitioners have developed a variety of processes to inform and educate the public and to seek their input and advice. Participation may be either indirect (as in electing representatives, responding to public opinion surveys, and contributing financial resources to political organizations) or direct (as in participating on advisory committees or in interest groups, presenting information at public hearings, and so on). Table 4.1 presents one way to think about the spectrum of opportunities for citizen participation, including the objectives of such participation, the role of public officials, and the promise to citizens. The column on the far right, "Civic Entrepreneurs," recognizes that a growing movement exists in which citizens, with or without the authority of government, are convening public forums for multiple objectives.[20] This movement, which we address in chapter 6, raises an important set of questions about the efficacy of existing institutional arrangements for public engagement and dispute resolution.

TABLE 4.1 Citizen Participation Spectrum

Objective	Inform and Educate	Seek Input and Advice	Build Agreement	Empower Citizens	Civic Entrepreneurs
Role of public officials	Provide information to help citizens understand problems, options, or solutions, and then decide.	Consult individuals or a diverse group of people, and then decide.	Work with a diverse group of stakeholders, and share problem-solving responsibility.	Delegate the decision to citizens.	Varies
Promise to citizens	We will keep you informed.	We will keep you informed; listen to, acknowledge, and try to incorporate your concerns into the decision; and provide feedback on how your input influenced the decision.	We will work with you side by side to formulate solutions and will incorporate any recommendations into the decisions to the maximum extent possible; we will not abdicate our authority to make decisions.	We will attempt to implement your recommendations consistent with relevant laws and policies.	Citizens take the initiative and convene public forums for multiple objectives. Issue-specific. Place-specific. Ongoing forums.

Low	Medium	High	Highest

Degree of Citizen Influence

Is Public Participation Working?

Table 4.2 (at the end of the chapter) presents a variety of tools and techniques that are available to achieve different public participation objectives. Although many of these tools and techniques provide innovative means for public participation, the ongoing challenge for public officials is to integrate the conflicting values and interests of citizens with the complex scientific and technical aspects of environmental decisions.

Symptomatic of this challenge, public participation under NEPA and similar state acts has been criticized from every angle. While many proposals are publicly scrutinized and processed with relatively little fanfare, project proponents sometimes complain of unwarranted and costly delays. The public argues that it is not given ample time to reflect and comment or that comments are collected but not heeded. For their part, agencies say that public participation requirements strain already limited budgets and staff time. Typically, only citizens with an identifiable stake in an issue or decision participate in the process, thereby biasing "public opinion." These criticisms raise an obvious question about whether public participation is working in these circumstances, yet there has been surprisingly little critical analysis of the effectiveness of public participation under NEPA and state environmental policy acts.[21]

One recent study evaluated the effectiveness of public participation under the Montana Environmental Policy Act (MEPA), and its results are representative of other studies. In 1999, the Montana legislature asked the state's Environmental Quality Council to study the efficacy of the twenty-eight-year-old Montana Environmental Policy Act, a state statute that mirrors NEPA. As part of that larger study, the Montana Consensus Council surveyed citizens, project proponents, and agency officials to evaluate the effectiveness of public involvement under MEPA.[22] Survey respondents agreed that public involvement in MEPA decisions is good policy but that, in practice, it needs to be improved. People said that the purpose of public involvement is not clear, and so the quality of public involvement processes varies from one agency to the next and from case to case. Saying that agencies could do more to encourage public participation, citizens complained that agencies meet the letter of the law but not its spirit by burying public notices of upcoming MEPA processes in one-inch classified ads at the back of newspapers. Agencies said that public comment is rarely well informed or substantive, but citizens argued that agencies don't provide adequate, timely information in plain language. Citizens also said that agencies favor economic and scientific information, too often ignoring comments that convey less tangible social, cultural, aesthetic, and natural values. Finally, one of the key concerns voiced by many citizens and project proponents alike was that agencies solicit comments but then don't seem to listen. Agencies, they said, rarely show whether comments were carefully considered or how they were incorporated into the final decision. They felt that part of the process should be more transparent and interactive.

While the "notice and comment" approach to public participation is a significant improvement over the earlier practice of simply providing access and information, participants are often dissatisfied with the process and its outcomes. Too often, agencies see the public comment period as an opportunity to "sell" their preferred approach at information fairs and public hearings, rather than actually listening to what the public has to say. The public's response to such tactics is predictable: suspicion that the agency has already made its decision, and frustration at not being heard. David Mathews, in *Politics for People*, helps explain this dissatisfaction by suggesting that something is missing in politics as usual, namely "a diversity of perspectives, listening, and careful weighing of trade-offs . . . the ability to keep an open mind, to stand in another person's shoes, to change, and to make decisions with others."[23] In short, we lack opportunities for public deliberation. Most, if not all, of our public institutions seem to foster a self-centered, adversarial approach to public dialogue. We have very few places where citizens and leaders with diverse viewpoints can engage in public deliberation.

Daniel Kemmis, in *Community and the Politics of Place*, goes further by arguing that our dissatisfaction with existing institutional arrangements for public decision making can be traced back to the philosophical differences between Madison and Jefferson.[24] The debate over the location of power in public life has always been, in Kemmis's terms, between Jefferson's preference for "face-to-face" democracy and Madison's preference for a "procedural republic," one of the defining characteristics of our current system.

Potential Tools—Clarifying Roles, Negotiated Rulemaking, and Engaging Unaffiliated Citizens

To improve the practice of public participation in western resource decisions, it may be useful to start with an assertion—adapted from Daniel Yankelovich's *The Magic of Dialogue*[25]—that the point of engaging citizens in dialogue is that adding the value-rich perspectives of the public to the information-rich perspectives of experts allows us to create more effective public policy. Based on the research reported above, we know that citizens want understandable information, a clear role, a significant and meaningful role, a better understanding of how things work, respect, and responsiveness.

These objectives can be achieved by promoting a variety of public participation processes that are transparent, participatory, interactive, and accountable. To move in this direction, public officials and agencies should
start by adopting the principles of public participation articulated by the International Association for Public Participation (IAP2):

1. The public should have a say in decisions about actions that affect people's lives.
2. Public participation includes the promise that the public's contribution will influence the decision.
3. The public participation process communicates the interests and
   meets the process needs of all participants.
4. The process seeks out and facilitates the involvement of those
   potentially affected.
5. The process involves participants in defining how they participate.
6. The process communicates to participants how their input affected the decision.
7. The process provides participants with the information they
   need to participate in a meaningful way.[26]

To its credit, the Bureau of Land Management (BLM) incorporated many
of these principles when it began a resource management planning process
for the Dillon Field Office in southwest Montana (as briefly described in
chapter 3). In 2001, BLM officials hired the Montana Consensus Council to
survey stakeholders to determine how they would want to participate in the
planning process. This was a landmark step; for the first time on a project of
this scale, the BLM was asking citizens to help design the process by which
they would exchange information and ideas with the agency and shape the
resulting resource management plan. Surveys were mailed to more than
1,000 people and organizations, and facilitators interviewed more than 100
stakeholders face-to-face in like-minded groups.

Not surprisingly, some people said they were most comfortable participating in the familiar NEPA process. Others were worried that an intensive
public participation process with a citizen working group would likely lead
to burnout over the course of a multiyear planning effort. In the end, the
BLM agreed to convene small citizen work groups, under the auspices of the
preexisting Resource Advisory Council, to study and make recommendations on specific issues, such as Wild and Scenic River designations, areas of

critical environmental concern, and travel management. By focusing on one issue at a time, these groups were able to complete their work in three to eight months, while the Resource Advisory Council provided coordination from one issue to the next and continuity during the prolonged planning process.

This example suggests that it is valuable to create opportunities for citizens to participate throughout the public decision-making process. Table 4.3 illustrates one way to integrate more meaningful opportunities for public participation into the standard decision-making process articulated by NEPA—from beginning to end. In March 1999, the Center for the Rocky Mountain West and others convened a workshop to explore how collaborative processes might improve decision making under NEPA.[27] Building on the work of the 1999 workshop, the U.S. Institute for Environmental Conflict Resolution created a panel of experts in 2002 to develop recommendations on how collaborative strategies can best be incorporated into NEPA.[28] The Environmental Protection Agency's new policy on public involvement, and the recommendations from the Committee of Scientists on national forest management planning, likewise encourage opportunities for "early and meaningful public involvement."[29]

Incorporating the IAP2 principles into standard operating procedures will require public officials, particularly scientific and technical experts, to rethink and revise their role in the decision-making process. Historically, agencies have played a well-defined role with clear expectations—decision maker and technical expert. As decision-making processes become more participatory and transparent, public officials understandably struggle to define their appropriate role.

Clarify the Roles of Public Officials

Based on an examination of sixty-five cases, Julia Wondolleck and Clare Ryan offer a useful framework for thinking about the different roles that public officials play in effective collaborative processes.[30] They conclude that public officials should play three distinct and essential roles: stakeholder, partner, and decision maker (or leader).

In the cases reviewed, public officials who were effective began by acknowledging that their agencies had a stake in the issues and proceedings. As public servants, they were entrusted to pursue the mandates set upon their agencies through the political process. This means that public officials should responsibly advocate their agencies' interests in public deliberations.

TABLE 4.3 Public Participation under NEPA: A Checklist of Strategies

Key Project Steps	Strategies
Project conception	• Consult an experienced facilitator or mediator to help determine what type of public participation may be appropriate and when. • If some type of public participation may be appropriate, include resources (time, money, and staff) in your project plan and budgets.
Preproject analysis	• Use an impartial third party to assess the situation or conflict. • Identify parties, issues, and options on how to proceed. • Allow citizens to help design a public participation process that will meet their needs and interests within the constraints under which the agency must operate.
Develop proposed action	• Consult stakeholders—citizens and other officials—in developing a proposed action; seek agreement on the proposed action. • Interview parties one-on-one; convene stakeholder groups; convene a broad-based, multiparty group. • Foster mutual education through joint fact finding and exchanging information.
Scoping	• Consider different processes for gathering public input and advice (public meetings, open houses, surveys, stakeholder meetings, study circles, and so forth). • Use an impartial facilitator to convene and manage large, controversial public meetings.
Validate the issues	• Based on the public input and advice, consult stakeholders—either individually or through an inclusive working group—to foster a common understanding of NEPA significant issues.
Develop alternatives	• Convene a working group of stakeholders to develop alternatives. • Encourage citizens and other stakeholders to develop and submit their own alternative. • Use stakeholders as a sounding board to ensure that the range of alternatives responds to NEPA issues and unresolved issues.
Identify preferred alternatives	• Use expert panels and stakeholder groups to help analyze alternatives. • Use agreed-upon criteria to evaluate alternatives.

TABLE 4.3 Continued

Key Project Steps	Strategies
Identify preferred alternatives (cont.)	• Clarify the distinction between facts (science) and values (goals or desired future conditions).
Analyze EA or DEIS public comments	• Convene a working group of stakeholders to review public comments, clarify dominant themes, validate or revise NEPA issues, and identify criteria for the selected alternative.
Select an alternative	• Before the responsible official announces the selected alternative, he or she may consult stakeholders to confirm decision and rationale.
Appeal	• Resolve outstanding issues through informal, nonadversarial processes of negotiation and mediation.
Litigation	• Consult Department of Justice and Office of the General Counsel on available options to resolve disputes. • Seek opportunities for settlement negotiations, mediation, and/or arbitration.
Post decision	• Convene a working group to monitor and evaluate implementation and to suggest appropriate changes to the plan of action.

Those who were effective also recognized that other people with diverse views and interests shared a stake in the issue at hand. To effectively resolve the dispute or shape a mutually agreeable solution, people—including public officials—worked together as partners in the problem-solving process. Among other things, this means providing scientific and technical information (a role that agencies have historically played) and sharing responsibility to identify solutions to common problems (a role that agencies seem reluctant to play).

Finally, public officials who were effective realized that, in addition to participating as a stakeholder and a partner, they were also the final decision maker. As the ultimate authority, the agencies not only have the legitimacy to convene such processes but also provide leadership when the other participants look to them for guidance, direction and, at the appropriate time, decisions.

According to this study, public officials who participated in a peripheral manner, such as by only providing technical data and expertise or by serving solely in an oversight capacity, were far less effective in helping the participants reach and implement an agreement. Furthermore, and contrary to common practice and conventional wisdom, Wondolleck and Ryan say that the roles of facilitator and agency representative are not compatible. Other participants expect public officials to actively represent their agencies, undistracted by the duties of facilitation. Also, to be credible and impartial to each of the participants, the facilitator should have no substantive stake in the process or outcome. As the ultimate decision makers, agency officials clearly do have a stake. Switching between the two roles can be difficult at best, and also leads to perceived or real conflicts of interest and complaints of bias or undue agency influence on other interests at the table.

Seeing public officials as stakeholders, partners, and decision makers is certainly a richer and more useful way of thinking than pigeonholing public officials as decision makers and experts. And, with more training and experience, public officials are likely to become more comfortable and effective in these new roles. But public officials must want to embrace these new roles and must demonstrate the will to give citizens a greater voice in shaping policies that affect their lives.

Unfortunately, according to Daniel Yankelovich in *The Magic of Dialogue,* "the political will is just about nil." He argues that "elites," including public officials, pay lip service to meaningful public participation, but in practice many don't want to do it, and they see no compelling reasons why they should. Yankelovich suggests that the resistance of elites stems from two sources: "One is a fear of losing status through sharing the power of policy making with the mass public. The other is a blind spot—an unthinking assumption that the public's views are so ill informed, narrowly self-interested, unrealistic, and moralistic that they cannot add anything of value to the decision-making process."[31] Indeed, a public official at a recent land use planning conference in the West remarked, publicly, that one of his colleagues had characterized the public as "stupid," and that he, as the technical expert, should be allowed to make decisions and do his job. Robert Moses, as reported in *The Powerbroker,* frames this sentiment only slightly more elegantly: "I love the public. It's people I hate."[32]

These are harsh words and certainly do not characterize the intentions or practice of all public officials or natural resource managers. (Some public officials are simply trying to live up to what they see as their mandate to represent the larger public interest, without necessarily seeking public advice on what that interest is.) But this elitist attitude does exist in some corners as a carryover from decades of scientific specialists holding authority to make decisions and resolve disputes among competing interests. Yankelovich concedes that "the picture is not as discouraging as these attitudes might suggest. Powerful forces at work in the society are pressuring elites to develop a more dialogic relationship with the public. Also, when we dig beneath the surface attitudes of elite's resistance, we find grounds for hope."[33]

On the one hand, Yankelovich and others see hope in emerging models of leadership that place an emphasis on building relationships. Variously referred to as relational, facilitative, and collaborative leadership, this style emphasizes "cooperating, conducting dialogue, crossing boundaries, seeking alignment on a shared vision, tolerating complexity, and developing networks of relationships." It sharply contrasts with the traditional model of command-and-control leadership, according to Yankelovich, where decision makers articulate objectives, select a "preferred alternative," and rely on the familiar carrot-and-stick or decide-and-defend strategies to battle toward implementation.[34]

On the other hand, it is arguably a more difficult challenge to address why public officials resist integrating ideas and information from citizens into the policy-making process. It is challenging in the first instance because this resistance is in part founded on legitimate concerns. Yankelovich asserts: "It is romantic nonsense to assume that people who haven't given a moment's thought to an issue are going to be able to make a constructive contribution to it. And regarding many issues, the public has not given them a moment's thought."[35] In the MEPA study, agency officials consistently raised concerns about the ability of citizens to make informed comments and suggestions.

But this is exactly where genuine dialogue—as conducted under the IAP2 principles—can effectively supplement other opportunities for citizen participation, such as polls, debates, referenda, lobbies, and interest groups. Dialogue gives citizens (and public officials) an opportunity to mutually learn more about the issues, the different interests, and the consequences of alternative courses of action. It is a solution to the problem of an uninformed citizenry. In a busy, diverse democracy such as ours in the United States, it may be the best solution.[36] While such an approach may be practical and desirable to address any number of western resource issues, it does become somewhat more challenging when addressing federal lands and resources. The challenge here is how to effectively integrate "national interests," defined by the concerns of 295 million people, many of them unaffiliated with any identifiable interest group and many of them unaware of the stake they hold in these resources. Later in this chapter, we talk about some promising proxies or strategies to capture the input and advice of a representative sample of unaffiliated, rank-and-file citizens.

The most insidious obstacle to more meaningful citizen participation, according to Yankelovich, is "a set of deeply rooted but erroneous assumptions built into our culture's dominant mode of knowledge."[37] Most public officials, including natural resource professionals, assume that knowledge is synonymous with information. From this perspective, it makes sense that citizens have less knowledge (information) than experts and professionals. Moreover, the paradigm of expert decision making assumes that (1) policy making requires expert knowledge, (2) expert knowledge involves specialized factual information, and (3) citizens cannot usefully contribute to policy making because they lack this specialized information. These assumptions, Yankelovich argues, and the degree to which they are unexamined and taken for granted, are far more influential in undercutting the motivation of public officials to engage in dialogue with citizens than mere reluctance to share power.

There are, however, cures for what ails us. As discussed in chapter 3, one promising approach to improving citizen participation in public decision making, and to overcome concern about the public's allegedly inferior level of information and understanding, is joint fact finding. Another worthwhile approach is negotiated rulemaking.

Foster Negotiated Rulemaking

Government agencies with regulatory authority typically codify those regulations through a process known as administrative rulemaking. In the traditional rulemaking process, the agency develops a draft of the proposed rule and then seeks input and advice from citizens. Agencies may occasionally consult the people affected by the proposed regulations, informally and one stakeholder at a time, as it prepares the proposed rule.

Negotiated rulemaking, in contrast, provides an opportunity for the stakeholders and agency representatives to jointly prepare the text of a proposed rule *before* the agency submits the rule to the formal rulemaking process.[38] In a typical negotiated rulemaking process, a facilitator helps stakeholder and agency representatives discuss the issues, understand one another's interests and constraints, and develop mutually agreeable solutions. This group can also help shepherd a proposed rule through the formal rulemaking process, explaining and defending its components to decision makers. In some cases, negotiations continue after the formal public comment period to allow adjustments during implementation of the rule.

The idea of negotiated rulemaking, also known as regulatory negotiation or "reg-neg," first emerged in 1982; a year later, the Federal Aviation Administration became the first federal agency to use negotiated rulemaking, successfully revising rules governing flight and rest time for domestic airline pilots.[39] To date, the U.S. Environmental Protection Agency is the most consistent and committed user of negotiated rulemaking at the federal level, accounting for about one-third of all federal reg-negs. At least seven states have also enacted negotiated rulemaking legislation, but there has been little systematic analysis of activity at the state level.

Montana adopted a negotiated rulemaking statute in 1993 and has used it sparingly for a number of reasons.[40] One of the state's earliest and most successful uses of negotiated rulemaking revolved around recreational access to state school trust lands. When Montana became a state in 1889, the U.S. government set aside two sections of every township to support public education. The Montana constitution requires the Land Board to manage these 5.2 million acres to maximize the financial return to the school trust. The Department of Natural Resources and Conservation (DNRC) leases most of these lands to farmers and ranchers. DNRC allows lessees to manage the land, a practice that has fostered feelings of ownership and exclusive use among many lessees.

In the 1950s, recreationists argued that school trust lands belong to the public and should be open to recreational use. A multiple-use policy was written into state statutes in the 1970s, but in 1979 the Land Board authorized lessees to deny hunting access. In 1988, a coalition of recreationists filed suit against DNRC and the Land Board to secure access to school trust lands. DNRC tried to negotiate a settlement, but negotiations broke down in 1990. The state district court recommended that the parties address the issue through legislation. In response, House Bill (HB) 778 was drafted and passed in the 1991 legislature. The bill allowed certain types of recreational use (hunting and fishing) of state school trust lands and required recreationists to buy a $5 license to compensate the trust.

In 1993, recreationists petitioned the Land Board to allow other types of recreation in accordance with HB 778. The Land Board voted to expand allowable uses to include not only hunting and fishing but also hiking, bird watching, and berry picking. The lessees responded by closing nearly 2 million acres of private land to recreationists. The closures occurred during the peak of fall hunting season. The lessees believed that, in supporting HB 778, they had agreed to give up their right to control access by hunters and anglers in return for recreationists abandoning their request for expanded access. The recreationists argued that the lessees never had a right to control access.

In October 1993, the Land Board asked the lessees and recreationists to sit down and resolve the issue within sixty days. The parties agreed and created an ad hoc committee composed of four representatives each from the Montana Wildlife Federation and the Montana Stockgrowers Association, and one representative from the Montana Farm Bureau. The committee invited the Montana Consensus Council to convene and facilitate negotiations.

In a series of meetings from November 1993 through January 1994, the committee worked out agreements on key provisions in the rules. The parties agreed that lessees could condition or deny access to state land for selected management reasons. They identified recreational uses that could cause problems for lessees, including motorized vehicles, fires, pets, horses, camping, and concentrated uses. The parties also developed a process for resolving site-specific disputes, and they agreed to a moratorium on any legislative, administrative, or judicial activity to amend the agreement. They also agreed to reconvene in December 1994 to assess these and other emerging guidelines. The issue of when and how people should notify lessees before recreating on leased land proved to be more difficult to resolve. The committee requested and received an extension of the sixty-day deadline, but the issue remained unresolved when the committee presented its consensus recommendations to the Land Board on January 18, 1994.

The board tentatively adopted the recommendations, tabling consideration of the notification procedures. DNRC and the committee then worked side by side to revise the existing administrative rules based on the negotiated agreement, prepare an environmental assessment, and hold four public hearings on the proposed rule. During this time, the Consensus Council shuttled among the participants to seek agreement on the notification issue. The day before the Land Board's next meeting, the committee finally agreed that recreationists should personally notify a lessee prior to staying overnight, using horses, or discharging firearms on leased land. If the lessee was unavailable, the recreationist could leave a note in a drop box at the lessee's ranch.

Based on the agreement negotiated among the participants, the Land Board adopted the revised administrative rules on June 6, 1994. The lessees gained increased control over access to leased land under specified conditions, while recreationists gained increased access to state school trust land.

Although negotiated rulemaking has proven to be an effective tool for drafting widely accepted, durable regulations, it is not appropriate in all circumstances for several reasons.[41] First, many agencies rely on informal conferences and consultations as a means of obtaining the viewpoints and advice of interested persons. Cary Coglianese, a professor at the John F. Kennedy School of Government at Harvard University and one of the most outspoken critics of negotiated rulemaking, argues that the performance of negotiated rulemaking has failed "in large part because of the strength of agencies in using less intensive methods of negotiation and public input in the context of conventional rulemaking. These methods, which include individual meetings, public hearings, and ongoing advisory committees, provide agencies with information about technical aspects of regulation as well as the interests of affected parties." If other, less-intensive methods of public participation are effective—particularly from the perspective of citizens and stakeholders—the more formal process of negotiated rulemaking may be unnecessary.

Second, some agencies and participants have noted that the process is cumbersome and resource intensive. Agencies often hire a facilitator to manage the process, and participants can expect to attend regular meetings for up to a year or more. Between meetings, they have documents and data to review and proposals to generate and ponder. Stakeholders and agency staff alike may dedicate hundreds of hours and substantial funds to follow a rule from start to finish. Professor Coglianese claims that only 1 percent of all administrative rules promulgated by the federal government from 1983 through 1996 were developed through negotiated rulemaking, largely because of the costs and uncertainties associated with the process. Proponents of the process respond that, when used in appropriate situations, the long-term benefits of reg-neg—more effective rules and stakeholder buy-in, with fewer recurring problems—more than outweigh the short-term costs and uncertainties.

Third, negotiated rulemaking may actually foster conflict stemming from determining membership on committees, the consistency of final rules with negotiated agreements, and the potential for heightened sensitivity to adverse aspects of rules. Given that reg-neg is designed to shape a proposed rule, which is then subject to the formal process of public review and comment, the sponsoring agency may need to amend the proposed rule to accommodate new interests and information. Such amendments may require a deviation from the consensus proposal, which may create additional tension. These are all legitimate concerns about the appropriate use of negotiated rulemaking. However, most of them can be addressed by relying on the simple principle of allowing citizens and stakeholders to be actively engaged throughout every step of the process: jointly defining the problem, creating the committee, hosting informal public meetings, and responding to public comments.

Finally, some administrative agencies have not engaged in negotiated rulemaking because the appropriate situation has not emerged. Philip Harter, one of the architects of negotiated rulemaking, suggested that these processes should be reserved for "highly complex, politicized rules— the very kind that stall agencies when using traditional or conventional procedures."[42] When used in this type of situation, according to Harter, reg-neg has been remarkable in fulfilling its promise to develop administrative rules that are substantively better, more widely accepted, and less likely to appeal. The value of reg-neg is not only that it provides another opportunity for public participation but also—and perhaps more importantly—that it allows direct negotiations among stakeholders and the agencies.

Still in its infancy, negotiated rulemaking will no doubt be improved in the years to come. By documenting cases and disseminating best practices, scholars and mediators are helping public officials and others better understand when reg-neg is appropriate and how to design and coordinate such processes to ensure their effectiveness.

Experiment with Strategies to Engage "Unaffiliated Citizens"

Citizen juries represent another innovative approach to bringing citizens more directly into the process of shaping policy, thereby building agreement and preventing disputes.[43] The brainchild of Ned Crosby and the Minneapolis-based Jefferson Center, a *citizen jury* consists of a group of citizens selected at random and stratified to represent the relevant community. Jurors are typically paid to participate in a five-day session, during which they listen to and question testimony from experts on the issues under consideration and from people representing diverse points of view. Ultimately, the jurors make recommendations on the policy questions or "charge" articulated by the project sponsors. Crosby suggests that the process works better on value questions than technical issues, which means that it might be applicable to disputes over such highly charged western issues as the reintroduction of wolves or grizzly bears, limits to growth, and other value-based disputes.

This "social contract" approach to public decision making, as described by Crosby, is similar to other experiments, such as the Danish Consensus Conference, the Future Search Conference, the Wisdom Council, and deliberative polling.[44] These processes share several common characteristics: being open to public scrutiny, relying on face-to-face communication, emphasizing the importance of respectful dialogue and good information, involving a cross section of the community, and being fair and neutral. The intent of all of these techniques is to generate informed input from unaffiliated, rank-and-file citizens, people who might not otherwise participate in public dialogue and decision making.

The Jefferson Center has used citizen juries for addressing environmental issues related to the impacts of agriculture on water quality, ranking environmental risks and priorities, and restructuring Minnesota's electric utility industry. One of the center's early projects consisted of five regional citizen juries considering the effects of farm chemicals and nutrients on Minnesota's famous lakes and rivers. Each regional jury presented findings on the significance of the issue, the need for action, how much money should be spent to address the problem and who should pay, and recommendations for specific action. Three members from each of the regional juries then sat on a statewide jury to refine those recommendations into a final report.

Crosby and others conclude that this project was a modified success.[45] Both regional and statewide panelists found it very difficult to reach any conclusions. In addition, panelists expressed concern that the facilitators of the statewide panel were not as impartial and nonpartisan as the moderators of the regional panels. Nonetheless, the sponsoring organizations enacted some of the recommendations that came out of the citizen jury. As a result, the Minnesota legislature agreed to spend an additional $10 million to address nonpoint sources of pollution and to implement a tree-planting program.[46] The sponsoring organizations and the Minnesota legislature, however, did not adopt the majority of the jurors' recommendations. This lack of responsiveness suggests that citizen-driven processes need to be carefully timed and strategically linked to established decision-making processes if they hope to influence public policy.[47]

For example, Governor Mike Leavitt of Utah initiated a collaborative polling process in 2002 to determine if citizens wanted to create a 620,000-acre San Rafael National Monument in Emory County. Leavitt took this approach after witnessing the controversy sparked by Secretary of Interior Bruce Babbitt and President Bill Clinton when they used executive orders to create several national monuments in the West, including Utah's Grand Staircase–Escalante, with little or no public input.

Working with faculty from the Kennedy School of Government at Harvard University, Governor Leavitt was poised to sponsor a "collaborative polling" project.[48] In this process, an experienced facilitator or mediator works with government and interest group representatives to design a survey of public opinion about a proposed action. The questionnaire provides relevant information and perspectives on the proposal to allow participants to reach informed judgments. After reviewing the background information, the participants—who are randomly selected from the appropriate population—are asked to indicate their level of support for each policy option presented. A typical questionnaire takes about thirty minutes to complete and provides decision makers and interest groups alike with accurate information about the degree of public support for alternative solutions to public problems.

Ironically, as the collaborative polling effort was getting under way, Emory County sponsored a nonbinding referendum on November 5, 2002, in which citizens narrowly defeated the San Rafael proposal, with 1,883 votes in favor and 2,151 against.[49] To his credit, Governor Leavitt had said all along that he would not forward a proposal to the Bush administration without local support, and thus the proposal to endorse the San Rafael as a national monument essentially died under the county vote. Mark Williams, president of the Southeastern Utah Off-Highway Vehicle Club, said people didn't want a monument rammed through: "People were just fed up with the way this was done. They wanted to be involved." Many people apparently believed the monument would limit access to the San Rafael Swell. "They were afraid of something like the Grand Staircase Monument," Williams said. "They didn't want that in their back yard."[50] Whether the outcome might have been different using a collaborative polling process is anyone's guess. The value of this case is that it illustrates the need to be timely and strategic in using innovative means to capture the input and advice of unaffiliated, rank-and-file citizens.

Citizen juries, collaborative polling, and similar strategies can also be cumbersome and expensive. It takes a lot of effort to ensure that the jury is a random, demographically representative sample of the general population, to recruit and prepare expert witnesses, and to prepare documents and follow-up strategies. There are other limitations as well. People volunteer, or "self-select," to be jurors, and so the jury will likely be more biased than its counterpart in the judicial system. Jurors and facilitators may struggle to effectively understand scientific and technical information and concepts and then communicate them to the ultimate decision makers. But despite these limitations, citizen juries and similar "social contract" approaches to public participation can play an important role in preventing and resolving western resource disputes because they strive to be inclusive, informed, and deliberative. Decision makers and other public leaders should seek out opportunities to adapt and experiment with these models to resolve western resource issues.

The familiar "notice and comment" approach to public participation represents the first attempt to integrate an interest-based approach to dispute resolution into the governance of western resources. Unfortunately, this strategy has proved to have limited effectiveness, in part because it is embedded within the culture of scientific management. Scientific and technical experts gather the input and advice of citizens and interest groups and then unilaterally make decisions or resolve disputes based on the authority Congress or some other legislative body has delegated to them.

"The conundrum of public participation," says Patrick Field, one of our colleagues at the Consensus Building Institute, "is the same as the search for 'good' science. Which public is involved, when, how, and why? Similarly, which science is used? The integration of science and citizens is doubly difficult."[51]

While the practice of public participation is not without problems, this strategy represents a step in the direction of creating more inclusive, informed, deliberative approaches to building agreements and resolving disputes. Based on a strong philosophical foundation, it is increasingly being improved with the addition of several innovative approaches to public participation. Nevertheless, when citizens feel disenfranchised, they turn to other strategies to promote their interests, foster social change, and resolve disputes over western resources.

TABLE 4.2. The IAP2 Public Participation Toolbox: Techniques to Share Information

Technique	Always Think It Through	What Can Go Right	What Can Go Wrong
PRINTED PUBLIC INFORMATION MATERIALS			
• Fact Sheets • Newsletters • Brochures • Issue Papers	• KISS!—Keep It Short and Simple • Make it visually interesting but avoid a slick sales look • Include a postage-paid comment form to encourage two-way communication and to expand mailing list • Be sure to explain public role and how public comments have affected project decisions. Q& A format works well	• Can reach large target audience • Allows for technical and legal reviews • Encourages written responses if comment form enclosed • Facilitates documentation of public involvement process	• Only as good as the mailing list/distribution network • Limited capability to communicate complicated concepts • No guarantee materials will be read
INFORMATION REPOSITORIES			
Libraries, city halls, distribution centers, schools, and other public facilities make good locations for housing project-related information	• Make sure personnel at location know where materials are kept • Keep list of repository items • Track usage through a sign-in sheet	• Relevant information is accessible to the public without incurring the costs or complications of tracking multiple copies sent to different people • Can set up visible distribution centers for project information	• Information repositories are often not well used by the public

	Tips	Advantages	Disadvantages
TECHNICAL REPORTS			
Technical documents reporting research or policy findings	• Reports are often more credible if prepared by independent groups	• Provides for thorough explanation of project decisions	• Can be more detailed than desired by many participants • May not be written in clear, accessible language
ADVERTISEMENTS			
Paid advertisements in newspapers and magazines	• Figure out the best days and best sections of the paper to reach intended audience • Avoid rarely read notice sections	• Potentially reaches broad public	• Expensive, especially in urban areas • Allows for relatively limited amount of information
NEWSPAPER INSERTS			
A "fact sheet" within the local newspaper	• Design needs to get noticed in the pile of inserts • Try on a day that has few other inserts	• Provides community-wide distribution of information • Presented in the context of local paper, insert is more likely to be read and taken seriously • Provides opportunity to include public comment form	• Expensive, especially in urban areas
FEATURE STORIES			
Focused stories on general project-related issues	• Anticipate visuals or schedule interesting events to help sell the story • Recognize that reporters are always looking for an angle	• Can heighten the perceived importance of the project • More likely to be read and taken seriously by the public	• No control over what information is presented or how

(Continued)

TABLE 4.2. Continued

Technique	Always Think It Through	What Can Go Right	What Can Go Wrong
BILL STUFFER			
Information flyer included with monthly utility bill	• Design bill stuffers to be eye-catching to encourage readership	• Widespread distribution within service area • Economical use of existing mailings	• Limited information can be conveyed • Message may get confused as from the mailing entity
PRESS RELEASES			
	• Fax or e-mail press releases or media kits • Foster a relationship of editorial board and reporters	• Informs the media of project milestones • Press release language is often used directly in articles • Opportunity for technical and legal reviews	• Low media response rate • Frequent poor placement of press release within newspapers
NEWS CONFERENCES			
	• Make sure all speakers are trained in media relations	• Opportunity to reach all media in one setting	• Limited to news-worthy events
TELEVISION			
Television programming to present information and elicit audience response	• Cable options are expanding and can be inexpensive • Check out expanding video options on the internet	• Can be used in multiple geographic areas • Many people will take the time to watch rather than read	• High expense • Difficult to gauge impact on audience

INFORMATION CENTERS and FIELD OFFICES			
Offices established with prescribed hours to distribute information and respond to inquiries	• Provide adequate staff to accommodate group tours • Use brochures and videotapes to advertise and reach broader audience • Consider providing internet access station • Select an accessible and frequented location	• Provides opportunity for positive media coverage at groundbreaking and other significant events • Excellent opportunity to educate school children • Places information dissemination in a positive educational setting • Information is easily accessible to the public • Provides an opportunity for more responsive ongoing communications focused on specific public involvement activities	• Relatively expensive, especially for project-specific use • Access is limited to those in vicinity of the center unless facility is mobile
EXPERT PANELS			
Public meeting designed in "Meet the Press" format. Media panel interviews experts from different perspectives.	• Provide opportunity for participation by general public following panel • Have a neutral moderator • Agree on ground rules in advance • Possibly encourage local organizations to sponsor rather than challenge	• Encourages education of the media • Presents opportunity for balanced discussion of key issues • Provides opportunity to dispel scientific misinformation	• Requires substantial preparation and organization • May enhance public concerns by increasing visibility of issues

(Continued)

TABLE 4.2. Continued

Technique	Always Think It Through	What Can Go Right	What Can Go Wrong
BRIEFINGS			
Use regular meetings of social and civic clubs and organizations to provide an opportunity to inform and educate. Normally these groups need speakers. Examples of target audiences: Rotary Club, Lions Clubs, Elks Clubs, Kiwanis, League of Women Voters. Also a good technique for elected officials.	• KISS!—Keep it Short and Simple • Use "show and tell" techniques • Bring visuals	• Control of information/presentation • Opportunity to reach a wide variety of individuals who may not have been attracted to another format • Opportunity to expand mailing list • Similar presentations can be used for different groups • Builds community good will	• Project stakeholders may not be in target audiences • Topic may be too technical to capture interest of audience
CENTRAL INFORMATION CONTACT			
Identify designated contacts for the public and media	• If possible, list a person not a position • Best if contact person is local • Anticipate how phones will be answered • Make sure message is kept up to date	• People don't get "the run around" when they call • Controls information flow • Conveys image of "accessibility"	• Designated contact must be committed to and prepared for prompt and accurate responses • May filter public message from technical staff and decision makers • May not serve to answer many of the toughest questions

CENTRAL INFORMATION CONTACT

Providing access to technical expertise to individuals and organizations	• The technical resource must be perceived as credible by the audience	• Builds credibility and helps address public concerns about equity • Can be effective conflict resolution technique where facts are debated	• Limited opportunities exist for providing technical assistance • Technical experts may counter project information

INFORMATION HOTLINE

Identify a separate line for public access to prerecorded project information or to reach project team members who can answer questions/ obtain input	• Make sure contact has sufficient knowledge to answer most project-related questions • If possible, list a person not a position • Best if contact person is local	• People don't get "the run around" when they call • Controls information flow • Conveys image of "accessibility" • Easy to provide updates on project activities	• Designated contact must be committed to and prepared for prompt and accurate responses

INTERVIEWS

One-to-one meetings with stakeholders to gain information for developing or refining public involvement and consensus-building programs	• Where feasible, interviews should be conducted in-person, particularly when considering candidates for citizens committees	• Provides opportunity for in-depth information exchange in non-threatening forum • Provides opportunity to obtain feedback from all stakeholders • Can be used to evaluate potential citizen committee members	• Scheduling multiple interviews can be time consuming

(Continued)

TABLE 4.2. Continued

Technique	Always Think It Through	What Can Go Right	What Can Go Wrong
IN-PERSON SURVEYS			
One-on-one "focus groups" with standardized questionnaire or methodology such as "stated preference"	• Make sure use of result is clear before technique is designed	• Provides traceable data • Reaches broad, representative public	• Expensive
RESPONSE SHEETS			
Mail-in forms often included in fact sheets and other project mailings to gain information on public concerns and preferences	• Use prepaid postage • Include a section to add name to the mailing list • Document results as part of public involvement record	• Provides input from those who would be unlikely to attend meetings • Provides a mechanism for expanding mailing list	• Does not generate statistically valid results • Only as good as the mailing list • Results can be easily skewed
MAILED SURVEYS AND QUESTIONNAIRES			
Inquiries mailed randomly to sample population to gain specific information for statistical validation	• Make sure you need statistically valid results before making investment • Survey/ questionnaire should be professionally developed and administered to avoid bias • Most suitable for general attitudinal surveys	• Provides input from individuals who would be unlikely to attend meetings • Provides input from cross-section of public, not just activists • Statistically tested results are more persuasive with political bodies and the general public	• Response rate is generally low • For statistically valid results, can be labor intensive and expensive • Level of detail may be limited

TELEPHONE SURVEYS/ POLLS

Random sampling of population by telephone to gain specific information for statistical validation	• Make sure you need statistically valid results before making investment • Survey/questionnaire should be professionally developed and administered to avoid bias • Most suitable for general attitudinal surveys	• Provides input from individuals who would be unlikely to attend meetings • Provides input from cross-section of public, not just those on mailing list • Higher response rate than with mail-in surveys	• More expensive and labor intensive than mailed surveys

INTERNET SURVEYS/ POLLS

Web-based response polls	• Be precise in how you set up site; chat rooms or discussion places can generate more input than you can look at	• Provides input from individuals who would be unlikely to attend meetings • Provides input from cross-section of public, not just those on mailing list • Higher response rate than other communication forms	• Generally not statistically valid results • Can be very labor intensive to look at all of the responses • Cannot control geographic reach of poll • Results can be easily skewed

COMPUTER-BASED POLLING

Surveys conducted via computer network	• Appropriate for attitudinal research	• Provides instant analyses of results • Can be used in multiple areas • Novelty of technique improves rate of response	• High expense • Detail of inquiry is limited

(Continued)

TABLE 4.2. Continued

Technique	Always Think It Through	What Can Go Right	What Can Go Wrong
COMMUNITY FACILITATORS			
Use qualified individuals in local community organizations to conduct project outreach	• Define roles, responsibilities, and limitations up front • Select and train facilitators carefully	• Promotes community-based involvement • Capitalizes on existing networks • Enhances project credibility	• Can be difficult to control information flow • Can build false expectations
FOCUS GROUPS			
Message-testing forum with randomly selected members of target audience. Can also be used to obtain input on planning decisions.	• Conduct at least two sessions for a given target • Use a skilled focus group facilitator to conduct the session	• Provides opportunity to test key messages prior to implementing program • Works best for select target audience	• Relatively expensive if conducted in focus group testing facility
DELIBERATIVE POLLING			
Measures informed opinion on an issue	• Do not expect or encourage participants to develop a shared view • Hire a facilitator experienced in this technique	• Can tell decision-makers what the public would think if they had more time and information • Exposure to different backgrounds, arguments, and views	• Resource intensive • Often held in conjunction with television companies • 2–3 day meeting

SIMULATION GAMES			
Exercises that simulate project decisions	• Test "game" before using • Be clear about how results will be used	• Can be designed to be an effective educational/ training technique, especially for local officials	• Requires substantial preparation and time for implementation • Can be expensive
TOURS			
Provide tours for key stakeholders, elected officials, advisory group members, and the media	• Know how many participants can be accommodated and make plans for overflow • Plan question/ answer session • Consider providing refreshments • Demonstrations work better than presentations	• Opportunity to develop rapport with key stakeholders • Reduces outrage by making choices more familiar	• Number of participants is limited by logistics • Potentially attractive to protestors
OPEN HOUSES			
An open house to allow the public to tour at their own pace. The facility should be set up with several stations, each addressing a separate issue. Resource people guide participants through the exhibits.	• Someone should explain format at the door • Have each participant fill out a comment sheet to document their participation • Be prepared for a crowd all at once—develop a meeting contingency plan • Encourage people to draw on maps to actively participate • Set up stations so that several people (6–10) can view at once	• Foster small group or one-on-one communications • Ability to draw on other team members to answer difficult questions • Less likely to receive media coverage • Builds credibility	• Difficult to document public input • Agitators may stage themselves at each display • Usually more staff intensive than a meeting

(Continued)

TABLE 4.2. Continued

Technique	Always Think It Through	What Can Go Right	What Can Go Wrong
COMMUNITY FAIRS			
Central event with multiple activities to provide project information and raise awareness	• All issues, large and small, must be considered • Make sure adequate resources and staff are available	• Focuses public attention on one element • Conducive to media coverage • Allows for different levels of information sharing	• Public must be motivated to attend • Usually expensive to do it well • Can damage image if not done well
COFFEE KLATCHES			
Small meetings within neighborhood usually at a person's home	• Make sure staff is very polite and appreciative	• Relaxed setting is conducive to effective dialogue • Maximizes two-way communication	• Can be costly and labor intensive
MEETINGS WITH EXISTING GROUPS			
Small meetings with existing groups or in conjunction with another event	• Understand who the likely audience is to be • Make opportunities for one-on-one meetings	• Opportunity to get on the agenda • Provides opportunity for in-depth information exchange in non-threatening forum	• May be too selective and can leave out important groups

COMPUTER-FACILITATED WORKSHOP		
Any-sized meeting when participants use interactive computer technology to register opinions	• Understand your audience, particularly the demographic categories • Design the inquiries to provide useful results • Use facilitator trained in the technique	• Immediate graphic results prompt focused discussion • Areas of agreement/ disagreement easily portrayed • Minority views are honored • Responses are private • Levels the playing field	• Software limits design • Potential for placing too much emphasis on numbers • Technology failure
PUBLIC HEARINGS		
Formal meetings with scheduled presentations offered	• Avoid if possible	• Provides opportunity for public to speak without rebuttal	• Does not foster constructive dialogue • Can perpetuate an us vs. them feeling
DESIGN CHARRETTES		
Intensive session where participants redesign project features	• Best used to foster creative ideas • Be clear about how results will be used	• Promotes joint problem solving and creative thinking	• Participants may not be seen as representative by larger public

(Continued)

TABLE 4.2. Continued

Technique	Always Think It Through	What Can Go Right	What Can Go Wrong
CONSENSUS BUILDING TECHNIQUES			
Techniques for building consensus on project decisions such as criteria and alternative selection. Often used with advisory committees. Techniques include Delphi; nominal group technique, public value assessment, and many others.	• Use simplified methodology • Allow adequate time to reach consensus • Consider one of the computerized systems that are available • Define levels of consensus, i.e., a group does not have to agree entirely upon a decision but rather agree enough so the discussion can move forward	• Encourages compromise among different interests • Provides structured and trackable decision making	• Not appropriate for groups with no interest in compromise • Clever parties can skew results • Does not produce a statistically valid solution • Consensus may not be reached
ADVISORY COMMITTEES			
A group of representative stakeholders assembled to provide public input to the planning process	• Define roles and responsibilities up front • Be forthcoming with information • Use a consistently credible process • Interview potential committee members in person before selection • Use third party facilitation	• Provides for detailed analyses for project issues • Participants gain understanding of other perspectives, leading toward compromise	• General public may not embrace committee's recommendations • Members may not achieve consensus • Sponsor must accept need for give-and-take • Time and labor intensive

TASK FORCES			
A group of experts or representative stakeholders formed to develop a specific product or policy recommendation	• Obtain strong leadership in advance • Make sure membership has credibility with the public	• Findings of a task force of independent or diverse interests will have greater credibility • Provides constructive opportunity for compromise	• Task force may not come to consensus or results may be too general to be meaningful • Time and labor intensive
PANELS			
A group assembled to debate or provide input on specific issues	• Most appropriate to show different news to public • Panelists must be credible with public	• Provides opportunity to dispel misinformation • Can build credibility if all sides are represented • May create wanted media attention	• May create unwanted media attention
CITIZEN JURIES			
Small group of ordinary citizens empanelled to learn about an issue, cross examine witnesses, make a recommendation. Always non-binding with no legal standing.	• Requires skilled moderator • Commissioning body must follow recommendations or explain why • Be clear about how results will be used	• Great opportunity to develop deep understanding of an issue • Public can identify with the "ordinary" citizens • Pinpoint fatal flaws or gauge public reaction	• Resource intensive

(Continued)

TABLE 4.2. Continued

Technique	Always Think It Through	What Can Go Right	What Can Go Wrong
ROLE-PLAYING			
Participants act out characters in pre-defined situation followed by evaluation of the interaction	• Choose roles carefully. Ensure that all interests are represented. • People may need encouragement to play a role fully	• Allows people to take risk-free positions and view situation from other perspectives • Participants gain clearer understanding of issues	• People may not be able to actually achieve goal of seeing another's perspective
SAMOAN CIRCLE			
Leaderless meeting that stimulates active participation	• Set room up with center table surrounded by concentric circles • Need microphones • Requires several people to record discussion	• Can be used with 10 to 500 people • Works best with controversial issues	• Dialogue can stall or become monopolized
OPEN SPACE TECHNOLOGY			
Participants offer topics and others participate according to interest	• Important to have a powerful theme or vision statement to generate topics • Need flexible facilities to accommodate numerous groups of different sizes • Ground rules and procedures must be carefully explained for success	• Provides structure for giving people opportunity and responsibility to create valuable product or experience • Includes immediate summary of discussion	• Most important issues could get lost in the shuffle • Can be difficult to get accurate reporting of results

WORKSHOPS

An informal public meeting that may include presentations and exhibits but ends with interactive working groups	• Know how you plan to use public input before the workshop • Conduct training in advance with small group facilitators. Each should receive a list of instructions, especially where procedures involve weighting/ranking of factors or criteria	• Excellent for discussions on criteria or analysis of alternatives • Fosters small group or one-to-one communication • Ability to draw on other team members to answer difficult questions • Builds credibility • Maximizes feedback obtained from participants • Fosters public ownership in solving the problem	• Hostile participants may resist what they perceive to be the "divide and conquer" strategy of breaking into small groups • Several small-group facilitators are necessary

FUTURE SEARCH CONFERENCE

Focuses on the future of an organization, a network of people, or community	• Hire a facilitator experienced in this technique	• Can involve hundreds of people simultaneously in major organizational change decisions • Individuals are experts • Can lead to substantial changes across entire organization	• Logistically challenging • May be difficult to gain complete commitment from all stakeholders • 2–3 day meeting

Source: Reproduced with permission of the International Association for Public Participation.

NOTES

1. Theodore Lowi, *The End of Liberalism: Ideology, Policy, and the Crisis of Public Authority* (New York: Norton, 1969).

2. David Mathews, *Politics for People: Finding a Responsible Public Voice* (Urbana: University of Illinois Press, 1994).

3. Jean-Jacques Rousseau, "The Social Contract," in *The Social Contract and Discourse on the Origin of Inequality*, ed. Lester G. Crocker (New York: Washington Square Press, 1967).

4. Jeremy Bentham, *A Fragment on Government and an Introduction to the Principles of Morals and Legislation*, ed. Wilfrid Harrison (New York: Oxford University Press, 1967).

5. John Stuart Mill, *Considerations on Representative Government*, (New York: Bobbs-Merrill, 1958).

6. Mill, *Considerations on Representative Government*.

7. Thomas Jefferson, *The Political Writings of Thomas Jefferson* (New York: Liberal Arts Press, 1955).

8. Daniel Kemmis, *Community and the Politics of Place* (Norman: University of Oklahoma Press, 1990).

9. Alexander Hamilton, James Madison, and John Jay, *The Federalist Papers* (Cutchogue, NY: Buccaneer Press, 1995). As a protégé of Jefferson, Madison believed in the values of a "republican" form of government. However, he also believed that a "politics of engagement" is most appropriate at a local or perhaps even a regional scale; it would not likely be an effective model of governance at a national scale. It should also be kept in mind that the founding fathers were responding, at least in part, to the failures of the loose confederation of thirteen states, which were governed more along the lines Jefferson envisioned than the "procedural republic" that the Federalists established.

10. Terry L. Cooper, "Citizen Participation," in *Organization Theory and Management*, ed. Thomas D. Lynch (New York: Marcel Dekker, 1983), 13–45.

11. John Dryzek, *Deliberative Democracy and Beyond: Liberals, Critics, Contestations* (New York: Oxford University Press, 2000).

12. Frank Fischer, *Citizens, Experts, and the Environment: The Politics of Local Knowledge* (Durham, NC: Duke University Press, 2000).

13. The history of public participation in the United States is not well documented. This section draws on the work of Thomas C. Beierle and Jerry Cayford, *Democracy in Practice: Public Participation in Environmental Decisions* (Washington, DC: Resources for the Future, 2002); Samuel Trask Dana and Sally K. Fairfax, "Citizen Activism in Forest and Range Policy in the 1970s," in *Forest and Range Policy: Its Development in the United States*, 2nd ed., 295–311 (New York: McGraw-Hill, 1980); Hanna J. Cortner and Margaret A. Moote, *The Poli-*

tics of Ecosystem Management (Washington, DC: Island Press, 1999), 1–35; and Stuart Langton, *Citizen Participation in America: Essays on the State of the Art* (Lexington, MA: Lexington Books, 1978).

14. James L. Creighton, "Public Participation in Federal Agencies' Decision Making in the 1990s," *National Civic Review* (Fall 1999): 249–58.

15. W. R. Derrick Sewell and Timothy O'Riordan, "The Culture of Participation in Environmental Decisionmaking," in *Natural Resources for a Democratic Society: Public Participation in Decision Making*, ed. Albert E. Utton et al., 1–5 (Boulder, CO: Westview, 1976).

16. Lowi, *The End of Liberalism.*

17. Sherry Arnstein, "A Ladder of Citizen Participation," *Journal of the American Institute of Planners* (July 1969): 216–24.

18. See Clive S. Thomas, ed., *Politics and Public Policy in the Contemporary American West* (Albuquerque: University of New Mexico Press, 1991).

19. Roderick Nash, *Wilderness and the American Mind* (New Haven, CT: Yale University Press, 1967).

20. Carmen Sirianni and Lewis Friedland, "Civic Environmentalism," in *Civic Innovation in America: Community Empowerment, Public Policy, and the Movement for Civic Renewal*, 85–137 (Berkeley: University of California Press, 2001).

21. One of the most recent and better evaluations of public participation in environmental decision making is Thomas C. Beierle and Jerry Cayford, *Democracy in Practice: Public Participation in Environmental Decisions* (Washington, DC: Resources for the Future, 2002). See also O'Connor Center for the Rocky Mountain West and Institute for Environment and Natural Resources, *Reclaiming NEPA's Potential: Can Collaborative Processes Improve Environmental Decision Making?* (March 2000); Council on Environmental Quality, *The National Environmental Policy Act: A Study of Its Effectiveness after Twenty-Five Years* (Washington, DC: Council on Environmental Quality, Executive Office of the President, 1997); and Lynton Keith Caldwell, *The National Environmental Policy Act: An Agenda for the Future* (Bloomington: Indiana University Press, 1998).

22. Matthew McKinney and Will Harmon, "Public Participation in Environmental Decision Making: Is It Working?" *National Civic Review* 91, no. 2 (Summer 2002): 149–70.

23. Mathews, *Politics for People.*

24. Kemmis, *Community and the Politics of Place.*

25. Daniel Yankelovich, *The Magic of Dialogue: Transforming Conflict into Cooperation* (New York: Simon & Schuster, 1999).

26. International Association for Public Participation, "Core Values for the Practice of Public Participation," http://www.iap2.org.

27. Center for the Rocky Mountain West and Institute for Environment and Natural Resources, *Reclaiming NEPA's Potential.*

28. U.S. Institute for Environmental Conflict Resolution, *Report and Recommendations on NEPA Pilot Projects* (August 21, 2001).

29. See U.S. Environmental Protection Agency, *Public Involvement Policy* (March 2003). On the final recommendations of the Committee of Scientists, see U.S. Department of Agriculture, *Sustaining the People's Land: Recommendations for Stewardship of the National Forests and Grasslands* (March 15, 1999).

30. Julia M. Wondolleck and Clare M. Ryan, "What Hat Do I Wear Now? An Examination of Agency Roles in Collaborative Processes," *Negotiation Journal* (April 1999): 117–33.

31. Yankelovich, *The Magic of Dialogue,* 170.

32. Robert A. Caro, *The Powerbroker: Robert Moses and the Fall of New York* (New York: Vintage Books, 1975).

33. Yankelovich, *The Magic of Dialogue,* 170.

34. Yankelovich, *The Magic of Dialogue,* 172.

35. Yankelovich, *The Magic of Dialogue,* 174.

36. Steven E. Daniels and Gregg B. Walker, *Working through Environmental Conflict: The Collaborative Learning Approach* (Westport, CT: Praeger, 2001).

37. Yankelovich, *The Magic of Dialogue,* 175.

38. Matthew J. McKinney, "Negotiated Rulemaking: Involving Citizens in Public Decisions," *Montana Law Review* 60 (1999): 499–539.

39. Public Law No. 101-648 (1990) 5 U.S.C. Section 561-570 (1998).

40. McKinney, "Negotiated Rulemaking."

41. These limitations and critiques of negotiated rulemaking are a synthesis of the work of McKinney, "Negotiated Rulemaking"; Cary Coglianese, "Assessing Consensus: The Promise and Performance of Negotiated Rulemaking," *Duke Law Journal* 46 (1997); and Philip J. Harter, "Fear of Commitment: An Affliction of Adolescents," *Duke Law Journal* 46 (1997).

42. Philip J. Harter, "The Actual Performance of Negotiated Rulemaking: A Response to Professor Coglianese" (unpublished, undated draft article on file with the authors).

43. Ned Crosby, "Using the Citizens Jury Process for Environmental Decision Making," in *Better Environmental Decisions: Strategies for Governments, Business, and Communities,* ed. Ken Sexton et al., 401–18 (Washington, DC: Island Press, 1999).

44. For an overview of different approaches to engaging unaffiliated citizens, see http://www.democracyinnovations.org; and James S. Fishkin, *The Voice of the People: Public Opinion and Democracy* (New Haven, CT: Yale University Press, 1995).

45. Ned Crosby et al., "Citizens Panels: A New Approach to Citizen Participation," *Public Administration Review* (March/April 1986): 170–78.

46. Lawrence Susskind and Liora Zion, *Can America's Democracy Be Improved?* (working paper of the Consensus Building Institute, August 2002).

47. On this note, see also David Getches, "Some Irreverant Questions about Watershed-based Efforts," in *Across the Great Divide: Explorations in Collaborative Conservation and the American West,* ed. Philip Brick, Donald Snow, and Sarah Van de Wetering, 180–87 (Washington, DC: Island Press, 2001).

48. This illustration, and the description of collaborative polling, is based on personal conversations with Dr. Keith Allred, associate professor at the John F. Kennedy School of Government at Harvard University, and a short paper he has written titled "Collaborative Polling: An Innovative Public Input Process" (undated).

49. Christopher Smart, "Proposal for San Rafael Monument Fails in Emery," *Salt Lake Tribune,* November 6, 2002.

50. Smart, "Proposal for San Rafael Monument Fails in Emery."

51. Personal conversation with Patrick Field, vice president of North American Dispute Resolution.

5

Citizens Strike Back

A s described in chapter 4, the 1960s and 1970s saw a dramatic increase in the number and variety of opportunities for citizens to participate in the process of making decisions and resolving disputes over natural resources in the West. Most of these efforts, however, indirectly reinforced the scientific management paradigm. They embedded the requirements of public participation into the long-established administrative framework of expert decision making. To counteract and challenge this deeply embedded approach to governing western resources, citizens used ballot initiatives and, beginning in the 1970s, the courts to increase their influence in public decision making.

This chapter focuses on the role of citizen ballot initiatives and litigation in resolving western resource disputes. Litigation and the courts have been a very important instrument in shaping western resource policy. Citizen ballot initiatives, by contrast, have played a lesser role. Together, however, these two strategies illustrate a certain degree of backlash by citizens against the highly centralized, expert-driven model of decision making that characterized the governance of western resources after World War II. In the hands of environmental advocates and, later, industry and development advocates, ballot initiatives and litigation have evolved from reactive stopgap tactics to more proactive and strategic measures.

Citizen Ballot Initiatives

Litigation is sometimes referred to as the "forum of last resort" because it often comes after attempts to provide meaningful public participation during legislative and administrative proceedings. In contrast, citizen ballot initiatives seek to influence the outcome of a policy issue at the front end. The process allows citizens to petition to place proposed statutes or constitutional amendments on the ballot or before the legislature. Under the direct initiative, citizens can take a statute or amendment directly to the ballot. Indirect initiatives, by contrast, go to the legislature first and then to the ballot. Some states allow one or the other, and some allow both. In addition, some states allow only statutory initiatives and prohibit constitutional initiatives (proposals to change the state's constitution). Ballots sometimes also include "referendums," which are laws passed by the legislature and sent to voters for ratification.

The Genesis of the Initiative Process

The use of initiatives to enact statutes or amend constitutions is often referred to as "direct democracy" and is contrasted with "representative democracy." In structuring our existing system of representative democracy, James Madison sought to avoid the dangers of too much citizen participation—what he referred to as the "mischiefs of factions," wherein citizens unite under a common interest that may be adverse to the rights and interests of other citizens. Madison supported the republican form of government, arguing that it would "refine and enlarge the public views, by passing them through the medium of a chosen body of citizens, whose wisdom may best discern the true interest of their country, and . . . will be least likely to sacrifice it to temporary or partial considerations."[1] Article IV, section 4 of the U.S. Constitution guarantees the republican form of government to individual states. This "procedural republic" is designed to weigh and balance competing interests.[2]

In contrast to representative democracy, initiatives reserve direct lawmaking power to the voters. In the 1600s, citizens of New England could propose ordinances and put other issues to a vote at town meetings. This idea also sprouted in Switzerland, where several provinces, or "cantons," adopted the initiative and referendum approach in response to perceived legislative corruption between 1830 and 1890. In 1891, South Dakota became the first state to allow citizen initiatives, and Oregon was the first to enact a law using the initiative process, in 1904. Between 1898 and 1918, nineteen states—most of them west of the Mississippi River—adopted the initiative process. (Ironically, perhaps, the progressive movement spawned both scientific management and the populist-inspired initiative process, two fundamentally different approaches to governance, each attempting to cure widespread corruption.) Only six states west of the Mississippi do not have some form of direct democracy, while east of the Mississippi only eight states have adopted some form of direct democracy. Since 1918, only five states have adopted the initiative and referendum process, including Mississippi in 1992. But interest is again growing. During the 2001–2002 biennium, seventeen states saw legislation to authorize initiatives and referendums. Today, the movement seems to be the strongest in Minnesota and New York.

The Use of Initiatives

Citizen initiatives were popular from 1910 to 1919 and then were used infrequently after World War II. In the 1970s, a new tide of public distrust of political leaders and government rekindled citizens' interest in the use of initiatives. In the United States, 183 statewide votes on initiatives took place during the 1970s, 253 in the 1980s, and 383 in the 1990s.[3]

Initiatives have proven to be a powerful tool for change, ushering in women's suffrage, direct primaries, term limits, new taxes as well as limits on taxation, and other reforms.[4] The first use of a citizen initiative to address an environmental issue was in 1970, the same year the National Environmental Policy Act (NEPA) was signed into law and Americans celebrated the first Earth Day.[5] That year, Oregonians voted on an initiative to ban dams on certain rivers in the state. Since then, environmental groups have used the initiative process in attempts to promote open space, fight nuclear power, limit the right to hunt (initiatives appeared on the ballots in Colorado, Oregon, Washington, and Idaho), mandate recycling, and oppose electricity deregulation (in California, Massachusetts, and Montana).

As more and more people move to the West for its open space and abundant opportunities for outdoor recreation, initiatives are increasingly used to challenge the region's traditional economic industries of agricultural, timber, and mining, and to otherwise promote environmental quality. In 1988, two initiatives appeared on the ballot in South Dakota to require reclamation of mined land and impose a sales tax on metallic minerals. Voters defeated both initiatives. In 1990, another initiative, which ultimately failed, would have limited the amount of land that could be subject to large-scale gold and silver mining in South Dakota.

In 1990 and 1992, initiatives were passed to regulate solid-waste disposal in South Dakota. In California, environmental groups promoted two ambitious initiatives in 1990. Proposition 128, otherwise known as "Big Green," addressed a variety of issues, including ozone depletion, oil spills, recycling, pesticide use, and logging. It debuted with an 80 percent approval rating but was defeated when 64 percent of citizens voted against it. Proposition 130, referred to as "Forests Forever," would have banned clear-cutting throughout California had it passed.

In 1994, Oregon citizens voted against a citizen initiative that proposed to restrict open-pit mining by banning the use of cyanide. In Montana, eight environmental groups promoted Initiative 122 in 1996. The proposed Clean Water and Public Health Protection Act would have required mining operations to remove iron, manganese, and other "toxins" and "carcinogens" from wastewater through special treatment.

In 1996, environmental groups unsuccessfully promoted the Oregon Clean Streams Initiative, which would have restricted livestock grazing on state lands and along certain riparian areas. In 1998, citizens in Colorado and South Dakota approved initiatives to limit hog farms. On election day 2000, voters across the country considered a wide range of ballot initiatives that affect the pace, quality, and shape of growth in their states and communities.[6] According to a report published by The Brookings Institution, voters faced 553 state and local ballot initiatives related to growth. Of these, more than 70 percent passed, although not every "yes" vote indicates that citizens supported smart growth ideas and policies. The initiatives considered by voters in 2000 dealt with open space preservation, transportation investments, and the connection between economic development and growth management.

Looking at the historic use of ballot initiatives in the West from 1990 through 1996, there is apparently an inverse correlation between the frequency of use and success. In short, voters approve a higher percentage of initiatives when they see fewer of them. Idaho ballots, for example, carried only 11 initiatives from 1990 through 1996, and voters enacted 45 percent of them. The trend was similar in Montana (28 initiatives, 57 percent enacted), Nevada (14 initiatives, 50 percent enacted), and Washington (78 initiatives,

47 percent enacted). Arizona voters, on the other hand, considered 112 initiatives and approved only 38 percent. Other states with high numbers of initiatives saw similar results, including California (151 initiatives, 28 percent enacted) and Oregon (207 initiatives, 33 percent enacted).

Some critics point to these numbers and complain that western states are being overrun with citizen initiatives. "We don't want to become like California," says Utah state senator John Valentine, "with so many ballot initiatives it's chaos."[7] Yet the actual numbers tell a different story. California has seen only 258 initiatives since 1911.[8] Oregon leads all states for the most statewide initiatives (318 between 1904 and 2000) and boasts the highest average initiative use (6.6 per general election). Oregon even holds the record for the most initiatives in a single year—27 appeared on the 1912 ballot.[9] Yet these "records" pale next to the number of draft laws and amendments considered by state legislatures in a single session. During the 1999 session alone, for example, the Oregon assembly entertained more than 3,300 bills.[10] In fact, in the century since the first use of initiatives in the United States, fewer than 2,000 have appeared on statewide ballots, and less than half were approved by voters.[11]

Citizen initiatives have not been used to address some of the West's most contentious natural resource issues, such as federal land management or water allocation, mostly because attempts to provide for a national initiative have failed, even though polling demonstrates its popularity with a majority of voters.[12] Nevertheless, citizen initiatives have been used to address a variety of western resource issues, and they are a direct challenge to both our representative system of democracy and the scientific management model of decision making.

Why the Resurgence?

The rise of citizen initiatives suggests that our current "procedural republic" does not meet the basic needs and interests of citizens who want to be meaningfully involved in public decisions. Voters have grown increasingly cynical and distrustful of elected officials and of government in general. Many feel disenfranchised by representative democracy and are dissatisfied with the level of discourse and outcomes offered by Congress and state legislatures. Citizen initiatives provide an opportunity for more people to be directly involved in formulating public policy.

Initiatives are also a very powerful agenda-setting strategy. Even if an initiative is not approved by voters, its appearance on the ballot raises public awareness and understanding and promotes public dialogue on an issue that legislatures and other public officials may be reluctant to address (such as term limits, smoking bans, abortion, gay rights, and so on). People of all political persuasions bring initiatives to the ballot, attempting to legalize marijuana and expanding animal rights, for example, but also requiring the use of the English language in public classrooms and banning same-sex marriages. Because they address controversial issues and to some extent reflect what's on the popular mind, many initiatives garner significant media attention, helping to publicize the initiative process as well. Also, according to the Initiative and Referendum Institute, voter turnout typically runs 3 to 7 percent higher when an initiative is on the ballot.[13] Perhaps voting for an initiative is attractive because it offers more certainty in the outcome—what you vote for is what you get—than a vote cast for a candidate, who may or may not live up to promises made during the campaign.

Today, citizen initiatives are big business. Consultants are hired to convene focus groups, draft the initiatives, and design and run the campaign. Professional petitioners are typically paid $1 to $2.50 per signature to qualify initiatives for the ballot; on a busy street corner, a single petitioner may collect up to 500 signatures a day. In an initiative-heavy election year, total spending on initiative campaigns can easily exceed $100 million. In 1996, mining interests spent $2 million to defeat an antimining initiative in Montana, and proponents and opponents together spent $35 million in Florida on an initiative to restore the Everglades with funding from a new sugar tax. In 1998, an initiative to allow video gambling machines in tribal reservations in California set the national record. The tribes spent $66.9 million to promote the initiative, but opponents were able to defeat the measure with a "mere" $21 million.[14]

Arguments against the Initiative Process

As the use of citizen initiatives continues to increase, it is not surprising that some people are beginning to speak out against them. Citizens, businesses, local government groups, and past and present legislators from Maine to California, including Arizona, Colorado, and Oregon, are actively studying the ballot initiative process in search of reforms.[15]

While most people agree that citizen initiatives were intended to be a grassroots tool to shape public policy and hold government officials accountable, opponents claim that the tool has been usurped by special interests to push their agendas. Reflecting on the use of citizen initiatives in

Nevada in 2002, a *Reno Gazette-Journal* editorial asserted that initiatives on the two most controversial issues—the definition of marriage and the decriminalization of marijuana—were paid for and pushed by out-of-staters.[16] Based on a study of California's Proposition 209 (which proposed to remove race and gender as a basis for college admission), Lydia Chavez concludes that the initiative process is used by wealthy special interest groups to bypass the process of representative democracy and to change laws to satisfy their narrow self-interests.[17] In a review of the past century of experience with initiatives, Brigham Young University professor David Magleby says that initiatives are voted on by middle- and upper-class elites. He claims that less educated, poorer, and younger voters either don't vote at all or skip voting on initiatives, which are often more complicated than other election items.[18]

Some critics question the public's ability to understand complex public policy issues, raising a second argument against the use of citizen initiative processes—that they do not promote fully informed, vigorous debate about the merits of public policy choices and consequences. After examining the use of citizen initiatives in California, Peter Schrag concluded that some of California's toughest public policy issues are being addressed not through a "comprehensible legislative process in which priorities are evaluated against one another, but through a crazy quilt of ad hoc decisions that defies rational budgeting, intelligent policy formulation, and civic comprehension."[19] Many observers and lawmakers say that initiatives offer voters simplistic solutions—simple yes or no decisions—on very complex issues. Oregon legislator Lane Shetterly, a member of the National Council of State Legislatures' Task Force on Initiatives and Referendums, says that "voters don't have to make the same kinds of tough decisions legislators face in balancing competing needs with limited resources."[20] The potential "shallowness" of public deliberation on an initiative sometimes leads to pitched battles about the initiative's title—which can be quite misleading—because too often this is all that most voters will see.

David Broder, a longtime journalist and observer of politics, argues that the lack of interaction and public dialogue in the citizen initiative process limits the exchange of information and the ability to build a common understanding of the issues.[21] He argues that minority viewpoints and interests are not likely to be adequately considered in the process, and that citizen initiatives tend to respond to the short-term needs and interests of society (whatever is sexy at the moment) and may compromise not only public policy (for example, by raiding the treasury or shifting the tax burden from one constituency to another) but also the long-term stability and effectiveness of our democracy.

Potential Tools—Improving the Initiative Process and Deliberative Democracy

A number of ways exist for improving citizen initiatives to respond to the limitations outlined above. Based on a recent report by the National Council for State Legislatures, it may be wise to consider the following:

- Adopt an indirect initiative process, allowing the legislature or attorney general an opportunity to review, amend, and possibly enact an initiative before it goes on the ballot.
- Increase public information and education about initiatives, including ballot pamphlets and public hearings with supporters and opponents. In Montana, Secretary of State Bob Brown convened a public debate on the initiatives and referendums on the November 2002 ballot.
- Require petitioners to gather signatures throughout a state, rather than on the busiest corner in the most populated city. Such reforms have proven difficult to implement. In August 2000, Utah's Supreme Court struck down a ballot initiative provision requiring signatures of 10 percent of voters in twenty of twenty-nine counties for a petition to qualify for the ballot.[22] Nine months earlier, Idaho courts struck down a provision requiring signatures of 6 percent of voters in half of the state's counties (a decision that is now being reviewed by the Ninth Circuit Court of Appeals). Montana voters approved similar requirements in the November 2002 election, although these too may be challenged in court.[23]
- Provide incentives to limit the use of "big money" in the initiative process by requiring fewer signatures and encouraging the use of volunteer signature gatherers.
- Impose a single subject requirement for initiative proposals.

In addition to improving the citizen initiative process itself, alternatives are also available that address the needs and interests of citizens to be more meaningfully involved in shaping public policy. Most discussions about the merits of "representative" versus "direct" democracy seem to suggest that these are the only two options for governing and that we must choose between them. A third option, which attempts to integrate the best features of both strategies, is what some people refer to as "deliberative" democracy, defined in part as public processes that are inclusive, informed, and deliberative. Unlike direct democracy, which provides limited opportunities for face-to-face interactions, deliberative democracy emphasizes the quality of public interactions and the opportunities to talk and think together.

We discussed one example of this type of strategy—citizen juries—in chapter 4. Another strategy is the use of "policy dialogues." Similar to negotiated rulemaking, the essence of a policy dialogue is to involve affected parties in the development of policy options or recommendations in which they have interest.[24] According to John Ehrmann and Michael Lesnick, who helped pioneer this strategy in the 1980s, "the process provides a sense of 'ownership' in the policy formulation process for all the parties and provides the agency with an opportunity to profit from the ideas generated by the interaction of various interests, rather than merely hearing the respective positions through the traditional lobbying process."[25] When used in appropriate situations, policy dialogues can help prevent disputes by meaningfully engaging people in the formulation of solutions to common problems.

The Colorado-based Keystone Center facilitated the National Policy Dialogue on Ecosystem Management, resulting in a consensus definition of ecosystem management and suggestions for implementing ecosystem management on the ground locally and at the national public policy level. The center has also successfully convened policy dialogues on water quality issues, Superfund reform, incentives for private landowners to protect endangered species, and the environmental impacts of ski areas.

As the use of policy dialogues to formulate policy options and recommendations on natural resource issues in the West increases, it is important to explicitly address several key variables in the design and coordination of such a process: Who should participate? What issues should be discussed? Who should decide these first two questions? How should the ad hoc policy dialogue be linked to the formal decision-making process? Fortunately, there is an ever-expanding literature on "best practices" to answer these and other questions, which we examine in chapter 7.

Litigation

When ballot initiatives, dialogue, and other strategies fail, or when citizens or watchdog organizations aren't satisfied with the direction of scientific management, disputes often land in court. Some advocacy groups also use litigation as an initial, tactical response to a situation, to delay action and garner media and popular attention to a cause. When an issue revolves around questions of statutory rights or legal precedence, the courtroom is the most logical place to seek answers.[26]

A Brief History of Citizen Lawsuits

In the late 1960s, two federal land management agencies were seriously considering a proposal by Walt Disney Enterprises to build a destination ski resort in the Mineral King valley. The valley is located in the southern part of the Sierra Nevada Mountains, in Sequoia National Forest. It also happens to be a congressionally designated game refuge. Conservationists had long wanted to include this same area in adjacent Sequoia National Park.

In 1969, the Sierra Club filed a lawsuit seeking an injunction to prohibit the Forest Service from issuing the permits needed for the development, and prohibiting the U.S. Department of the Interior from issuing permits for a power line and road across part of Sequoia National Park to service the development.[27] The environmental groups asserted that issuing the permits and approving the development would violate several federal statutes and regulations governing the use of national forests, refuges, and parks.

To justify its lawsuit, the Sierra Club had to show that it had a special interest in Mineral King valley and had to prove that its interest would be adversely affected if the ski resort were developed. In legal terminology, these two conditions are required to establish the "standing" of the plaintiff. Without such standing, a lawsuit alleging a violation of a statute or regulation would be dismissed out of hand.

The Sierra Club sought to meet this test by claiming that it is a membership organization "with a special interest in the conservation and sound maintenance of the national parks, game refuges and forests of the country."[28] The federal district court in California agreed that the environmental group's interests would be harmed by the proposed development and issued a preliminary, temporary injunction against issuance of the permits.

Attorneys for the two federal land management agencies appealed the decision, and the Ninth Circuit Court of Appeals ruled that the Sierra Club's interests were not "sufficiently direct" to establish standing. The Club appealed to the U.S. Supreme Court, which agreed to hear the case. In 1972, the Supreme Court agreed with the Ninth Circuit, concluding that the Sierra

Club did not have an identifiable interest that would be injured by the proposed development, and thus that it did not have standing.

The kicker, and what has proved to be the foundation for natural resource and environmental litigation in the past thirty years, was in a footnote to the Supreme Court's decision. The Court pointed out that members of the Sierra Club apparently recreated in the Mineral King valley. It further noted that the district court might allow the Club to amend its original complaint, alleging that the proposed ski resort would injure the recreational interests of individual members. The implication was that a history of recreational use by some of its members would be sufficient to allow an organization to file a lawsuit on behalf of its members.

When the case returned to the lower court, the judge allowed the Sierra Club to amend its complaint. In addition to asserting that its members used the Mineral King valley for recreational interests, the Club also claimed that the agencies violated a provision in the National Environmental Policy Act—passed by Congress in 1969 in the midst of this lawsuit—which requires the agencies to consider several alternatives to the proposed action, including maintaining the status quo.

Although the Mineral King case is widely regarded as the foundation that allows citizens and organizations to file lawsuits to enforce federal statutes and regulations, a decision on the merits of the case was never made. During the intervening years, it became clear that the best use of Mineral King was not as a ski resort. No court ever ruled on the question of whether the Sierra Club's revised complaint was sufficient to establish standing, and the lawsuit was dismissed in 1977. In 1978, Congress passed legislation making Mineral King part of Sequoia National Park.

Vawter Parker, president of Earthjustice Legal Defense Fund, the nation's largest nonprofit environmental law firm, says that the importance of *Sierra Club v. Morton* is hard to overstate. However, he suggests that the origins of citizen lawsuits can be traced back to an earlier opinion written by Justice William O. Douglas in 1967.

In *Udall v. Federal Power Commission*, the Supreme Court considered a dispute over whether private utilities, municipal utilities, or possibly the federal government should build and operate dams at multiple sites in Hells Canyon, a mile-deep cut between northeastern Oregon and Idaho through which the Snake River winds north toward the Columbia River. While much of the dispute centered on the merits of private versus public providers of power and specific dam sites, Justice Douglas focused instead on the impact of dams on salmon and steelhead and on recreation, wondering if the Snake River could withstand any more dams at all. This being 1967, he was slightly ahead of his time. Writing the majority decision, Justice Douglas said that "the importance of salmon and steelhead in our outdoor life as well as in commerce is so great that there certainly comes a time when their destruction might necessitate a halt in so-called 'improvement' or 'development' of waterways."[29] In deciding to grant or deny authority to build a dam, Douglas continued, "the test is whether the project will be in the public interest. And that determination can be made only after an exploration of all the issues relevant to the 'public interest,' including future power demand and supply, alternate sources of power, the public interest in preserving reaches of wild rivers and wilderness areas, the preservation of anadromous fish for commercial and recreational purposes, and the protection of wildlife."[30]

In 1967, the Supreme Court did not address the merits of private or public sources of electricity. Rather, Justice Douglas, writing for the majority, ordered the commission to reopen the hearings to consider the possibility that the public interest might be best served by denying a permit to anyone. Using a provision in the Federal Power Act (passed in 1920) requiring the commission to adopt a plan that develops or improves waterways for commercial and "other beneficial public uses, including recreational purposes," Douglas transformed the commission's single-purpose mandate to promote commercial development into a multiple-use mandate. This ruling anticipated two of the most compelling requirements of the National Environmental Policy Act, which was passed two years after the Court's decision: the obligation of a federal agency (1) to examine *all* of the social, economic, and environmental issues relevant to the public interest and (2) to consider what is now known as the "no action" alternative. Of course, if an agency chose to ignore these requirements, people without a demonstrated economic interest in the outcome had no standing to complain—until the Mineral King case, that is.

Legislatively, the citizen suit was born in section 304 of the Clean Air Act as amended in 1970.[31] Proponents of the idea originally argued that it was a way to hold untrustworthy agencies accountable. After the Senate Judiciary Committee suggested that such a provision would burden an already overcrowded court with a large number of lawsuits, proponents suggested that citizen suits were the answer to the enforcement agencies' inevitable lack of resources to address all statutory violations. Citizens were allowed to sue, but only after notifying appropriate regulatory agencies and giving them an opportunity to sue first. In 1976, Congress applied the "coup de grace," according to several well-known federal land scholars, when it amended the Administrative Procedures Act by abolishing sovereign immunity for most purposes, giving further rise to the use of citizen suits against federal land management agencies.[32] Other provisions allow recovery of attorney's fees from the agency if the citizen group prevails in court. This makes it financially feasible for nonprofit groups to take on the economic burden of litigation.

Once embedded in the Clean Air Act, and refined and clarified by the Mineral King case and the Administrative Procedures Act, the citizen suit clause was included in nearly all federal environmental and natural resource statutes. The Endangered Species Act of 1973, for example, states that "any person may commence a civil suit on his own behalf to enjoin any person, including the United States . . . who is alleged to be in violation of any provision of this Act."[33] This brief history of citizen suits reveals that many of the most notable cases and issues that established the right of citizens to sue the government not only were located in the American West but addressed distinctly western resource issues.

The Value of Litigation

In a world with so many other options for influencing public policy and decision making, why would some groups choose to litigate? The most likely answer is that litigation is the "big stick" that gets results when "walking softly" doesn't.

In a story published in the *Helena (Montana) Independent Record,* environmental activist Sara Jane Johnson says that "filing a lawsuit really is the only public involvement that isn't ignored."[34] Johnson has a Ph.D. in biology and worked for the U.S. Forest Service for six years. During the past ten years, as the founder of her own nonprofit conservation organization, she has appealed almost every timber sale proposed for the Helena National Forest. She claims that the Forest Service is "not following their own forest plan." She goes on to say: "I want to make a difference. So this is my new strategy: going to court. I'm only here because nothing else worked. The Forest Service has no one but themselves to blame."

Not quite, according to Tom Clifford, supervisor of the Helena National Forest. He says that Johnson never sits down to participate in any of the planning processes but instead allows everyone else to work out a compromise and then goes over their heads with her appeals and lawsuits. In one situation, the Clancy/Unionville wildfire prevention project, Clifford and his staff worked for five years with people who live near the project and people who ride motorized vehicles, hike, or otherwise recreate there. Together, they crafted an agreement to log and perform controlled burns, in an effort to minimize the danger of large wildfires nears homes south of Helena, and to limit off-road vehicle access. When Clifford presented the final plan, Johnson filed a formal appeal, along with five other environmental organizations based in Bozeman and Missoula, Montana, and in Oregon. They feared that the proposed plan would destroy or degrade mature and old-growth forests and would threaten the security and cover for big-game species.

Also filing appeals from the opposite side of the multiple-use spectrum were the Capital Trail Vehicle Association and the Montana 4x4 Association, who were upset that the plan closed ninety-one miles of established trails—old logging roads—in the project area. In what is perhaps the most intriguing piece of this story, the Montana Wilderness Association, never one to shy away from the use of litigation, publicly disagreed with the other environmental groups' protests, arguing that Clifford's efforts and the plan were "a model of public involvement."

Johnson says that she doesn't plan on litigating every timber sale, but she'll be using the courtroom more often because it's the only place she feels her voice is being heard. Clifford would rather see everyone sit down together and come up with some kind of compromise.

The Montana Environmental Information Center (MEIC), one of the most outspoken environmental groups in Montana, says it uses litigation to hold agencies accountable. John Ray, a professor at Montana Tech University and a former chair of MEIC's board of directors, argues that governmental agencies frequently fail to promote the public interest by not implementing environmental laws and policies. The reasons for this, Ray suggests, are "the nature of the bureaucratic personality," which Ray says is motivated by self-interest and the desire to gain power, status, money, and prestige, as well as by "the dictates of the bureaucratic structure." Agencies, he says, tend to promote the interests of client groups—the industries and user groups the agencies are supposed to regulate—over the public interest because those clients can bestow political power. Also, Ray points to a "revolving employment door" between the agencies and the client groups, which often leaves the fox guarding the henhouse. These client groups tend to benefit over the public interest when bureaucrats misuse their discretionary decision-making authority, Ray says. MEIC and other watchdog organizations then must use the rule of law to assert public control over agency actions and "guard the public from the guardians."[35]

In a recent example of such legal action, environmental groups sued the U.S. Department of the Interior to prevent it from permitting oil and gas exploration in the Dome Plateau region on the eastern boundary of Utah's Arches National Park. The Bush administration hoped to expedite proposals to drill on public lands throughout the West after Congress stymied the president's plan to drill in Alaska's Arctic National Wildlife Refuge. The environmental groups said that the Bureau of Land Management's environmental assessment for the project was inadequate. Although a federal judge granted a preliminary injunction to block seismic testing on the Dome Plateau, he warned plaintiffs that the merits of their case were "questionable."[36] A lawyer for the Southern Utah Wilderness Alliance, one of the plaintiffs, said, "There's no doubt it's an uphill battle any time you challenge a federal agency . . . but . . . a favorable decision could have very serious but positive ramifications for us in these other cases."[37]

On a more philosophical plane, the Center for Biological Diversity also uses litigation to pursue and achieve its interests. The Center argues that the natural world is under assault from human overpopulation and resource consumption, both of which are driving a massive and rapid extinction of species around the globe as well as the destruction of traditional cultures.[38]

Based on this premise, the Center believes that the health and vigor of human societies and the integrity and wildness of the natural environment are closely linked: "Beyond their extraordinary intrinsic value, animals and plants, in their distinctiveness and variety, offer irreplaceable emotional and physical benefits to our lives and play an integral part in culture. Their loss, which parallels the loss of diversity within and among human civilizations, impoverishes us beyond repair."[39] To promote biological diversity, the Center conducts the scientific studies necessary to prove what's at risk and uses those studies to petition agencies and litigate under the Endangered Species Act, the National Environmental Policy Act, the Resource Planning Act, and the National Forest Management Act. The Center is widely criticized and praised for its ability to limit and redirect growth and development in the American West.

The Ecology Center, a nonprofit conservation group based in Missoula, Montana, regularly appeals timber sales and other decisions on national forests in the Northern Rockies. Most recently, the group successfully appealed a sale that would have cut 700 acres of old growth in the Lewis and Clark National Forest.[40] The Ecology Center also joins forces with other organizations to share court costs and present a unified front on certain cases. Several groups filed a suit when the U.S. Environmental Protection Agency and the Montana Department of Environmental Quality were dragging their feet on recovery plans for polluted Montana waterways. According to the judge, development of the recovery plans would have taken more than 100 years at the rate the agencies were moving before the lawsuit.

These anecdotes illustrate that litigation can be a valuable strategy to address disputes over western resources. At its best, litigation provides an independent, formal arena for public participation where an impartial third party—a judge—governs both the process and its outcomes. It empowers individuals and small organizations to challenge agency decisions and hold public officials accountable. Apart from the political process, it is the only legal check on agency actions. Litigation allows the plaintiff to set the agenda, rather than reacting to an agenda established by a government agency. Even if outright victory is unlikely, the mere filing of a lawsuit may give an environmental or other organization important leverage. It usually forces action; when one side brings a suit and makes allegations, the other side must respond. Frequently, legislative intent and standards are clarified through litigation. Even when a lawsuit fails, legislators may step in to change the laws governing agency actions.

In some cases, litigation creates a safe space for agency staff and others to bring the best available scientific and technical information to bear on the dispute, thereby dulling the influence of arbitrary political decisions. (Indeed, some citizen suits are initiated with the quiet cooperation of agency personnel frustrated by the intrusion of partisan politics into decisions.) Along these lines, litigation can be a means of educating the public about a particular issue. It can also galvanize public opinion and serve as an effective vehicle to strengthen an organization—increasing membership and revenues—by demonstrating its vigilance, dedication, and competency. Litigation is also valuable because it is a process that is well understood; it goes forward under highly structured rules that are well known by the parties. Laws that are clear and specific tend to generate court decisions that are also clear and specific. Litigation can also establish precedents and thereby shape future actions and decisions.

Limitations of Litigation

Environmental watchdogs insist that lawsuits and appeals are often the only way to compel industry and government agencies to comply with laws designed to protect western lands and resources. But industry and agencies have long complained that "excessive" and "frivolous" lawsuits impede progress and hamper good faith efforts to build understanding and trust among stakeholders. They also say the courts are overburdened with "unwarranted" cases. Federal judges and the Supreme Court justices are beginning to heed these complaints and have gradually raised the standards a suit must clear to be heard in court, often citing constitutional requirements that the courts limit themselves to suits that involve specific "cases" and "controversies."[41]

Other observers have noted that litigation to achieve environmental objectives sometimes backfires.[42] In 2000, the U.S. Fish and Wildlife Service said it was so busy responding to lawsuits filed by environmental groups that it did not have enough money to add any more wildlife to the endangered species list for nearly a year. "We just don't have the staff or the funding necessary to do anything that isn't ordered by a court," said an agency spokesperson.[43] In January 2002, then-director of the U.S. Fish and Wildlife Service Jamie Rappaport Clark placed a moratorium on additions to the endangered list, saying the agency's resources were being gobbled up by critical habitat designation. Said Clark: "Critical habitat has turned our priorities upside-down. Species that are in need of protection are having to be ignored. This is a biological disaster."[44]

One emerging consequence of a perceived overuse of litigation is to limit or restrict the conditions under which agency decisions can be appealed. During the 2001 session, the Montana legislature reduced to sixty days the appeal period on decisions under the Montana Environmental Policy Act (MEPA). In the 2003 session, legislators considered a bill to restrict or limit the ability of citizens to appeal decisions under MEPA.[45]

In August 2002, Senate majority leader Tom Daschle quietly added a provision to a counterterrorism bill just days before Congress adjourned for its summer recess. The provision had nothing to do with counterterrorism; rather, it exempted some logging projects in the Black Hills National Forest from environmental regulations and lawsuits. Loggers, two environmental groups, and the Forest Service jointly developed and agreed to the provision, which included no chance for public participation or appeal. The western

and overwhelmingly Republican response to the Black Hills rider was pre-
dictable: apply Senator Daschle's model to the entire national forest system.
Using Daschle's language practically verbatim, Montana congressman Den-
nis Rehberg drafted just such a bill—the National Forest Fire Prevention
Act—specifically exempting actions taken under the act from scrutiny under
NEPA, the National Forest Management Act, and the Appeals Reform Act.[46]

In August 2002, under the guise of fire prevention, the Bush administration also began to float a number of proposals—collectively known as the
Healthy Forests Initiative—to streamline public and environmental review
prior to logging, drilling, and other activities in national forests. On November 27, 2002, the administration announced a set of proposed regulations
that would reduce the number of scientific and environmental reviews required to develop new forest management plans, restrict public input, and
allow agencies to disregard form letters and preprinted postcards.[47]

According to the *Washington Post*: "Administration officials say the
change is needed to speed up an overly burdensome, time-consuming
process in which it is too difficult to make justified changes in national forest policies."[48] The Forest Service claims that the expedited process will be
simpler, easier to understand, and more efficient. "The streamlined studies
would cost about one-third less, saving the government $1 billion over 10
years," Forest Service officials say. According to the Forest Service, "this new
rule cuts out a lot of red tape" and will "better harmonize the environmental, social and economic benefits" of national forests.[49]

On December 11, 2002, the Bush administration announced another set
of plans to eliminate certain types of projects from environmental and public review under the National Environmental Policy Act.[50] Using a provision
under NEPA that allows "categorical exclusions," the Bush administration
would allow forest-thinning projects and wildfire restoration projects to go
forward without environmental review and with no opportunity for citizen
appeal or litigation. Administration officials continue to argue that the proposed changes will simplify the process, make it easier for people to understand, require people to get involved earlier in the process, and improve the
ability to manage forests and reduce wildfires. Some forest managers agree,
saying that proposed projects are in fact reviewed and that only those which
would have minimal or no environmental impact are approved.

The Bush administration and some state legislatures believe that limiting
public participation by fast-forwarding environmental reviews and restrict-
ing the ability to appeal decisions will improve the management of western

resources. But the General Accounting Office (GAO) of the federal government concluded that very few projects to reduce wildfire threats on the national forests are delayed for a lengthy time because of challenges and appeals.[51] According to the GAO report, released in spring 2003, only 180 out of 762 projects were appealed. Of those 180 projects, 142 were processed within the standard ninety-day review period. The other appealed projects took longer than ninety days because of staff shortages, a backlog of appeals, or the need to give the parties time to negotiate a resolution. The report shows that 95 percent of the 762 Forest Service projects to reduce wildfire hazards were ready for implementation within the standard ninety-day review period. This conclusion supports the findings of a similar study conducted by Northern Arizona University's Ecological Restoration Institute and contradicts the claim made by the Forest Service that almost half of such projects were appealed.[52]

Attempts to curtail environmental review, public participation, and appeals are symptoms of the problems that underlie the governance of western resources. Commenting on the Black Hills rider, Daniel Kemmis says: "While wildfire is clearly a major problem for the West, it is only the symptom of a much deeper problem. Even if all forest health issues were magically resolved tomorrow, nothing would have been done to restore our public land management system to health. That system is deeply diseased, and it cannot be cured by treating symptoms."[53]

Our focus here is not to diagnose and offer prescriptions on problems related to federal lands governance per se. For our purposes, the Black Hills rider, the Bush Healthy Forests Initiative, and the criticism surrounding proposals to limit public participation and opportunities for citizen appeals and lawsuits demonstrate the potentially destructive nature of too little meaningful public participation and too much litigation. Many observers agree that the sheer number of civil cases is paralyzing our judicial system. One commentator suggests that the burgeoning caseload facing many state and federal courts renders the right to a speedy trial practically meaningless. Another growing concern is the cost of litigation, not only in monetary terms but, perhaps more importantly, in limiting one of the ideals of this country's judicial system, equal access.

Litigation is also frequently criticized as incapable of resolving disputes in a way that parties feel is fair and effective. By definition, the process results in winners and losers. Depending on the issues, the losers may not go away but may simply reload and carry the dispute to another venue—

administrative, judicial, and then perhaps to a legislative body. While more than 90 percent of all civil lawsuits are settled prior to a jury or court decision, the process of settlement is "awkward, time-consuming, and expensive." Defendants complain that delays and legal fees are just preludes to the "inevitable settlement."[54]

Another obvious limitation of litigation as a means to dispute resolution is that the disputants turn to a third party—a judge—for a decision, rather than trying to resolve the issue on their own. In complex environmental disputes, this raises the risk that the decision will be made without as full an understanding of the issues as is available to the stakeholders themselves.

In the same way that court procedures can take advantage of the best available scientific and technical information, they may also constrain the introduction of evidence and thereby limit the use of the best available information. Litigation focuses on historical facts or events that have transpired between the parties to a lawsuit, not the larger and more relevant body of "social facts." In this respect, litigation provides no room for planning. Judges base their decisions on "antecedent facts." In social policy, it is critical to plan for the future based in part on the knowledge of past experience.

Litigation and the courts may reinforce the influence of the scientific management model by deferring to agency expertise on matters of statutory interpretation and the facts of the case, and by allowing broad delegations of authority to the executive branch under the nondelegation clause of article I of the U.S. Constitution. However, federal judges have become increasingly willing to second-guess agency expertise using the "hard look" doctrine, which is a more stringent standard of judicial review than the long-established "rational base" test. In these cases, the courts are playing a more activist role in shaping policy, making administrative decisions, and resolving disputes. In this respect, when judges interpret statutes and analyze evidence, they often develop and enforce their own—possibly misguided—concept of the public interest.

Another limitation is that litigation is piecemeal. It only deals with the case presented, thereby resulting in incremental decision making, which may not adequately consider the larger policy questions. And courts act only when litigants call. It is a passive, reactive forum and does not initiate action when needed. It is the "forum of last resort." Generally, it is much easier for the plaintiff to prevail by showing that the agency in question committed an error of procedure rather than a bad policy decision. It follows, then, that much litigation is directed at narrow procedural and legal issues, instead of the underlying policy question.

In the context of western resources, courts are faced with the underlying problem that Congress has promulgated conflicting mandates. How should the courts weigh and balance the multiple, conflicting interests of multiple use, preservation, and so on? With some exception (namely the public trust doctrine), neither Congress, executive agencies, nor the courts have provided helpful directions or standards on how to resolve such disputes. As we've seen in the Klamath situation, even a single agency—the U.S. Fish and Wildlife Service—appears unable to reconcile its conflicting responsibilities to manage upstream wildlife refuges and protect downstream habitat for endangered anadromous fish.

Finally, the basis for a decision or resolution is "rights." The court is usually faced with the questions "Does one party have a legal right?" and "Does another party have a duty?" This focus on rights and duties tends to stifle discussion of alternative solutions that might integrate the underlying interests. It does not necessarily include a consideration of costs, and it eliminates, for all practical purposes, any consideration of interests.

Potential Tool—Alternative Dispute Resolution

As a result of the limitations associated with the use of litigation, people are increasingly turning to alternative methods of preventing and resolving disputes. Collectively referred to as alternative dispute resolution (or ADR), these processes include various forms of negotiation, mediation, and arbitration. Proponents argue that ADR can reduce the number of pending lawsuits and address many of the weaknesses associated with the traditional process of adjudication. Specifically, proponents argue that ADR reduces the backlog of cases, makes a better use of court resources by allowing judges to dedicate more time to lawsuits that require court or jury deliberations, and facilitates early and direct communication among the disputants, thereby improving their understanding of the issues and interests. Other proponents believe that ADR procedures can (1) sustain and improve relationships by minimizing acrimony, frustration, and adversarial confrontation; (2) foster fairer and more effective outcomes by involving the disputants directly in the decision-making and dispute resolution process; and (3) generate more flexible and creative remedies that satisfy the real needs and interests of the parties.

In one recent case, a judge ordered the use of mediation to resolve a dispute over a proposal for one of the largest timber sales in Montana history. In the summer of 2000, wildfires burned more than 300,000 acres in the Bitterroot National Forest. In an attempt to expedite the decision-making process and quickly implement a forest restoration plan, the Forest Service limited public participation and bypassed its own internal appeals process. In December 2001, Undersecretary of Agriculture Mark Rey approved the plan to remove 176 million board feet of timber from 46,000 acres on the Bitterroot. Shortly after the restoration plan was approved, seven environmental groups filed a lawsuit decrying the plan's impact on watersheds and wildlife habitat and contesting the agency's refusal to accept administrative appeals. A U.S. district judge sided with the plaintiffs, saying that the process violated the public's right to be involved in decision making. "It is presumptuous," the judge wrote in his decision, "to believe that the agency's final decision has a perfection about it that would not be illuminated by interested comment, questioning, or requests for justification of propositions asserted in it."[55] He granted a temporary injunction against the logging plan until the Forest Service complied with its own established appeals process.

When the Forest Service appealed that decision, the court ordered the agency to enter into mediation—with the undersecretary and regional forester present in Missoula—to settle the dispute. Another federal judge presided over the two-day mediation, and environmental groups and loggers negotiated a new plan with the Forest Service to salvage 55 million board feet of timber, prohibiting removal of any trees over 22 inches in diameter and protecting 15,000 acres of roadless area in the bargain.[56] But as the timber sale moved forward, the Forest Service filed a motion in district court, arguing that the 22-inch size limit applied only to living trees, and that loggers should be allowed to cut 199 dead trees in the larger-size class. In June 2003, a federal judge denied the agency's request.[57]

Mandating the use of mediation to resolve such a dispute over natural resources is rare, but the use of negotiation, mediation, and other forms of dispute resolution to resolve court-connected disputes is well established. For example, in 1996, Montana's Supreme Court adopted Rule 54, which requires mediation in worker's compensation cases, specific domestic relations disputes, and civil cases seeking a money judgment or monetary damages. During the three-year period from 1997 through 1999, 1,820 cases were appealed to the Montana Supreme Court, and 698 of those cases were referred to mediation under Rule 54. Of the 698 cases, 169 were settled, for a success rate of about 24 percent. Other studies demonstrate a similar degree of success.

Section 164(e) of the Clean Air Act mandates negotiation to resolve selected types of disputes among tribes, states, and the Environmental Protection Agency. The provision has been used only four times since 1977, raising questions about the value of requiring the use of more cooperative approaches to dispute resolution.[58]

The literature on using ADR to resolve court-connected disputes suggests that the likelihood of success can be improved by adhering to six key principles:

1. Recognize that each dispute is unique and that any ADR process should be tailored to match the specific situation. Provide a range of different types of ADR processes.
2. Rather than mandating the use of ADR, give judges the discretion and tools to apply it in appropriate cases. As far as possible, allow the parties to enter the ADR process voluntarily; some people see mandatory participation as undue pressure to settle.
3. Select a neutral third party when a mediator or facilitator is needed—someone credible and trustworthy to all parties in the dispute. Clearly define the neutral party's role, responsibilities, and liabilities. Provide ongoing training and education for court-connected ADR practitioners.
4. When recommending that parties settle a dispute through ADR, the court must clearly identify who should participate, define expectations for "good faith" participation, and specify sanctions to ensure compliance.
5. Be aware of power imbalances among the parties. Some states avoid the use of mediation in domestic violence cases, for example, because of likely power imbalances between the abusers and the victims. In less extreme cases, mediators can take responsibility for protecting the weaker interests.
6. Ensure that settlements include a plan for implementing and monitoring the agreement.[59]

Litigation is an important strategy in resolving western resource disputes, particularly where the case will likely set a precedent or in disputes over fundamental values. It also acts as an incentive for the parties to enter mediation or negotiation to avoid a less favorable outcome in court. Indeed, many natural resource lawsuits are settled before going to trial. But it may be possible to improve the role of litigation by further integrating opportunities for principled negotiation, mediation, and other forms of "alternative" dispute resolution into the process of litigating and appealing decisions. In this respect, litigation can provide the incentive for disputing parties, including public officials, to come to the ADR table and seek agreement and resolution. Also, the use of ADR does not preclude litigation—if the issues cannot be resolved after a good faith ADR effort, the parties can continue with litigation.

Citizens want to be involved in shaping public policy that affects their lives. As this chapter illustrates, they are willing to use whatever means are available to make sure their voices are heard. When other avenues are closed to them, or have reached a point of diminishing returns, citizens can rely on ballot initiatives and litigation to draw attention to their cause and perhaps even prevail over entrenched interests. But these are relatively expensive, combative processes, and other approaches can be more inclusive, informed, and deliberative—and can also produce better substantive outcomes.

NOTES

1. Alexander Hamilton, John Jay, and James Madison, *The Federalist*, no. 10, p. 21.
2. Daniel Kemmis, *Community and the Politics of Place* (Norman: University of Oklahoma Press, 1982).
3. Jennifer Drage Bower, "The Initiative: Take It or Leave It," *State Legislatures* (June 2002): 22–23.
4. Regarding tax-related initiatives, see Dane Waters, *A Century of Citizen Lawmaking: An American Experiment in Self-Governance*, Initiative and Referendum Institute, http://www.iandrinstitute.org.
5. Becky Watson, "Direct Democracy: Anti-mining Initiatives" (paper delivered at the 1999 Mining Lawyers Conference, Lake George, New York).
6. Phyllis Myers and Robert Puentes, *Growth at the Ballot Box: Electing the Shape of Communities in November 2000* (Washington, DC: Brookings Institution, 2001).
7. Donna Kemp Spangler and Bob Bernick Jr., "Initiative Chaos Coming to Utah?" *Deseret News*, August 28, 2002, http://www.deseretnews.com.
8. Initiatives Database, Hastings Law Library, University of California Hastings College of the Law, http://holmes.uchastings.edu.
9. Initiative and Referendum Institute database, http://www.iandrinstitute.org/.

10. Oregon State Legislature, "Citizen's Guide to the Oregon Legislative Process," http://www.leg.state.or.us/citizenguide/home.htm.

11. M. Dane Waters, *A Century of Citizen Lawmaking: An American Experiment in Self-Governance*, Initiative and Referendum Institute database, http://www.iandrinstitute.org/.

12. Jack Kemp, *An American Renaissance: A Strategy for the 1980's* (New York: Berkley Publishing Group, 1981), 187–89.

13. Waters, *A Century of Citizen Lawmaking*.

14. Michelle DeArmond (Associated Press), "Californians Reconsider Gambling," *Las Vegas Review-Journal*, February 29, 2000, http://www.reviewjournal.com/lvrj_home/2000/Feb-29-Tue-2000/business/13058387.html.

15. See Jennifer Drage Bowser, "The Initiative—Take It or Leave It? *State Legislatures* (June 2002): 22–23, which highlights a number of reform movements around the country. See also Montana Consensus Council, *Citizen Initiative Dialogue Agreement Document* (August 9, 2000), which summarizes the results of a facilitated negotiation on improving the citizen initiative process in Montana.

16. "Initiatives Abused by Special Interest," *Reno Gazette-Journal*, November 3, 2002.

17. Lydia Chavez, *The Color Bind* (Berkeley: University of California Press, 1998).

18. David B. Magleby, "Let the Voters Decide? An Assessment of the Initiative and Referendum Process," *University of Colorado Law Review* 66 (1995): 13.

19. Peter Schrag, *Paradise Lost: California's Experience, America's Future* (New York: New Press, 1998).

20. Bowser, "The Initiative—Take It or Leave It?"

21. David S. Broder, "A Republic Subverted," in *Democracy Derailed: Initiative Campaigns and the Power of Money* (New York: Harcourt, 2000), 1–21.

22. Spangler and Bernick Jr., "Initiative Chaos Coming to Utah?"

23. Constitutional Amendments C-37 and C-38, "Montana Secretary of State Bob Brown, 2002 Ballot Measures," http://sos.state.mt.us/css/ELB/Ballot_Measures.asp.

24. John R. Ehrmann and Michael T. Lesnick, "The Policy Dialogue: Applying Mediation to the Policy-Making Process," *Mediation Quarterly* 20 (Summer 1988): 93–99.

25. Ehrmann and Lesnick, "The Policy Dialogue."

26. For general background on this topic, see Samuel Trask Dana and Sally K. Fairfax, "Citizen Activism in Forest and Range Policy in the 1970s," in *Forest and Range Policy: Its Development in the United States*, 311–20 (New York: McGraw-Hill, 1980); and Robert B. Keiter, "Ecological Policy and the Courts: Of Rights, Processes, and the Judicial Role," *Human Ecology Review* 4, no. 1 (1997): 2–8.

27. *Sierra Club v. Morton*, 405 U.S. 727 (1972).

28. *Sierra Club v. Morton.*

29. *Udall v. Federal Power Commission,* 387 U.S. 438 (1967). As quoted in Vawter Parker, "Natural Resources Management by Litigation," in *A New Century for Natural Resources Management,* ed. Richard L. Knight and Sarah F. Bates, 209–20 (Washington, DC: Island Press, 1995).

30. *Udall v. Federal Power Commission.*

31. Jeffery G. Miller, *Citizen Suits: Private Enforcement of Federal Pollution Control Laws* (New York: Wiley Law Publishers, 1987), 1–15.

32. George C. Coggins, Charles F. Wilkinson, and John D. Leshy, *Federal Public Lands and Resources Law,* 5th ed. (New York: Foundation Press, 2002), 303.

33. *Endangered Species Act* 16 *U.S. Code* 1531.

34. Eve Byron, "Working through a Log Jam," *Helena Independent Record,* March 4, 2002, http://www.helenair.com.

35. John W. Ray, "Bureaucracy, Public Policy, and Environmental Protection," *Down to Earth* (newsletter of the Montana Environmental Information Center, November 2002), 16.

36. Eric Pianin, "Judge Halts Utah Oil Project; Environmentalists to Argue against Exploring Region," *Washington Post,* November 1, 2002, http://www.washingtonpost.com.

37. Pianin, "Judge Halts Utah Oil Project."

38. Center for Biological Diversity, http://www.biologicaldiversity.org.

39. Center for Biological Diversity, http://www.biologicaldiversity.org.

40. Ecology Center, Ecosystem Defense Program, http://www.wildrockies.org/TECI/programs/defense.html.

41. William Glaberson, "Novel Antipollution Tool Is Being Upset by Courts," *New York Times,* June 5, 1999.

42. Tom Knudson, "Litigation Central: A Flood of Costly Lawsuits Raises Questions about Motive," *Sacramento Bee,* April 24, 2001.

43. "No More Endangered Species?" *Helena Independent Record,* November 22, 2000, 8c.

44. Knudson, "Litigation Central."

45. See "Montana House Bill 437," http://data.opi.state.mt.us/bills/2003/billhtml/HB0437.htm.

46. The National Forest Fire Prevention Act, HR 5214, sponsored by Congressman Dennis Rehberg. Paradoxically, nine months earlier, Rehberg had sponsored a bill to create a United States Consensus Council (HR 3305). As of this writing, both bills are still under consideration.

47. See "President Announces Healthy Forests Initiative" (remarks by the president in Central Point, Oregon, August 8, 2002), http://www.whitehouse.gov.releases. See also Sherry Devlin, "Forest Bill Sails Through," *Missoulian,* October 31,

2003. The provisions streamlining public participation for areas in the "wild-land-urban interface" (Sec. 104 (d)(1)) were included in the Healthy Forests Restoration Act, signed into law December 2003 (H.R. 1904).

48. Mike Allen, "Bush to Shorten Forest Environmental Reviews," *Washington Post,* November 28, 2002, A1.

49. Allen, "Bush to Shorten Forest Environmental Reviews."

50. Mike Soraghan, "White House Forest Plan to Thin Out Logging Rules," *Denver Post,* December 12, 2002; Laura Paskus, "Bush Undermines Bedrock Environmental Law," *High Country News,* October 28, 2002, http://www.hcn.org/servlets/hcn.Article?article_id=13467. See also Matt Jenkins, "Forest Planning Gets a Facelift," *High Country News,* December 23, 2002, http://www.hcn.org/servlets/hcn.Article?article_id=13611.

51. See Eve Byron, "GAO: Appeals Don't Seriously Delay Forest Projects," *Helena Independent Record,* September 16, 2003.

52. Hanna J. Cortner et al., *Designing a Framework for Evaluating the Impacts and Outcomes of Forest Service Appeals* and *Analyzing USDA Forest Service Appeals: Phase 1, The Database* (Ecological Restoration Institute, March 2003), http://www.eri.nau.edu; U.S. Forest Service, *The Process Predicament: How Statutory, Regulatory, and Administrative Factors Affect National Forest Management* (June 2002).

53. Daniel Kemmis, "Daschle's Move Proved a Bigger Point," *Headwaters News,* August 25, 2002.

54. Benjamin Sokoly, *Institutionalization of Court-Annexed ADR: An Examination of Five States' Provisions* (unpublished, undated manuscript on file with the authors).

55. Katherine Q. Seelye, "Judge Overrules Decision Allowing Logging of Burned Trees," *New York Times Online,* January 10, 2002, http://www.fire.uni-freiburg.de/media/news_01102002_us2.htm.

56. "Deal Limits Logging, Protects Habitat in Montana's Bitterroot NF," *Cyberwest,* February 7, 2002, http://www.cyberwest.com/cw21/bitterroot_logging.shtml.

57. Sherry Devlin, "Ruling Protects Dead Bitterroot Trees," *Missoulian,* June 27, 2003, http://www.headwatersnews.org/miss.treerule.html.

58. See Maureen Hartmann and Matthew McKinney, "Resolving Disputes under Section 164(e) of the Clean Air Act: Experience and Lessons Learned" (working paper on file with the authors, September 3, 2003).

59. Benjamin Sokoly, *Institutionalization of Court-Annexed ADR.*

6

This Land Is Our Land

The previous two chapters explained how public participation and litigation in the public interest are designed to improve the scientific management model of resolving disputes by requiring opportunities for citizen
participation throughout the process. Citizen initiatives, by contrast, provide an opportunity to do an end run around the administrative state. And
negotiation and consensus building, which are addressed in chapter 7, are
for the most part ad hoc forums designed to supplement the legislative, executive, and judicial processes.

In this chapter, we examine another approach to resolving disputes and
making decisions over western resources. The essence of this strategy is devolution, or decentralizing the authority to make decisions. Unlike the other
strategies that have emerged during the past century, devolution explicitly
questions the legitimacy of centralized, scientific management. It raises the
fundamental issues of who should decide how western resources are used
and how disputes should be resolved.

Before examining the rationale behind devolution as it is promoted
today, let us review the history of earlier efforts to decentralize the authority
over natural resources in the West.

Efforts to Decentralize Control over Western Resources

The West has long been the home of pioneering people who, rather than waiting for government to solve problems, assume the responsibility for creating forums to address a variety of western resource issues. Indeed, this was the spirit behind the "claims clubs" formed by settlers in the 1800s who banded together to discourage outsiders and newcomers from bidding on land that club members wanted for themselves. More often than not, the claims clubs were one step ahead of federal surveyors, and the allocation of nationally owned lands fell to local interests. Similarly, westerners have joined forces to assert greater local control over federal land management, water, and fish, wildlife, and parks. A closer look at these attempts reveals that the call to devolution has shifted over the past century from specific issues, such as grazing access and predator control, to an overarching movement to strip authority from the federal government and give it to the states or counties.

Federal Land Management

Under the current model of governance over federal lands, the federal government—Congress in particular—has legal primacy or control.[1] State and local governments have no legal authority to make or enforce decisions over the use of natural resources that fall under the complex web of laws governing the use of federal lands and resources, even when those decisions implicate the interests of state and local jurisdictions. While there have been a few experiments that share the authority to make decisions and resolve disputes, these efforts have not significantly changed the balance of power between the federal government and state and local governments.[2] Laws such as the National Environmental Policy Act, the Endangered Species Act, and the Federal Land Policy and Management Act require little more than consultation with state and local jurisdictions and stop well short of giving states and local communities the ability to veto decisions by the federal government.

While this model of governance provides some assurance that national goals will be achieved, it is not surprising that westerners have opposed national ownership and management of federal lands for at least a century.[3] In 1909, westerners organized the Western Conservation League and the National Domain League to, respectively, "destroy federal tenantry by . . . freeing the natural resources from the clutches of the Eastern socialists" and to

"restore the rights of farmers, stockmen, and miners to the public domain."
In response, the U.S. Forest Service established state conservation commissions in 1909 that led, at least briefly, to greater acceptance of national resource policy among western citizens and officials.

Several years later, when the Forest Service proposed to increase grazing fees, Senator Stanfield (R-Oregon) convened a series of public hearings throughout the West that did not block the proposed increase but resulted in the creation, by President Herbert Hoover in 1929, of the Committee on the Conservation and Administration of the Public Domain.[4] The committee, composed largely of representatives from the national livestock association, concluded that federal grazing lands were being ruined and should be regulated by the people who know how best to use such resources—the residents of the western states themselves. The committee recommended that the states should be given the remaining public domain on one condition: the federal government should retain title to the mineral estate.

Needless to say, the general reaction of western people was mixed; on the one hand, they appreciated the offer to assume ownership and authority of the surface rights, but on the other, they disagreed with the recommendation to leave mineral rights under the jurisdiction of the federal government. Conservationists, worried that western interests would exploit national resources, opposed any such transfer of ownership, authority, or responsibility. Attempts to implement the commission's recommendations bogged down in a battle among critics within the federal agencies, states, stockmen, and conservationists.

Realizing that national control of federal lands in the West was inevitable, stock growers redirected their energies to the task of designing a management framework that simultaneously acquiesced to federal jurisdiction and allowed for as much local control as possible. The result was the Taylor Grazing Act of 1934, which directed the secretary of the interior to establish grazing districts, create advisory boards of local stockmen, and allocate range rights according to the principle of first in time, first in right.

Not completely satisfied with the implementation of the Taylor Grazing Act, Senator Pat McCarran of Nevada introduced a resolution in the Senate (in 1940) on behalf of western stockmen criticizing the new Grazing Service and calling for a study, including field hearings in the West. Four years later, the study concluded that state ownership of public lands was preferable to national control and that private ownership should be the long-term objective for western rangelands.[5]

According to Daniel Kemmis, the effort to decentralize control over federal lands in the West lay largely dormant between 1950 and 1975. The movement was reinvigorated in the late 1970s as something of a backlash to the adoption of the National Environmental Policy Act (1970), the Clean Water Act (1972), the Endangered Species Act (1973), and other pieces of environmental legislation.[6] Given the preponderance of federal lands in the West, the provisions of this national framework for environmental protection came to roost more heavily on this region than on any other.

In 1976, another federal law—the Federal Land Policy and Management Act (FLPMA)—further fueled interest in decentralizing control of western lands. FLPMA expressly affirmed the national government's intent to keep lands admistered by the Bureau of Land Management (BLM) in public ownership. With very few exceptions, the national government's policy since the mid-1800s had been to consider the federal government as a temporary steward of federal lands until they were claimed and privatized.[7] In response to this basic shift in policy, the Nevada state legislature passed Assembly Bill 413 in 1979, claiming all Nevada land administered by the BLM as state property. This bill, later referred to as the Sagebrush Rebellion bill, rested on the "equal footing" doctrine of the U.S. Constitution, which says that a new state must enter the Union on an "equal footing" with other states. The legislators argued that states dominated by federal lands couldn't possibly operate economically or in any other way on an equal footing with other states. According to the state deputy attorney general who helped draft the legislation, such an overwhelming presence limits the state's sovereignty.

By the end of 1980, Nevada, Utah, Wyoming, New Mexico, and Arizona had all enacted bills claiming federal public lands as state property. Hawaii, Alaska, and Idaho passed "supportive resolutions," while Washington State passed similar legislation and put it before citizens in a referendum. In 1981, President Ronald Reagan appointed James G. Watt (formerly with the Mountain States Legal Foundation, a nonprofit legal center dedicated to promoting private property rights and limited government) as secretary of the interior. Rather than grant ownership of federal lands to the states, Watt aimed to provide opportunities for westerners to be more meaningfully involved in decisions over federal lands and resources. Nevadans, led by state senator Norman Glaser, worried that Watt's approach might undermine the enthusiasm for their movement.

Not content to sit by and hope Watt's approach would in fact nullify the movement, environmentalists went to court and persuaded U.S. district court judge Edward Reed to reject Nevada's Sagebrush bill. Reed declared that "no state legislation may interfere with Congress' power over the public domain."[8] This legal defeat, combined with the loss of political momentum caused by Watt's approach, took a great deal of steam out of the movement.

When the "rebellion" next surfaced, proponents' claims of sovereignty over western lands had shifted from state to county jurisdiction. Realizing that taking ownership of federal lands would be very expensive, this next move asserted control over federal lands and resources without assuming the financial responsibilities of ownership. In 1991, Catron County, New Mexico, published its *Interim Land Use Policy Plan*. The plan asserted county jurisdiction over all federal and state lands, waters, and wildlife within its borders; prohibited wilderness designation; required county approval for all actions on state and federal lands; and stated the county's intent to protect the "custom and culture" of the area. The introduction of the plan started with the demand that all lands not designated as "specific lands" be "relinquished to the citizens, echoing the disposal policies of the nineteenth century to transfer federal lands to private ownership."

From Catron County, the so-called "county supremacy" movement spread rapidly across the West. By 1993, the National Federal Lands Conference claimed to have as many as 200 counties enrolled in the movement. The basic argument of county supremacy advocates is that federal lands were not reserved to the United States at the time of statehood. Moreover, they say, federal laws allow deference to local "custom and culture," which some westerners prefer to define almost entirely as the local extractive or resource-dependent industries, such as logging, mining, ranching, and farming.[9] Once these customs and cultures are identified, federal agencies must by law and regulation defer to them to allow counties to determine their own policy.

Other observers of the western scene argue that the phrase "custom and culture" does not appear in any of the statutes regulating federal land and resource agencies.[10] Moreover, they point out, the Property Clause of Article IV of the U.S. Constitution grants Congress and no other entity—certainly not states or counties—control over federal land and resources.

During the last half of the 1990s, the county supremacy movement, like so many earlier attempts to denationalize western federal lands, began to fade. In 1995, the U.S. government filed suit against Nye County, Nevada, in response to their Catron County–like land use plan. Federal attorneys argued that resolutions in the plan were unconstitutional, and that the federal government has sovereignty over federal lands. In 1996, the U.S. district court ruled against Nye County, saying that the federal government "owns and has the power and authority to manage and administer the unappropriated public lands and National Forest Service lands in Nye County."[11] A year later, federal agencies and the county entered into a settlement agreement that established a framework for working together to resolve disputes and manage public natural resources.

After these failed attempts to transfer sovereignty from the national government to state or local governments, disgruntled westerners resorted to more symbolic gestures. In January 2000, protestors paraded through Elko, Nevada, with nearly 10,000 shovels sent from across the West.[12] The shovels were symbols of solidarity with locals who wanted to reopen 1.5 miles of gravel road on national forest land. Federal officials gated the end of the road after the Jarbidge River jumped its banks in 1995 and washed out the roadbed. The U.S. Fish and Wildlife Service said that repairing the road would add silt to the river and harm the resident bull trout, listed as endangered in 1998. A federal judge sided with the government and ordered that the section of road remain closed. As a symbol of their frustration, the self-proclaimed Shovel Brigade erected a giant shovel in front of the county courthouse in Elko. More than 13,000 people paid $1 each to have their names engraved on the shovel. Then, on July 4, 2000, several hundred people from around the country joined the Shovel Brigade and removed a four-ton boulder—dubbed "Liberty Rock"—from the roadblock created by the U.S. Forest Service. Organizers were charged with trespassing, and a judge ordered parties into mediation. In the resulting settlement, Elko County and the federal agencies agreed to allow the county to rebuild the road if it paid for the work and adhered to all federal environmental laws to protect the bull trout.

Even in its formative days, the Shovel Brigade invigorated like-minded people around the West. Early in 2000, citizens in Libby, Montana, organized and then canceled an April 15 rally against President Clinton's environmental policies, which were characterized as the "environmental regime's war on the West." Despite the cancellation, three dozen people showed up and burned a United Nations flag in the spring rain. On June 21, 2000, several thousand lumber workers and motorized recreationists led a mock funeral procession through Missoula, Montana, complete with a coffin full of comments against Clinton's Roadless Area Initiative, which proposed to set aside more than 40 million acres as wilderness. Similar rallies were held during the Klamath Basin crisis, including a "Bucket Brigade" that emptied fifty buckets of water from an Upper Klamath Lake tributary into an irrigation canal. This symbolic protest garnered media coverage for the protestors' message: "Us now, you're next."[13] Interestingly, both the Jarbidge Shovel Brigade and the Klamath Bucket Brigade evolved into ongoing volunteer organizations aimed at preserving their communities.[14]

Water

Despite challenges over the years, westerners have maintained a significant amount of local control over water. As explained in chapter 1, the prior appropriation doctrine is fundamentally a grassroots, place-based system for resolving disputes and governing use of the resource. The most senior user of water, not necessarily the most upstream user, has the most control, and on down the line. This system is institutionalized throughout the West through a system of state-issued permits and administrative agencies. Until recently, broader regional or national interests had generally chosen not to interfere with state-run water management.

There have been a few notable exceptions. As California's cities grew, they reached farther afield to meet increasing demand for water. In 1906, Congress debated whether to allow Los Angeles to divert water from the Owens River on the east side of the Sierra Nevada. Locals wanted the water to stay put for irrigation and their own use. President Teddy Roosevelt ended the argument, declaring that "it is a hundred or a thousand fold more important to the state and more valuable to the people as a whole if [the water is] used by the city than if used by the people of the Owens Valley."[15] Similarly, in 1913, Congress approved San Francisco's proposal to dam Yosemite's Hetch Hetchy Valley to supply the city's water.

Today, Colorado's Front Range cities grapple with the same demand-and-supply crisis: 85 percent of the state's population lives east of the Continental Divide, and 75 percent of the state's precipitation falls on the western slopes. One proposed solution, labeled "The Big Straw," is to build a $5 billion, 200-mile-long, 10-foot-wide pipeline to suck water from the Colorado River at the Colorado-Utah border and pump it over the hill to Denver.[16] West-slope irrigators and conservationists are understandably concerned, but proponents of the scheme say existing water rights will be respected. Project proponents even go so far as to use the "local control" argument to justify rerouting nature's course from one end of the state to the other. If Colorado doesn't use the water allocated to it under the 1922 Colorado

River Compact, they warn, California may lay claim to it. Despite the doctrine's bias in favor of local interests and historic use, such out-of-basin calls on water (with little protection or recourse for local users) are not unusual under the prior appropriation system.

Today, one of the biggest challenges to local control over water is the looming presence of federal reserved water rights. Under the *Winters vs. United States* decision, these reserved rights were implicitly established when Congress set aside (or "reserved") lands for tribal use, wilderness, military bases, national parks and forests, and other public uses requiring the use of water to fulfill their purposes. Other water rights holders and water managers live with uncertainty because these federal reserved rights would have an early, if not senior, priority date, and the amount of water needed to fill these rights has yet to be determined.

Another challenge to the West's history of local control over water resources is the impact of federal regulatory powers. In 1990, the Environmental Protection Agency vetoed the proposed Two Forks dam on the South Platte River near Denver, citing concerns over compliance with the Clean Water Act.[17] Also, section 303(d) of the Clean Water Act requires the government to set limits on the amount of pollutants that a water body can receive and still meet water quality standards. These limits, known as total maximum daily loads (TMDLs), trigger regulatory action when pollutant levels are exceeded, either because of contaminated inflow or because of water withdrawals that reduce the water body's capacity for dilution.[18] Finally, as dramatically illustrated by the Klamath Basin situation, enforcement of the Endangered Species Act can limit historic diversions and uses of water. These and other federal regulatory requirements restrict the exercise of appropriative water rights issued under state water law and limit the discretion of states to define water rights.

Fish, Wildlife, and Parks

While Congress alone holds the power to manage public resources, it can delegate authority to the executive branch as well as to local and state governments. The best example of delegating authority to states is wildlife management, for which states are explicitly given authority to set seasons and limits and to enforce those regulations on federal and state lands.[19] The Clean Water Act and the Clean Air Act also provide opportunities for states to assume responsibility for federal programs and mandates. These arrangements are based on the principle of federalism, an approach to devolution that relies on legal and institutional checks and balances to ensure that states comply with overall national policy.

The notion that wildlife is owned by the government is an extension of the European concept that game animals belonged to the Crown.[20] In this context, ownership implies stewardship as well; the government's responsibility to protect wildlife was brought to the fore as hunters and trappers moved west and nearly wiped out bison, beaver, and other game and fur species. States took the lead in protecting their wildlife. California was the first western state to create its own fish and game agency, in 1878, and other western states soon had their own game agencies or commissions. Likewise, many states passed legislation to protect dwindling herds of big game; in 1879, Michigan enacted a ten-year moratorium on elk hunting, and Wyoming did the same for bison in 1890, four years before Congress acted to save bison from certain extinction. The original Lacey Act, enacted in 1900, protected game birds and other wild birds by prohibiting interstate shipping of wildlife taken in violation of a state game law.[21] This effectively ended commercial hunting, dramatically reducing the harvest of many species, and also strengthened the states' position as wildlife administrators.

By the 1930s, such organizations as the Boone and Crockett Club and the National Wildlife Federation had convinced decision makers that wildlife protection and restoration were dependent on providing viable habitat. Wildlife managers also recognized that many species ranged across lands under multiple jurisdictions, and that to be effective, management must be coordinated among states and between state and federal governments. In response, Congress passed the 1934 Fish and Wildlife Coordination Act, which authorized the secretary of the interior to cooperate with federal, state, and public or private agencies in "developing, protecting, rearing and stocking all species of wildlife, resources thereof, and their habitat."[22] In addition, the act provided that state wildlife agencies could administer wildlife resources on federal lands if those lands were no longer being used for their original purpose.

Other legislation soon followed. The 1937 Pittman-Robertson Act authorized the secretary of the interior to provide federal funding to state fish and wildlife departments for restoration projects, including acquiring and improving wildlife habitat.[23] The act stipulated that, to receive federal funds, state agencies must dedicate all hunting and fishing license revenues to fish and wildlife management. Similarly, the 1950 Dingell-Johnson Act authorized the secretary to allocate funds for state fish restoration and management plans and projects.[24] The Sikes Act (1960) grants similar power to the secretary of defense to develop cooperative wildlife management plans with other state and federal agencies.[25]

Congress also frequently delegates authority to the executive branch within the federal government. A general delegation of authority to a cabinet-level officer or agency head is customarily construed to include an implied ability to subdelegate authority down through the department or agency.[26] In 1995, then–secretary of the interior Bruce Babbitt took this idea to its logical end by creating resource advisory councils (RACs) composed of local citizens who offer guidance to the BLM on planning and management decisions. Babbitt announced the RAC concept in a teleconference, acknowledging, "We really do have to find some way to discharge national responsibility, but in the context of genuine local participation."[27] Today, some twenty-three RACs work with the BLM throughout the West. Although proponents hoped that RACs would wield considerable clout in shaping BLM decisions, the agency is free to heed or disregard RAC recommendations, and not every member of a RAC has been satisfied. In the eight years since RACs first began deliberating land and resource issues, their work has been variously denounced as a "rubber stamp" and a "dog and pony show."[28] Also, some observers say that RAC membership is rarely as balanced and diverse as required by law. In 2002, for example, the Colorado Environmental Coalition criticized the Department of the Interior for stacking Colorado's RACs to favor commodity interests over conservation interests.[29]

In the 1990s, the National Park Service attempted to go one step further and devolve authority to manage the Niobrara National Scenic River in western Nebraska down to a local citizen's council.[30] In 1991, despite local opposition, Congress designated portions of the Niobrara to become part of the national Wild and Scenic Rivers system. Much of the land along the river is private, and access sites include a state park and a national wildlife refuge, so Congress—encouraging the National Park Service to work closely with state and local officials in managing the area—created the Niobrara Scenic River Advisory Commission to help develop a management plan.

The commission, composed largely of local people, generated four options for managing the Niobrara, including one that envisioned a local council—composed of local landowners, businesspeople, and state and local governments—to oversee management of the area. After completing an environmental impact statement, the Park Service selected the option of a local council and in 1997 entered into an "interlocal agreement" with local governments in Nebraska to create the Niobrara Council. The council would assume full responsibility to make and enforce decisions to manage the resource, including the ability to implement zoning, regulate public access, resolve disputes among competing interests, and hire staff.

Eighteen months after the Niobrara Council was created, the National Parks and Conservation Association (NPCA) filed a lawsuit against the National Park Service claiming that the council had not done anything to protect or manage the Niobrara's resources, and that the Park Service had unlawfully delegated its responsibilities and authority to the local council. The NPCA also asked that the Park Service resume control over management of the area. The court concluded that the National Park Service cannot completely shift its responsibility to manage the Niobrara to a private actor, particularly one whose objectivity may be questioned on grounds of conflict of interest. The court further concluded that "delegations by federal agencies to private parties are . . . valid so long as the federal agency or official retains final reviewing authority."[31] In this case, however, the Park Service did not retain any oversight function or the ability to review and veto the council's actions or inactions. Today, the council continues to be an active partner in coordinating management of the national scenic river, but the Park Service bears final decision-making authority.

Land Use and Growth Management

The resistance of westerners to centralized authority is not limited to federal lands. Of the eleven states located entirely west of the 100th meridian, not including Alaska and Hawaii, only Oregon and Washington have adopted statewide land use planning and growth management programs. Most of the other western states have very small state offices, which provide technical assistance and advice to local communities. When these offices flirt with programmatic or statewide planning efforts, they are typically ignored or rebuked. According to a consortium of state planning directors in the West, the lack of more comprehensive and integrated systems of land use planning and growth management is due in large part to the region's culture of "local control."

The story of land use planning in Oregon is particularly striking. In 1973, the Oregon legislature created what is widely viewed as one of the most progressive statewide land use planning frameworks in the United States. As a result, over the years, housing costs—and public resentment—have risen in

Portland and other urban areas. In the more rural areas of the state, residents blame the land use regulations for decreasing land values. Building on this dissatisfaction, voters in the 2000 elections passed Measure 7, requiring state and local governments to compensate landowners whose property is affected by regulation. A team of academics concluded that the passage of Measure 7 was largely the result of misunderstanding and misinformation. The Oregon Supreme Court threw the measure out in October 2002, declaring it unconstitutional based on a technicality in phrasing.

In Montana, pro-development forces recently overturned a key provision of the state's existing growth policy law, which four years earlier had given local planners and officials the power to regulate development based on locally adopted growth policies. During the 2003 session, legislators passed a bill to amend the statute, stripping out any suggestion that county and local growth policies are binding. The new language stipulated that "a growth policy is not a regulatory document and does not confer any authority to regulate" development.[32] The bill's sponsor said that his intent was to cut down on lawsuits brought by environmentalists and to give local officials more flexibility. "When it comes to planning, the more local control the better," boasted Senator Daniel McGee. "Planning and land use regulation need to start from the bottom up."[33] Critics point out that McGee's bill was a top-down move that weakens local control over growth policies and will likely lead to more—not fewer—lawsuits. Removing local regulatory authority, they say, will "undermine the abilities of local governments to use their growth policies at all."[34] This debate is common throughout the West, wherever private property owners and developers fear losing unfettered use of their land—and, hence, what they see as its value—under zoning or planning laws. Planning advocates counter that local control is the best way to maintain property values while allowing the community to preserve its character and chart its own course.

Citizens Take the Reins

Despite limited legal authority, citizens from many walks of life are not waiting for federal, state, or local government to make decisions and resolve disputes over some of the West's most precious resources and landscapes.[35] Beginning in 1990, these "civic entrepeneurs," frustrated with the limited effectiveness of the approaches available for citizen participation in natural resource decisions, began experimenting with a new form of public participation. The essence of this new strategy—which is often referred to as community-based collaboration—is that citizens take the initiative and convene working groups around a particular community, watershed, ecosystem, or some other bioregion. These working groups often take the form of what one observer calls "coalitions of the unalike," meaning that they attempt to include a diversity of viewpoints and interests.[36] (One viewpoint that is sometimes left out is that of public officials. In some cases, agencies and officials are invited but choose not to participate. Other working groups, however, apparently prefer to do their work without the presence of public officials.)

Citizen-initiated forums often emerge to tackle a particular problem, and they occasionally continue because they provide something that is missing in other forums—a safe place for a mix of local citizens to exchange ideas and search for solutions to public problems. In short, these citizen-designed forums provide the type of civic engagement and face-to-face democracy advocated by Thomas Jefferson. More than 200 years since the founders framed our representative democracy, Don Snow argues that this citizen movement signals a sea change from Madison's federalism to Jefferson's deliberative democracy.[37] If we are losing faith in the ability of government agencies to arbitrate among competing interests, we are gaining a renewed confidence in our own ability as citizens and leaders to work together to shape and implement public policy.

Community-based collaboration tends to focus on the social, economic, and environmental values of a particular place, and it reinforces the ideology of local control and decentralized decision making. Because such forums are convened by and for citizens, it is not surprising that they are often designed to achieve a variety of objectives other than resolving disputes, including knowledge building, community building, and restoring working relationships.

A good example of such a community-based group is the Beaverhead County Community Forum in southwest Montana. In July 1994, Beaverhead County entered into a memorandum of understanding (MOU) with six federal and state land management agencies to promote a coordinated ecosystem approach to planning in the county. As the Interagency Steering Group, these seven agencies sponsored a workshop on community planning, which they asked the Montana Consensus Council to facilitate. More than fifty citizens and officials spent the day exploring how to better involve citizens in natural resource decision making in their county.

The workshop spawned the Beaverhead County Community Forum, a group of twenty-one citizens representing ranching, conservation, business, human services, recreation, private lawndowners, and government. Importantly, it was the citizens at the initial workshop who took the reins and decided to join forces as a way to gain greater influence in shaping government planning and decision making in their county. At first, the working group focused on helping the U.S. Forest Service successfully develop a landscape management plan for the nearby Gravelly Mountains. But then the forum continued to meet for another five years to address a wide range of community issues, from housing and economic development to health care and recreational crowding on local rivers. Eventually, after accomplishing much community improvement, the group disbanded, due in part to scarce funding and participant burnout.

Similar citizen-driven, community-based groups are scattered across the West. Some, such as the Quincy Library Group in California and the Applegate Partnership in southern Oregon, have become well-cited case studies for both proponents and opponents of community-based collaboration. Lesser-known efforts include the Malpai Borderlands Group (a grassroots coalition of private landowners and ranchers working closely with local conservation districts, universities, and federal and state agencies to restore and maintain the natural processes in the Borderlands region of southern New Mexico and Arizona); the Powder River Resource Council (an ad hoc group of farmers and ranchers, who initially met in 1973 over concerns about local strip mining for coal and are now working to preserve the western lifestyle and environment throughout eastern Wyoming); and the Diablo Trust (a community forum in northern Arizona, initially started in 1993 by ranchers and now "open to everyone," that encourages active participation in a land stewardship process using the founders' ranch lands as "hands-on" proving grounds for new, collaborative land management ideas).[38]

It may help here to pause and consider the place of community-based collaboration in the history of public dispute resolution or environmental conflict resolution. In the next chapter, we examine the history and use of negotiation, mediation, and consensus building to resolve disputes over natural resources and the environment. For now, it's useful to know that, since 1973, citizens and officials with diverse viewpoints have used a variety of collaborative processes to shape public policy, develop administrative rules, and resolve disputes. The philosophy and strategies of civic entrepreneurs— inclusive participation, joint fact finding, and so on—are to a large degree rooted in the theory and practice of public dispute resolution. The uniqueness of civic entrepreneurs, as mentioned at the beginning of this chapter, is the degree to which citizens take the lead in initiating and coordinating these efforts as well as the degree to which the efforts are designed around particular places or regions.

Building on the work of civic entrepreneurs throughout the West and drawing on experience with alternative dispute resolution processes, agencies like the U.S. Forest Service now assert that local, place-based collaborative processes are a way to address the "process predicament."[39] Agencies are increasingly training scientific and technical experts in the philosophy and techniques of collaborative problem solving and are exploring ways to incorporate collaboration into their existing decision-making process. (We will talk more about this development in chapters 7 and 8.) This effort on the part of public officials is a step in the right direction, but it is still embedded within the dominant culture of expert decision making. As explained by Daniel Kemmis, the philosophy of community-based collaboration and civic entrepreneurship is fundamentally at odds with the structure of scientific and technical decision making. "One is an inherently decentralized, democratic form of governing," Kemmis says, whereas "the other is inherently centralized and hierarchical."[40]

While it may be difficult if not impossible for agencies like the U.S. Forest Service to effectively integrate collaborative problem solving into their standard operating procedures, given their legal responsibilities and institutional culture, it is also difficult for civic entrepreneurs to go it alone. If the intent of civic entrepreneurs is to influence public policy, they must inevitably link their efforts to established decision-making processes. The theory of public dispute resolution suggests that this should be done as early in the process as possible, in order to build sufficient ownership among all stakeholders, including the decision makers and agencies needed to implement any outcome.[41] Building on this principle, David Getches, professor and dean of the School of Law at the University of Colorado and an experienced observer of western resource politics, argues that citizen-initiated forums are not likely to be effective without the involvement of government. In fact, a study by the law school's Natural Resources Law Center concludes that most watershed councils depend heavily on federal support—in the form of both direct funding and in-kind services—to do their work.[42]

The force of this conclusion is revealed by the fate of two high-profile attempts at homegrown collaboration and problem solving: the Applegate Partnership and the Quincy Library Group. The Applegate Partnership grew out of conflict over how to manage 500,000 acres of national forest in southern Oregon. In 1992, an unlikely coalition of environmentalists, loggers, and local businesspeople sat down to draft an ecosystem management plan for the Applegate watershed and then invited government officials to help refine the plan. As the process moved forward, conservation groups and the timber industry seemed poised to support the emerging plan. But then the partnership won the attention of President Clinton, whose Northwest Forest Plan included similar partnerships on ten "Adaptive Management Areas." Threatened by Clinton's forest plan, the timber industry challenged the process, saying that federal agency participation violated provisions of the Federal Advisory Committee Act. The suit was successful, and agency officials had no choice but to withdraw from the partnership. Other participants continue working together to this day, but the legal barriers between local community and government make it more difficult for the Applegate Partnership to implement changes in forest management.

In the case of the Quincy Library Group, the U.S. Forest Service itself blocked action, after initially supporting local collaborative efforts. In 1993, the usual suspects—environmentalists, timber interests, local businesses, and government officials (including the supervisor of the Plumas National Forest)—met to map out a "Community Stability Proposal" for managing 2.5 million acres on parts of Plumas, Lassen, and Tahoe national forests around Quincy, California. This alternative forest plan included protection for old-growth forest, endangered species habitat, and roadless areas, along with enough timber from selective logging to support local sawmills. The government appeared to welcome the plan—Secretary of Agriculture Dan Glickman authorized $4.7 million for the Forest Service to develop projects proposed by the group, and Forest Service chief Jack Ward Thomas said the agency would begin plans to implement specific proposals. But then the agency turned unresponsive, and nothing moved forward for two years. Apparently, Thomas disliked the project. "They're not properly chartered," Thomas was quoted as saying, "and they're sitting there cutting deals back and forth. . . . I like cooperation, but I don't like [Quincy participant and owner of Sierra Pacific Industries] Emmerson; who the hell turned over my national forests to him?"[43] Frustrated, the Quincy group took their ideas to Congress, which eventually—three years later—passed the Quincy legislation.

In both of these cases, the efforts of civic entrepreneurs were thwarted by government officials for three apparent reasons: (1) officials were not involved in or were removed from the process; (2) the processes became subject to partisan politics, in part because they were not adequately linked to the existing decision-making systems; and (3) the processes—even if well designed or intentioned—run counter to the established system of scientific and technical experts making decisions.

The work of civic entrepreneurs continues the 100-year-old effort of westerners to regain control of their communities and landscapes. In many respects, the emergence of community-based collaboration is the logical conclusion of devolved decision making, from federal to state to local government, and finally to citizens themselves. But this is an emergent phenomenon; it is still too early to offer any conclusive evidence on its effectiveness.[44] The increasing number of examples, and a growing literature of case studies and best practices, suggests that this movement is at least persistent, if not also effective. A recent study of forty-eight community-based collaborative processes in the Rocky Mountain West found that the participants valued the opportunity to influence federal land and resource decisions.[45] They also placed a high value on improved communication and working relationships among diverse stakeholders, even in processes where the outcomes were rated as less than satisfactory. This suggests that, even when on-the-ground solutions are difficult to come by, place-based forums help build a sense of community and civic engagement many people find missing in today's political climate.

Devolution through Privatization

Human nature being what it is, some people are less interested in the "civic" values of devolution than in the "entrepreneurial" opportunities. In their minds, the West remains a place where a private citizen should be able to stake a claim on public resources. Broader, more programmatic proposals to private public resources also continue to be popular among commodity interests, libertarians, and other "small-government" advocates.

As part of the Healthy Forests Initiative, for example, President Bush plans to privatize the management of large tracts of federal lands.[46] The plan, offered as a way to reduce the danger of forest fires by cutting more trees, provides broad authorization for "stewardship contracting," which basically means that private companies, local governments, and nonprofit groups could assume responsibility for thinning undergrowth and small trees that ostensibly fuel wildfires. To make the contracts appealing, the stewards would also be allowed to cut down larger trees that are more marketable (and, ironically, more fire resistant). Environmental groups claim that such a plan amounts to giving public resources to private companies.

The Bush administration is also considering a proposal to further privatize federal rangeland resources. In a speech to the National Cattlemen's Beef Association, BLM director Kathleen Clark announced the administration's plan to consider the local culture and economy when conducting environmental assessments of grazing on federal land; to allow ranchers to hold property interests in the fences, stock ponds, and equipment they put on publicly owned lands; and to extend to five years the amount of time a grazing allotment could go ungrazed before a rancher loses it under so-called "use it or lose it" rules.[47] While Clark asserts that the changes would enhance community-based conservation and promote cooperative stewardship of public rangelands, environmentalists claim that the proposals make grazing on public land a right rather than a privilege.

Other attempts to privatize western resources—and the philosophy behind such strategies—were examined in chapter 2.

Recurring Themes

The history of attempts to decentralize decision making for western natural resources is marked by three recurring themes. For the most part, these themes are consistent with this book's prescriptive framework.

The first theme is *community stewardship*, which is based on the premise that people living in a particular place share an identity and commitment to that landscape that compels them to generate effective solutions to social, economic, and environmental problems. Local people, according to this argument, tend to have the most incentive to sustain their communities and landscapes.

A second common theme among efforts to decentralize authority is *indigenous knowledge*, the idea that people who live in particular places have a good understanding of those places. Kemmis characterizes this as an "inescapable truth: that people who live on a landscape, who have struggled to sustain themselves and their families on its bounty and against its hardships, will have learned lessons about that place that nothing else can teach."[48] Local knowledge is, by definition, location specific. It is often anecdotal, passing from one generation to the next through oral traditions, and frequently cannot be generalized to other places. Given that different people and organizations have developed distinct ways of knowing, local knowledge is often perceived, right or wrong, as invalid and competing with more professional, scientific ways of learning.[49]

The third theme, which is based on the other two, revolves around the desire of local people to *control their own future*. The history of efforts to decentralize authority over western resources is defined, at least in part, by westerners claiming jurisdiction or sovereignty over western land and resources. In the mid-1800s, the framework for resolving disputes over western resources was completely decentralized. People with a direct interest in minerals, water, and range resources were allowed to resolve their own disputes through the principle of first in time, first in right. Then, around 1900, the national government imposed a highly centralized system for managing western resources and resolving disputes, effectively removing the people most affected by decisions from the decision-making process. While none of the alternative claims of sovereignty made so far has survived legal challenges, this fundamental question appears to be unresolved in the minds of many people who care about the West. They are now taking the initiative to create their own forums for public dialogue, dispute resolution, and resource management.

While these themes may accurately describe the motivations of people advocating devolution and decentralized control over the West's natural resources, not everyone agrees with the merits of these arguments.

Arguments against Devolution

In 1947, Bernard DeVoto reflected on the reality that the same westerners who supported free access to federal resources and federal subsidies for water development projects sought repeatedly to take the public domain away from the national government and turn it over to western states. DeVoto famously summarized this basic contradiction as "Get out and give us more money."[50] Today, the accusation that people supporting local control (particularly over federal lands and resources) are motivated by a sense of entitlement, if not outright greed, is combined with a number of more thoughtful, well-intentioned critiques of devolution and decentralized decision making (see box 6.1).

George Coggins, professor of law at the University of Kansas, argues that "much local decisionmaking has been narrow, greedy, and shortsighted," and that too often devolution means federal agencies abdicate their legal responsibilities at great cost to national interests.[51] As examples, Coggins

BOX 6.1   Arguments against Devolution

1. While far from perfect, the existing processes for citizen participation, public decision making, and public dispute resolution are not fundamentally flawed.
2. Devolving authority upon community-based collaborative groups:
   - is an abdication of responsibility under existing law and therefore is unlawful;
   - compromises the authority and accountability of public officials;
   - tends to favor local interests, result in co-optation, and may not adequately incorporate national interests;
   - may impede or contravene national laws and policies;
   - undermines established mechanisms of representative democracy, such as interest group organization, advocacy, and coalition building;
   - shifts the balance of power from national to local forums.
3. There is little to no historic evidence suggesting that the devolution of authority is a more effective way to make decisions and resolve disputes over land use, natural resources, and environmental protection.
4. The premises underlying local superiority are false or unproven. Community-based collaboration typically rests on the assumption that the people involved will behave reasonably and will seek mutually agreeable solutions. It also presumes that such solutions are readily available. In fact, however, most people are driven by self-interest. They will seek solutions that primarily favor their own interest. Some debates hinge on irreconcilable value differences—win-win solutions are not always possible.

cites the early-twentieth-century cronyism of grazing advisory councils that allocated federal forage allotments to the detriment of small ranchers and rangeland health, as well as the extermination of major predators from national parks to placate local livestock growers. Devolving decision making from federal officials to local citizens runs counter to all relevant laws, says Coggins. "No statute authorizes abdication of the authority," Coggins says. "It is illegal. Period."[52]

Skeptics of devolution also say that local control undermines established mechanisms of representative democracy, such as interest group organization, advocacy, and coalition building. In a 1995 memo to his board of directors, Sierra Club chairman Michael McCloskey warned that community-based collaboration on federal resource issues redistributes power away from urban and national interests. "Transferring power to a local venue," he wrote, "implies decision-making by a very different majority—in a much smaller population." Often in such forums, individual interests can veto local majority proposals, and so, McCloskey argued, "Only lowest common denominator ideas survive the process."[53]

Some skeptics have contested the notion that community-based forums are somehow "more democratic" than our national representative democracy. According to these skeptics, Congress had good reason to retain federal lands in the national interest, and westerners should not be given undue influence over those lands simply because they live there. In most debates over federal land and resource decisions, they say, "communities of interest"—on a national scale—are more relevant than "communities of place."[54]

Critics of devolution also point out that, while far from perfect, existing democratic and legal processes for citizen participation, public decision making, and public dispute resolution are fundamentally sound. Citizens at all levels have opportunities to be heard, and the legislative, executive, and judicial branches provide adequate checks and balances to ensure that decisions and actions on public issues reflect the public will.[55] Devolution, they say, doesn't solve any procedural problems but simply shifts them to a local level.

Potential Tools—Federalism, Compacts, and Trust Arrangements

As a method for resolving western resource disputes, devolution sits on the horns of a dilemma. On the one hand, there are limited conditions under which it is legally possible to devolve the authority over western resources to civic entrepreneurs, local officials, or even state governments. And, given the reservations of many people (particularly in the environmental community) about the various proposals by the Bush administration to decentralize decision making (in some cases, handing it to business and industry), it may not be politically desirable at this time to devolve authority over federal lands and resources. On the other hand, there is a growing awareness of the value of decentralizing and sharing some decision-making responsibility.

The challenge, then, is to design institutional arrangements where different political jurisdictions and interests can share decision-making and dispute resolution authority without completely devolving authority from one level of government to another, or from government to civic entrepreneurs. The Constitution provides little guidance on how to structure public decision-making and dispute resolution systems that share authority among multiple jurisdictions.[56] As discussed in chapter 3, this is particularly apparent when it comes to regional forms of governance to resolve transboundary natural resource issues.

During the past thirty years, however, a number of jurisdictions, from federal to state to local, have experimented with different ways to share decision-making authority.[57] Table 6.1 presents three basic models of shared decision making. These models are based on the premise that natural resource management is, in many cases, the responsibility of multiple jurisdictions and interests. Many of these models grow out of experience in trying to manage transboundary resources according to watersheds, ecosystems, bioregions, or other organically defined regions. While there are other approaches to regional collaboration, the models presented in this table are defined by the objective of sharing the authority to make and enforce decisions. Many other models, such as interstate councils, interstate commissions, and federal-state commissions, are not discussed here because their primary objectives are to provide mechanisms to coordinate resources, not to share authority per se.

Taken together, the three models or legal instruments suggest a common principle for designing institutional arrangements to share decision-making authority—what professor Archon Fung at the John F. Kennedy School of Government at Harvard University refers to as the principle of "accountable autonomy."[58] Fung suggests that wedding local autonomy with public accountability integrates the two competing forces behind devolution, allowing us to draw on the information and innovation of both citizens and officials who are closest to the problems of particular places while promoting broader (regional or national) social policies and goals.

TABLE 6.1 Models of Shared Decision Making

Type of Model	How It Works	Examples
Federalism	Federal authority is administratively delegated to states to achieve national goals and standards.	Clean Water Act Coastal Zone Management Act
	States develop and implement programs consistent with national criteria.	
	In some cases, states may veto proposed federal initiatives.	
Compacts	Formally negotiated agreements among sovereign powers, typically implemented through statute.	Lake Tahoe Regional Planning Agency (interstate compact) Columbia River Gorge Commission (federal-state compact)
Trust Arrangements	Authority is statutorily delegated to a "board of trustees" to achieve a defined set of public goals.	Valles Caldera National Preserve The Presidio

Federalism—National Goals, Local Implementation

The first model of shared decision making is often referred to as federalism and is illustrated by a number of federal environmental laws, including the Clean Water Act. Under this model, federal authority is administratively delegated to states and some Indian tribes with federally approved programs, thereby giving the states and tribes primary regulatory authority to implement federal directives. This model presumes that the resources in question are of national interest and begins with a nonnegotiable set of federal goals and standards. It then allows states and tribes to develop, implement, and enforce their own programs to achieve those goals and standards. The beauty of this model is that it is designed to achieve uniform national results while allowing significant freedom in how each state or tribe pursues those results.

One example of federalism is the Coastal Zone Management Act (1972). Under this law, the federal government delegates to states the authority to develop, implement, and enforce a program that meets national interests. States may or may not include the federal government in their deliberations and can veto proposals from the federal government that are inconsistent with the state plan. The federal government provides financial assistance (up to 90 percent) for state management plans that meet federal criteria, so clear and significant incentive exists for the states to work closely with the federal government. Subsequent federal activities in the coastal zone are required to be consistent with the state plans. Some states include local input as part of their coastal zone management plans, giving even small local governments an opportunity to impose substantial restrictions on federal activities.

Compacts—Negotiated Agreements among Sovereign Entities

A second strategy to share authority among multiple jurisdictions is through compacts. A compact is a formal, legally binding instrument that establishes a permanent arrangement among two or more jurisdictions on an issue of shared interest. In essence, a compact is a negotiated solution to a shared problem. Compacts may be used among states, between one or more states and the federal government, or between one or more states and a sovereign power (such as a tribal government).

Article I, section 10 of the U.S. Constitution authorizes the use of interstate compacts to resolve disputes among states. States initiate compact negotiations, which are ultimately ratified by Congress and state legislatures. Historically, interstate compacts were used to resolve boundary disputes between states; New York and Connecticut negotiated such disputes as early as 1644. Beginning in the twentieth century, interstate compacts have been a common approach "to resolve disputes between sovereign states over a shared waterway."[59] Congress has approved about thirty-five water-related compacts, more than twenty of them in the West.

For example, in 1969, Congress ratified a compact that created the country's first interstate environmental planning agency. After two decades of rapid growth around Lake Tahoe, California and Nevada joined forces to create the Lake Tahoe Regional Planning Agency (TRPA). The agency's mission is to preserve, restore, and enhance the unique natural and human environment of the Lake Tahoe region. The interstate compact, as revised in 1980, authorizes TRPA to adopt environmental quality standards and enforce ordinances. Today, to protect the region's water and air quality, wildlife habitat, and scenery, TRPA regulates land use, development density, rate of growth, land coverage, excavation, and changes to the scenic viewshed.

In addition to interstate compacts, federal-interstate compacts have been used to share decision-making authority among states and the federal government. Although the Compact Clause in Article I of the U.S. Constitution does not explicitly provide for federal involvement in the compacting process beyond ratification, the U.S. Supreme Court has recognized the legitimate value of such institutional arrangements.

The Delaware River Basin Compact, approved in 1961, was the first federal-interstate compact over natural resources. The 330-mile Delaware River originates in New York and flows along the borders of Pennsylvania, Delaware, and New Jersey before emptying into the Atlantic Ocean. The compact, which includes these four states and the federal government, requires the Delaware River Compact Commission to develop and maintain a comprehensive basin plan. This plan, in turn, is used to guide decisions on proposed projects. The commission must approve a proposed project if it "would not substantially impair or conflict with the comprehensive plan."[60] Commission decisions are binding, unless the U.S. president determines that portions of the comprehensive plan are not in the national interest.

More recently, in 1986, Oregon and Washington entered into a compact with the federal government "to establish a national scenic area to protect and provide for the enhancement of the scenic, cultural, recreational, and natural resources of the Columbia River Gorge; and . . . to protect and support the economy of the Columbia River Gorge."[61] Like the Delaware River Basin Compact, the Columbia River Gorge National Scenic Area Act requires that land use activities within the Scenic Area are consistent with a comprehensive management plan. This plan is periodically reviewed and revised by a twelve-member commission appointed by local, state, and federal officials. With its small staff, the commission also coordinates projects among county, state, tribal, and federal agencies and works with them to implement the management plan, primarily through local ordinances. The commission also certifies grants and loans to fund economic development in the gorge, monitors plan implementation, and hears appeals on land use decisions in the Scenic Area.

Trust Arrangements

A third, less common model of shared decision making is a trust arrangement, wherein a board of trustees is granted authority to manage public lands and resources. One of the earliest such experiments is the Whidbey Island National Historic Reserve in Puget Sound.[62] In 1978, Congressman Lloyd Meeds of Washington State was looking for a way to preserve open space and beach access adjacent to four units of the state park system on Whidbey Island without threatening property rights or the lifestyle of island residents. Meeds hit upon the idea of creating a national historic reserve out of the existing Central Whidbey Island Historic District. Traditionally a unit of the National Park Service, national reserves also require significant cooperation among federal, state, and local governments. In this case—the first *historic* reserve in the country—Congress delegated management of the reserve to an independent, volunteer board of trustees, composed largely of local officials. The National Park Service would provide technical assistance and funding. Actual transfer of administrative authority proved difficult because of legal questions and local concern that funding would dry up once the Park Service was no longer wholly responsible for the area. The transfer was completed after ten years of off-and-on negotiations and the drafting of a comprehensive management plan. The trust board was designated as a "unit of local government" under Washington's Interlocal Cooperation Act, which enabled the Park Service to relinquish management control to the board, whose chair serves as reserve coordinator. Today, the reserve is an "affiliated" unit of the Park Service, which means it remains eligible for federal funding and assistance.

A similar arrangement turned the private Baca Ranch into the Valles Calderas National Preserve. Its 89,000 acres of federal public lands in north-central New Mexico are home to forest and high country meadows, the headwaters of the Jemez River, a dormant volcano, and cultural and religious sites. In 2000, Congress purchased the land from a Texas oil family. Several influential politicians, however, had opposed acquisition of more public land in New Mexico. To win their approval, proponents suggested that the preserve be controlled by a presidentially appointed board of nine trustees. This board has almost complete power over what happens in the preserve, consistent with its statutorily defined mission: to "protect and preserve the scenic, geological, watershed, fish, wildlife, historic, cultural, and recreational values of the preserve, and to provide for multiple use and sustained yield of renewable resources within the preserve."[63] The ranch must remain a working cattle ranch and must attempt to be self-sufficient by 2017. A similar trust arrangement guides management of the Presidio in San Francisco, the oldest continuously operated military post in the United States, dating from 1776.

These three basic models or legal instruments have been adapted, and sometimes combined, by different jurisdictions and are often referred to by different names. The nuances and distinctions among different examples are perhaps less instructive than the observation that it is possible to create innovative institutional arrangements to share decision-making authority. Joint powers and interlocal agreements are common in the land use arena, as illustrated by the Massachusetts Environmental Joint Powers Agreement and the Salton Sea Management Authority.[64] Other examples, such as the Santa Fe Regional Planning Authority, the San Diego Association of Governments, the Boston Harbor Islands Park, the Appalachian Trail, the Cape Cod National Seashore, the Chesapeake Bay Commission, and the National Estuary Program under the Clean Water Act represent slightly different approaches, some designed to foster more cooperation and coordination while others are designed to share decision-making authority.[65] In most cases, federal, state, and other political jurisdictions jointly define goals and strategies, and approval by one sovereign is often contingent upon approval by the other participating sovereigns.

As a whole, the experience with various models of shared decision making may be too limited at this point to offer firm conclusions about the strengths and weaknesses of different approaches. Much remains to be learned about how different models deal with issues related to membership and participation, function and responsibility, and operational attributes, and how these variables of design influence the effectiveness of the institutional arrangement. In the final analysis, however, the most effective model of shared decision making for a given situation will most likely emerge by adapting the experiences of others to the unique needs and interests of the particular situation.

As many of the examples in this chapter illustrate, the West's call to devolve authority and decentralize decision making rises from a smoldering sense of self-determination among its citizens. In part, devolution is a backlash against the pattern of rhetoric and control exercised by officials inside the Beltway in Washington, D.C. In spring 2002, Secretary of Agriculture Ann Veneman visited Montana's Rocky Mountain Front, one of the most pristine landscapes in the lower forty-eight states. Veneman said that the Bush administration would not rule out the possibility of exploring for oil and gas reserves along the Front and on federal lands throughout the West. She also emphasized the administration's commitment to involving local communities in decisions affecting local forests.

On its face, this statement seems consistent with the much-touted "4 C's" policy of the Bush administration—communication, consultation, and co-operation all in the service of conservation. But Gloria Flora, who as a supervisor for the U.S. Forest Service imposed a moratorium on drilling along the Front, sees a paradox in the secretary's stance: a large majority of local people, Flora points out, have already made it clear that the Front should remain as it is, protected from the impacts of oil and gas exploration and extraction. Nevertheless, the Bureau of Land Management and the U.S. Forest Service announced in June 2003 their plan to conduct another environmental impact study—at a cost of about $1.2 million—on oil and gas development along the Front.[66]

Our recommendation to develop institutional arrangements to share decision-making authority is based on the recognition that local and regional interests are often sacrificed for national interests—or at least for national political objectives. Sharing authority is obviously contrary to more traditional models and strategies for making decisions and resolving disputes over western resources. Those with power, or with a vested interest in the existing legal and institutional structure, are not likely to embrace this recommendation in any proactive sense. The challenge, then, is to create opportunities for local interests to share decision-making authority, but not to the exclusion of national or other interests. While many civic entrepreneurs throughout the West instinctively gravitate toward this model, it is most likely to be applied only as a last resort or perhaps in experimental "pilot project" settings. The political will to use this model in appropriate circumstances, however, will emerge only as citizens continue to demand fair, effective, and efficient processes to resolve disputes over western resources. Our next chapter explores some of these possibilities.

NOTES

1. See George Cameron Coggins, Charles F. Wilkinson, and John D. Leshy, *Federal Public Land and Resources Law*, 5th ed. (New York: Foundation Press, 2002).

2. One example of shared decision making, which we will address later in this chapter, is the Columbia River Gorge National Scenic Area.

3. This section draws heavily on Daniel Kemmis, *This Sovereign Land: A New Vision for Governing the West* (Washington, DC: Island Press, 2001).

4. See R. McGreggor Cawley, *Federal Land, Western Anger: The Sagebrush Rebellion and Environmental Politics* (Lawrence: University Press of Kansas, 1993), 72.

5. Kemmis, *This Sovereign Land*, 51–52.

6. Nancy Marzulla, "Property Rights Movement: How It Began and Where It Is

Headed," in *A Wolf in the Garden: The Land Rights Movement and the New Environmental Debate*, ed. Philip D. Brick and R. McGreggor Cawley, 39–58 (Lanham, MD: Rowman & Littlefield, 1996).

7. Marzulla, "Property Rights Movement."

8. Marzulla, "Property Rights Movement," 40.

9. Karen Budd-Falen, "Protecting Community Stability and Local Economies: Opportunities for County Government Influence in Federal Decision and Policy Making Processes," in *National Federal Lands Conference: The Power and Authority of County Government* (Bountiful, UT: National Federal Lands Conference, 1993).

10. Scott Reed, "The County Supremacy Movement: Mendacious Myth Marketing," in *A Wolf in the Garden: The Land Rights Movement and the New Environmental Debate*, ed. Philip D. Brick and R. McGreggor Cawley, 87–104 (Lanham, MD: Rowman & Littlefield, 1996).

11. *United States v. Nye County*, 920f. Supp. 1108 (D. Nevada 1996).

12. See "Fed Up with Feds, 'Shovel Brigade' Opens Road," *USA Today*, July 6, 2000; Associated Press, "Government Sues Shovel Brigade," *Las Vegas Review-Journal*, August 11, 2000; and Associated Press, "President of Shovel Brigade Resigns," *Reno Gazette-Journal*, April 18, 2001.

13. Sarah Foster, "'Us Now, You're Next' Say Desperate Farmers; Massive 'Bucket Brigade' to Protest Court-ordered Water Shut-off," *WorldNetDaily*, May 7, 2001, http://www.worldnetdaily.com/news/article.asp?ARTICLE_ID=22718.

14. For example, see Klamath Bucket Brigade, www.klamathrelief.org.

15. Department of Water and Power, City of Los Angeles, http://web.ladwp.com/~wsoweb/Aqueduct/historyoflaa/hundred.htm.

16. Allen Best, "Drought Unearths a Water Dinosaur," *High Country News*, September 16, 2002.

17. See Ed Marston, "Water Pressure," *High Country News*, November 20, 2000.

18. U.S. Environmental Protection Agency, "Total Maximum Daily Loads," http://www.epa.gov/owow/tmdl/.

19. See Dale D. Goble and Eric T. Freyfogle, *Wildlife Law: Cases and Materials* (New York: Foundation Press, 2001).

20. Steven E. Daniels, Antony S. Cheng, and Mark G. Rickenbach, *The Fish and Wildlife Resource* (paper commissioned by the Western Consensus Council, October 27, 2001).

21. *Lacey Act*, 16 *U.S. Code* 701 (May 25, 1900).

22. *Fish and Wildlife Coordination Act*, 16 *U.S. Code* 661–667e (March 10, 1934).

23. *Pittman-Robertson Act*, 16 *U.S. Code* 669–669i (September 2, 1937).

24. *Dingell-Johnson Act*, 16 *U.S. Code* 777–777l (August 9, 1950).

25. *Sikes Act*, 16 *U.S. Code* 670a–670o (September 15, 1960).

26. See Coggins, Wilkinson, and Leshy, *Federal Public Land and Resources Law,* 244.

27. Tim Findley, "Participants Find 'RAC' Stands for 'Resource Advisory Charade,'" *Hatch (New Mexico) Courier,* http://www.electricnevada.com/pages97/ figleafs.htm.

28. Findley, "Participants Find 'RAC' Stands for 'Resource Advisory Charade.'"

29. Colorado Environmental Coalition, "Letter to Secretary Gale Norton on RAC Selection Process" (January 31, 2002), http://www.ourcolorado.org/alerts/ 041802_rac_letter.htm.

30. *National Parks and Conservation Association v. Stanton,* 54 F. Supp. 2d 7 (D.D.C. 1999).

31. *National Parks and Conservation Association v. Stanton,* Civil Action No. 98-615 (GL), U.S. District Court, Washington, D.C., memorandum opinion, undated.

32. *Montana Code Annotated,* sec. 7, 76-1-605, 2(a).

33. Jason Mohr, "Bills Address Growth," *Helena Independent Record,* February 17, 2003.

34. Jason Mohr, "Session Defines Growth Policies as Guidelines, Not Regulations," *Helena Independent Record,* April 21, 2003.

35. The most comprehensive assessment of this "movement" at a national level is Carmen Sirianni and Lewis Friedland, *Civic Innovation in America: Community Empowerment, Public Policy, and the Movement for Civic Renewal* (Berkeley: University of California Press, 2001). In particular, see pages 85–137 on "civic environmentalism." On the emergence of this movement in the West, see Daniel Kemmis, *Community and the Politics of Place* (Norman: University of Oklahoma Press, 1990); and Donald Snow, "Empire or Homelands? A Revival of Jeffersonian Democracy in the American West," in *The Next West: Public Lands, Community, and the Economy in the American West,* ed. John A. Baden and Donald Snow, 181–203 (Washington, DC: Island Press, 1997).

36. See Donald Snow, "Coming Home: An Introduction to Collaborative Conservation," in *Across the Great Divide: Explorations in Collaborative Conservation and the American West,* ed. Philip Brick, Donald Snow, and Sarah Van de Wetering, 1–11 (Washington, DC: Island Press, 2001).

37. Donald Snow, "Empire or Homelands? A Revival of Jeffersonian Democracy in the American West," in *The Next West: Public Lands, Community, and the Economy in the American West,* ed. John A. Baden and Donald Snow, 181–203 (Washington, DC: Island Press, 1997).

38. For more information on these and other collaborative groups, visit the Web site for the Center for the Rocky Mountain West at http://www.crmw.org/ and click on the link for "Regionalism in the West: Index."

39. Julia Wondelleck, "An Evaluation of the U.S. Forest Service Natural Resource

Conflict Management Training Program (Final Report)" (unpublished manuscript, School of Natural Resources, University of Michigan, 1986).

40. Kemmis, *This Sovereign Land*, 129–30.

41. Lawrence Susskind, Sarah McKearnan, and Jennifer Thomas-Larmer, eds., *The Consensus Building Handbook: A Comprehensive Guide to Reaching Agreement* (Thousand Oaks, CA: Sage, 1999).

42. David H. Getches, "Some Irreverant Questions about Watershed," in *Collaborative Conservation and the American West*, ed. Philip Brick, Donald Snow, Sarah Van de Wetering (Washington, DC: Island Press, 2001); Douglas S. Kenney et al., *The New Watershed Source Book: A Directory and Review of Watershed Initiatives in the Western United States* (Boulder: Natural Resources Law Center, University of Colorado School of Law, 2000).

43. Ed Marston, "The Timber Wars Evolve into a Divisive Attempt at Peace," *High Country News*, September 29, 1997, http://www.hcn.org/servlets/hcn. Article?article_id=3656.

44. The *Chronicle of Community*, a quarterly publication that was around for about five years, documented and evaluated the trend in citizen-driven, community-based collaborative processes. Although the *Chronicle* is no longer being published, some of its best work is included in Philip Brick, Donald Snow, and Sarah Van de Wetering, eds., *Across the Great Divide: Explorations in Collaborative Conservation and the American West* (Washington, DC: Island Press, 2001).

45. Matthew McKinney et al., *Community-based Collaboration on Federal Lands and Resources: An Evaluation of Participant Satisfaction* (Helena and Cambridge: Western Consensus Council and Consensus Building Institute, 2003).

46. Mike Soraghan, "Congress Rushing to Pass Forest-Privatization," *Denver Post*, February 12, 2003.

47. Mike Soraghan, "Eased Cattle-grazing Rules Sought," *Denver Post*, January 31, 2003; see also *Federal Register* 03-4933 (February 28, 2003).

48. Kemmis, *This Sovereign Land*, 55.

49. For an excellent summary of strategies to integrate local and professional knowledge, see Peter S. Adler and Juliana E. Birkoff, *Building Trust: When Knowledge from "Here" Meets Knowledge from "Away"* (Portland, OR: National Policy Consensus Center, n.d.).

50. Bernard DeVoto, "The West against Itself," *Harper's*, January 1947, 245.

51. George C. Coggins, "Regulating Federal Natural Resources: A Summary Case against Devolved Collaboration," *Ecology Law Quarterly* 25 (1999): 602–10.

52. Coggins, "Regulating Federal Natural Resources."

53. Michael McCloskey, "The Skeptic: Collaboration Has Its Limits," *High Country News*, May 13, 1996.

54. Douglas S. Kenney, "Collaborative Approaches to Environmental Protection:

Exploring the Concerns of the Skeptics" (paper prepared for the Western Consensus Council, 2001).

55. See Coggins, "Regulating Federal Natural Resources," and Kenney, "Collaborative Approaches to Environmental Protection."

56. John E. Thorson, *River of Promise, River of Peril: The Politics of Managing the Missouri River* (Lawrence: University Press of Kansas, 1994).

57. This section is based largely on the work of Hope M. Babcock, "Dual Regulation, Collaborative Management, or Layered Federalism: Can Cooperative Federalism Models from Other Laws Save Our Public Lands?" *Hastings West-Northwest Journal of Environmental Law and Policy* 3, no. 2 (1996): 193–208.

58. Archon Fung, "Accountable Autonomy: Toward Empowered Deliberation in Chicago Schools and Policing," *Politics and Society* 29, no. 1 (2001): 73–103.

59. Thorson, *River of Promise, River of Peril*, 123.

60. *Delaware River Basin Commission Comprehensive Plan* (Trenton, NJ: DRBC, 2001), 5.

61. *Columbia River Gorge National Scenic Area Act*, 16 *U.S. Code* 544–544p; see also Bowen Blair Jr., "The Columbia River Gorge National Scenic Area: The Act, Its Genesis and Legislative History," *Environmental Law* 17, no. 863 (1987).

62. This vignette is based on the thorough history of Ebey's Landing and Whidbey Island National Historic Reserve available from the National Park Service at http://www.nps.gov/ebla/adhi/adhit.htm. Of particular interest is chapter 4, "The Movement to Preserve Central Whidbey Island," and chapter 7, "Administrative Overview."

63. See Erika Trautman and Andy Lenderman, "Cooperating on the Valles Caldera," *High Country News*, December 31, 2001; see also "Valles Caldera National Preservation Act" (P.L. 106-248, 106th Congress, 2000), http://www.vallescaldera.gov/documents/prevAct.php.

64. *An Act Authorizing Environmental Joint Powers of Agreements*, ch. 491, *Acts of 1996, State of Massachusetts*; "Joint Powers Agreement Creating the Salton Sea Management Authority," http://www.sci.sdsu.edu/salton/JointPowersAgreeSS ManComm%20.html.

65. The Santa Fe Regional Planning Authority (RPA) works through a joint powers agreement to delegate decision-making authority between the city and the county. The RPA includes four county commissioners and four city council members. More information is available from the Santa Fe RPA, 128 Grant Avenue, Suite 108, Santa Fe, NM 87501.

66. "Agencies Plan New Study of Drilling Plan," *Helena Independent Record*, June 20, 2003, 10A.

7

Sharing Responsibility

"When it [the West] fully learns that cooperation, not rugged individualism, is the quality that most characterizes and preserves it, then . . . it has a chance to create a society to match its scenery."

—Wallace Stegner, *The Sound of Mountain Water* (1946)

In 1973, the options available to resolve natural resource disputes in the American West were once again expanded. That year, two mediators initiated and then facilitated a negotiation over a proposed flood control dam on the Snoqualmie River in Washington State. This effort is widely acknowledged as the first instance of environmental mediation in the United States, pioneering a new way to approach land, water, and other resource management disputes.[1] After a yearlong negotiation, an agreement was forged around plans to construct the dam (which was never built), manage floods, control land uses, and create a watershed coordinating council.

From this modest beginning, the use of negotiation, mediation, consensus building, and other collaborative problem-solving methods—in sum, the field of public dispute resolution—has grown dramatically in the past three decades. Today, citizens and leaders use these approaches to shape legislation, administrative rules, and intergovernmental agreements. As discussed in chapter 6, they are also employed by a number of citizen-initiated, place-based forums, including watershed councils, forestry partnerships, and ongoing community forums. People have used collaboration to address virtually every western resource, including water, range, timber, minerals, recreation, fish and wildlife, and preservation. It has also been used to address issues related to tribal activities, community growth and land use, air and water quality, and hazardous waste management.[2]

The idea of cooperative decision making and sharing responsibility for common problems has a rich and diverse history that goes back well beyond 1973.[3] The earliest arrivals in the New World brought with them the Christian tradition of peacemaking: "as far as it depends on you, live at peace with everyone."[4] Far from being the "alternative" it is often presented as today, this ethic was the norm. Religious congregations, ethnic groups, and some business circles embraced the values of individual responsibility, mutual trust, and avoidance of adversarial courts and lawyers. Many tribal cultures practiced their own brand of community-based problem solving, which often included ideas that today are incorporated into the restorative justice movement, such as community service and victim reparations.

More recently, the field of public dispute resolution has drawn inspiration from labor relations, small-group dynamics, the tradition of barn raising, and social activism. Practitioners have also drawn from the larger field of conflict resolution, including interpersonal, family, organization, community, commercial, and international areas of practice. The theory and practice of public dispute resolution has both benefited from and contributed to these other arenas.[5]

The rise of collaboration, negotiation, and consensus building parallels a growing dissatisfaction with other forms of decision making and dispute resolution. Simply put, over the past thirty years, citizens and decision makers alike have grown tired of recurring problems, hostilities and gridlock, and resource policies that sway back and forth and back again with every swing of the political pendulum. The old strategies are unable to resolve many of today's complex issues.

Defining Our Terms

Collaboration, from the Latin *com laborare*, means "to work together." Ideally, collaboration is based on the premise that if you bring together the appropriate people in constructive ways with good information, they will create effective, sustainable solutions to the problems they share in their organization or community. The essence of collaborative problem solving is to integrate the interests of people who have a stake in an issue or decision, usually referred to as stakeholders. Interests are needs, desires, concerns, and fears—the intangible items that underlie people's positions or the items they want.

Collaborative problem solving is a deeper, more intimate, and more inclusive kind of democracy—one that is more direct than representative, more consensual than majoritarian. It is a shift from a politics of hostility to one of civility, from advocacy to engagement, from confrontation to conversation, from debate to dialogue, and from divisiveness to community. David Chrislip and Carl Larson argue that initiating and sustaining successful collaborative initiatives are two of the key ways communities can develop "social capital" or a strong civic community.[6]

As defined here, collaboration shares many values and strategies with civic environmentalism, deliberative democracy, community-based conservation, and consensus building.[7] Given the degree to which some of these terms— particularly *collaboration* and *consensus building*—are used interchangeably, it helps to draw some distinctions. Collaboration is perhaps best understood as a social learning process in which people share knowledge, ideas, and experience through cooperative, face-to-face interaction. Whereas consensus building typically aims to reach some solution to a problem, collaboration may emphasize other objectives, such as developing knowledge and understanding, building a sense of community, and sharing resources. A collaborative problem-solving process may or may not be designed to reach consensus.

By contrast, consensus building is perhaps best understood as a particular form of collaborative problem solving, meaning that consensus shares many of the same traits as collaboration. However, whereas collaboration may or may not be designed to reach agreement or resolve a dispute, consensus processes are designed to seek agreement among all the people interested in or affected by a particular issue or situation. Consensus processes seek unanimous agreement, in contrast to processes where a decision is reached through voting (a power-based procedure where the majority rules) or is made unilaterally by a government agency or judicial body (typically a rights-based procedure). The process usually takes the form of interest-based negotiations among all affected parties. Consensus processes are further defined by a set of key theoretical and strategic elements, which are discussed below.

Collaboration may sound like a warm, fuzzy approach to public decision making, but in practice it works best when participants take a principled stand and advocate strongly for their own interests. Agreement is reached not by one side yielding to the other but by clarifying each side's interests and seeking a mutually satisfying solution through civil dialogue. Such an approach is consistent with both the communitarian leanings of liberals and the conservative ideology of voluntary, decentralized problem solving. Either way, despite its history of more adversarial approaches (such as first in time, first in right), the West has a long tradition of neighbor helping neighbor and of "good fences make good neighbors." Think of collaboration and consensus building as tools for installing helpful gates in those fences.

Why Collaboration and Consensus Building?

Although collaboration and consensus building are becoming more and more popular throughout North America, there seems to be more interest and use of such processes in the American West than in any other region. There are a number of reasons for this:

- The American West is changing.[8] For the past 100 years, the West has grown steadily (despite economic booms and busts), while population in most other regions of the country has fluctuated up and down. But now the West seems to be growing and changing faster than ever. The five fastest-growing states in the United States during the last ten years were Nevada, Arizona, Idaho, Utah, and Colorado. Between 1990 and 1998, the region's metropolitan areas grew by 25 percent and the nonmetropolitan, rural areas by 18 percent; both rates are significantly higher than other regions of the country. As illustrated by the 2000 presidential election, this growth in population is followed by an ideological trend. Rural counties overwhelmingly voted for Republican George Bush, while the more urban counties voted for Democrat Al Gore. Increasingly, agencies and decision makers are seeking effective ways to cope with the tensions and competing demands created by these schisms of liberal versus conservative, urban versus rural, and longtime residents versus newcomers.
- The economy of the West is also changing. In the past twenty years, high-tech, service-oriented industries have surpassed the West's traditional economic base of agriculture, forestry, mining,

and other natural resource extractive industries. This shift, coupled with an influx of new residents, places new pressures on the landscapes and communities in the West. Farming, ranching, forestry, and other resource industries are increasingly facing competition from subdivisions, second homes, resort communities, and recreational uses. The infrastructure of communities—roads, schools, and other basic services—is also lagging behind the changes. Collaboration offers a way to bridge these changes.

- These demographic and economic changes mean that more and more city dwellers are coming into contact with farmers, ranchers, miners, loggers, and other people who have historically made a living off the land. While they often share a common commitment to sustain communities and landscapes, a need exists for more effective processes to integrate the "old west" with the "new west."
- All of this change seems to foster a sense of loss among many longtime residents. The cumulative effect of this change is often stalemate and gridlock. Relatively speaking, it is easier to block a proposal or plan than it is to design and implement a sustainable solution that meets the needs and interests of as many people as possible. Collaborative problem solving offers a way out of this endless circle and a means to integrate the goals of maintaining a livelihood and sustaining the region's environmental quality.
- The passage of preservation-oriented laws in the 1970s led people to seek ways to integrate multiple-use values with the preservation values. These laws also spurred an incremental shift in many natural resource agencies away from a dominant focus on commodity production. The agencies now contend with a greater variety of interests and demands.
- Recognition of the transboundary nature of western natural resource issues is growing. The West's most compelling natural resource problems—responding to growth; preserving landscapes and endangered species; sustaining air and water quality; managing public and private lands; integrating local, state, federal, and tribal interests; and balancing economic development and environmental protection, to name just a few—not only involve multiple parties and multiple issues but also cut across jurisdictional boundaries, scientific disciplines, and cultural norms. These types of problems transcend the capacity of any single public or

private institution and call out for more integrated institutional arrangements that are characterized by their ability to learn and adapt to changing circumstances.[9] Short of creating new institutions or reforming old ones, the philosophy and strategies of collaborative problem solving can bring together the appropriate people, institutions, and disciplines to generate effective solutions to common problems.

- Stakeholders are increasingly dissatisfied with the disengaging, adversarial nature of the public decision-making processes. Many traditional forms of public participation foster a one-way flow of information, from decision makers to stakeholders. There is limited opportunity for sharing information and learning together, and citizens are often frustrated when the final decision does not reflect their input and advice. More formal dispute resolution processes, such as litigation, may provide clarity, set legal precedent, and offer a sense of closure, but such processes typically result in winners, losers, and impaired relationships. The underlying problems may also go unresolved. Collaboration is seen as a welcome alternative.

- The West's historic, chronic, and almost cultural distrust of government seems to be reaching a fever pitch as nearly all stakeholders raise concerns about the ability of local, state, and federal governments to solve public problems. In short, we are faced with a fundamental question of governance: Who decides? Who should have control over decisions and the consequences of those decisions? Stakeholder groups often favor collaboration because it offers them a transparent way to directly engage in the decision-making process. Agency officials may embrace collaboration as an opportunity to rebuild credibility and restore the public's trust.

Collaborative problem solving responds to these changes in two ways. First, it offers a *means* to bring citizens together with local, state, and federal officials as well as with national environmental groups to negotiate a more effective system of solving the West's natural resource problems. Second, the theory of collaborative problem solving offers a particular *vision* of governance—that is, it is a political philosophy that argues for allowing stakeholders to be meaningfully involved in defining problems and finding sustainable solutions. In chapter 8, we will discuss the desirability and feasibility of collaboration as a new form of governance, as a set of ideas for restructuring our current institutional arrangements.

The primary advantages of collaborative, consensus-seeking processes are summarized in box 7.1. Proponents argue that collaborative problem solving not only provides more meaningful dialogue among citizens and leaders with diverse viewpoints but also results in better decisions—ones that are more informed, more widely supported, more likely to be implemented, more effective in solving problems, and less likely to be appealed. Such processes build understanding, support, and the capacity to resolve shared problems in the future.

Involving the stakeholders in defining problems, searching for solutions, and making trade-offs increases the potential to focus on the real interests that are at stake, rather than on divergent opinions and positions. This, in turn, avoids the need for "winners" and "losers" and the hardening of positions, embitterment, and desire for retaliation that frequently characterize more conventional processes.

A collaborative approach encourages creativity in problem solving by bringing a diversity of knowledge and expertise together to resolve issues. This leads to greater flexibility in designing the terms of agreement, greater control over and predictability of the outcomes, and more informed and better solutions.

BOX 7.1 **Advantages of Collaborative, Consensus-seeking Processes**

- They ensure that all interests and viewpoints are represented and respected.
- They enable participants to work with one another face-to-face.
- They supplement existing public decision-making processes.
- They anticipate and resolve issues before individuals and organizations become polarized and engaged in more expensive processes to resolve disputes.
- They lead to better informed, more creative, and enduring solutions.
- They improve working relationships among diverse interests.
- They nurture our sense of community.

A consensus-based process increases the commitment to decisions. If the stakeholders have been part of a decision-making process, they are less likely to appeal or protest the decision and more likely to support its implementation. Future modifications of the decision may also be more achievable because the parties are aware of the initial assumptions and the basis for needed changes.

Collaborative processes can also establish channels of communication and build working relationships among diverse interests. These working relationships, in turn, can help individuals and groups begin to develop a sense of place and of belonging to the larger community.

Finally, consensus-based processes can improve trust in government by involving the public and stakeholders in decisions, providing proof that their concerns are being addressed. Public agencies, in turn, have the opportunity to educate the parties about the constraints under which they operate and the technical, administrative, and political complexity of collective choice and governance. All of these benefits can be realized even when consensus is not reached. Decision makers will become better informed about the real issues of contention, and the parties will develop a greater understanding and respect for one another's concerns and values, even if they cannot agree on ultimate solutions.

"Good Process" Is Inclusive, Informed, and Deliberative

In 1969, Dr. Charles H. W. Foster, professor emeritus at the John F. Kennedy School of Government at Harvard University, presented a paper at the annual meeting of the American Institute of Biological Sciences titled "The Case for Environmental Conciliation." In that paper, which is one of the very first articles written on the use of negotiation and mediation to resolve natural resource and environmental disputes, Dr. Foster urged people concerned about environmental protection to seriously consider the use of conciliatory approaches to making decisions and resolving disputes.[10] Since Dr. Foster's exploratory essay, and after more than thirty years of experience, the theoretical and strategic framework to resolve natural resource and other public policy disputes has been well established.

The essence of this approach to resolving disputes over natural resources—and the primary prescription of this book—is that one of the best ways to sustain communities and landscapes in the West is to integrate interests. By comparison to all of the other strategies we have examined, this approach to dispute resolution tends to be less costly than determining who is right, which in turn is less costly than determining who is more powerful. This does not mean that focusing on interests is invariably better than focusing on rights and power, but it tends to result in lower transaction costs, greater satisfaction with outcomes, less strain on relationships, and less recurrence of disputes.[11]

Interest-based strategies are more effective when they are inclusive, informed, and deliberative. By inclusive participation, we mean that an effort is made to meaningfully include all viewpoints and interests. It also suggests that participants are empowered by the presumption that their input and advice will be considered and will influence the outcome. An informed process is one in which all participants have an equal opportunity to share views and information. The process fosters mutual learning, common understanding, and consideration of a variety of options. It enables participants to jointly develop and rely on the best available information, regardless of the source. A deliberative dialogue occurs when people listen to one another, consider the rationale or reason for competing viewpoints (that is, the interests that underlie the positions), and seek solutions that accommodate as many interests as possible.[12]

This approach—integrating interests through inclusive, informed, deliberative dialogue—constitutes our normative sense of the word *confluence*. Up to this point, we have used the word in a descriptive sense, suggesting that there is a confluence of strategies available to resolve western resource disputes in the twenty-first century. But *confluence* is also an apt metaphor for the primary message of this book: *if you bring together the right people in constructive ways with good information, they will produce effective, sustainable solutions to the challenges and opportunities they face.*

As mentioned above, the principles, concepts, and strategies for how to effectively use collaborative, consensus-oriented processes are well established, and it is not our intention to repeat what is available in other books. However, it is important to provide an overview of the theoretical and strategic framework for convening and coordinating multiparty, interest-based negotiations. To do this, we have distilled many of the key ideas into a set of tables, relying heavily on the work of Professor Lawrence Susskind, founder of the Public Disputes Program at MIT-Harvard University and one of the chief architects of this theory.[13]

Figure 7.1 provides a general picture of the four phases of collaboration and consensus building. It is critical to first assess the situation, to genuinely

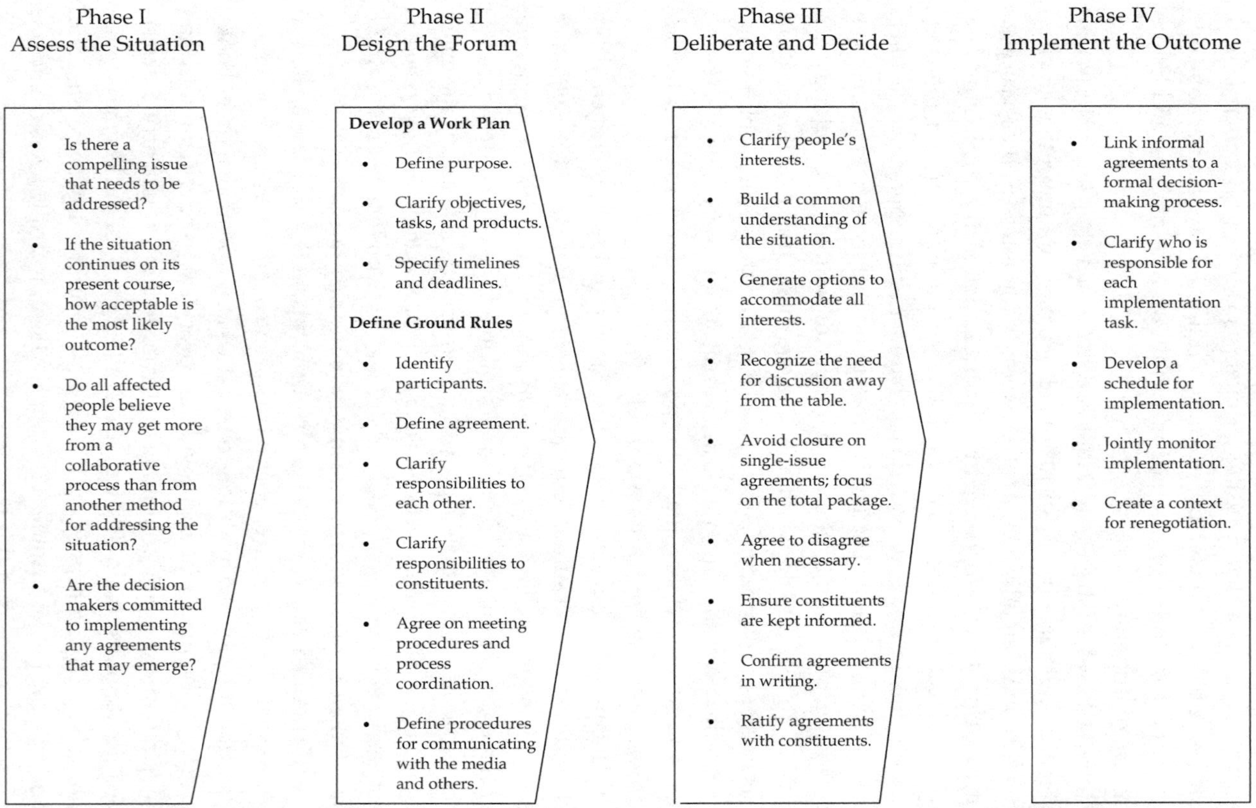

Phase I Assess the Situation	Phase II Design the Forum	Phase III Deliberate and Decide	Phase IV Implement the Outcome
• Is there a compelling issue that needs to be addressed?	**Develop a Work Plan**	• Clarify people's interests.	• Link informal agreements to a formal decision-making process.
• If the situation continues on its present course, how acceptable is the most likely outcome?	• Define purpose.	• Build a common understanding of the situation.	• Clarify who is responsible for each implementation task.
• Do all affected people believe they may get more from a collaborative process than from another method for addressing the situation?	• Clarify objectives, tasks, and products.	• Generate options to accommodate all interests.	• Develop a schedule for implementation.
• Are the decision makers committed to implementing any agreements that may emerge?	• Specify timelines and deadlines.	• Recognize the need for discussion away from the table.	• Jointly monitor implementation.
	Define Ground Rules	• Avoid closure on single-issue agreements; focus on the total package.	• Create a context for renegotiation.
	• Identify participants.	• Agree to disagree when necessary.	
	• Define agreement.	• Ensure constituents are kept informed.	
	• Clarify responsibilities to each other.	• Confirm agreements in writing.	
	• Clarify responsibilities to constituents.	• Ratify agreements with constituents.	
	• Agree on meeting procedures and process coordination.		
	• Define procedures for communicating with the media and others.		

FIGURE 7.1. Phases of Public Dialogue. (Prepared by the Public Policy Research Institute, The University of Montana [October 2003].)

understand the issue or problem at hand (for more on situation assessments, see chapter 9). Based on the assessment, a process can be tailored to best meet the needs of the people involved. These first two phases set the stage for the meat of the process—principled deliberation and agreement building. Finally, the agreement must be acted upon by implementing it and monitoring its progress.

Box 7.2 presents a set of best practices for participants, highlighting strategies to improve the effectiveness of participants and the constituents they represent.

BOX 7.2 Best Practices for Participants

What Compels People to Engage in Collaboration and Consensus Building?

1. First and foremost, people determine that they will achieve more of their interests through negotiation than through their "best alternative to a negotiated agreement" (BATNA). Your BATNA is what you would most likely achieve without an agreement.

2. Second, a number of variables might compel people to engage:
   - a crisis, threat, or opportunity;
   - a shared vision or goal;
   - frustration with inaction;
   - a sense of responsibility;
   - a mandate (keeping in mind that it is very hard to insist that people cooperate!).

What Enables Participants to Be Effective?[1]

1. Prepare.
2. Clarify your interests.
3. Know your BATNA—what would you most likely achieve if you don't reach agreement? If you can achieve your interests more efficiently and effectively through some other means, then you may not want to negotiate.
4. Agree on the purpose and scope of the negotiation. Make sure it is framed broadly enough to include your interests, so that you have a compelling reason to participate.

5. Pursue interests; don't be trapped by "positions."
6. Focus on substance and relationships. Recognize that every person has two kinds of interests: (1) in the substance of the issue and (2) in the relationship. Deal directly with both interests.
7. Generate options for mutual gain.
8. Search for ways to accommodate everyone's interests.
9. Separate inventing (creating value) from deciding (claiming value).
10. Beware of the "negotiator's dilemma" over revealing versus concealing information.[2]
    - Consider what information to disclose, and when.
    - Ask yourself: "If I share information about my interests or options, will other parties reciprocate?"
    - Ask yourself: "Should I share the information with some or all of the parties? Is there a particular sequence that would be most effective?"
11. Use objective criteria to evaluate options. Common criteria include fairness, efficiency, tradition, precedent, and best available information. Evaluate the options against the criteria, and deal in packages; be willing to trade across items that you value differently.
12. Be accountable to your constituents. Inform and educate them on a regular basis; seek their input and advice. Don't surprise them!
13. Consider follow-through. How will any agreement be implemented? Monitored? Evaluated? Adapted?

---

1. In addition to the work of Professor Susskind, this section draws on the "seven elements" framework explained in Roger Fisher and William Ury, *Getting to Yes: Negotiating Agreement without Giving In* (New York: Penguin Books, 1991). The seven elements include communication, relationships, interests, options, standards of legitimacy, alternatives, and commitments.
2. See David Lax and James Sebenius, *The Manager as Negotiator: Bargaining for Cooperation and Competitive Gain* (New York: Free Press, 1986).

Process managers (people who sponsor and convene collaborative, consensus-seeking processes) also need to understand best practices for playing their role effectively. Box 7.3 focuses on the key principles of assessing the situation up front: engaging all affected interests, allowing the

---

BOX 7.3   Best Practices for Process Managers

1. Assess the Situation.

- Identify stakeholders, issues, interests, and options.
- Determine if people agree that they are more likely to achieve their interest by using a collaborative process rather than any available alternative.
- Acknowledge that collaboration and consensus building are not appropriate in all situations.
- Emphasize that collaboration and consensus building are designed to supplement, not replace, the formal processes for making decisions.

2. Ensure That the Process Is Inclusive.

- Realize that natural resource disputes typically involve multiple parties.
- Involve people affected by the issue, those needed to implement any outcome, and anyone who may undermine the process and outcome if not included.
- Acknowledge and respect the diversity of viewpoints and interests.

3. Allow Participants to Design the Process.

- Acknowledge the complex structure of multiparty negotiation.
- Participants should agree on ground rules to govern the process, including:
  - the purpose and scope of the process;
  - the issues and objectives;
  - decision-making rules and fallback;
  - representation;
  - incorporation of new issues and stakeholders;
  - communication between meetings;
  - communication with the media.

- Recognize the dynamic nature of multiparty negotiations, and design flexibility into the process. Anticipate learning about the situation and different interests, and then adapt the process as appropriate.

4. Manage the Complexity of Group Interactions.

- Conveners or sponsors
- Coalitions
- Steering committees
- Working groups
- Task forces

5. Encourage Joint Fact Finding and Mutual Learning.

- Build a common understanding of the issues in question.
- Gather and interpret data and information together.
- Provide equal access to information.
- Allow all participants an opportunity to exchange ideas.

6. Insist on Accountability.

- Hold participants accountable to the ground rules they adopt.
- Ensure that the participants report to their constituents in a timely and responsible manner.
- Keep the public and decision makers informed of progress and accomplishments.
- Be trustworthy at all times.

7. Design Implementation Strategies.

- Clarify the participants' commitment to implement the agreement.
- Make sure constituents are aware and agree.
- Link the outcomes of the ad hoc process to the appropriate formal decision-making process.
- Identify roles and responsibilities.
- Monitor and evaluate implementation.
- Reconvene if and when necessary.
- Adapt the outcome as new information, interests, or other variables emerge.

process to be participant driven, compiling the right information, encouraging civil dialogue and deliberation, and facilitating implementation.

Applications in the West: A Brief Roundup

Between 1974 and 1984, mediation was used to resolve more than 160 natural resource and environmental disputes in the United States.[14] Since then, there have been so many cases in which some type of negotiation, mediation, or collaborative problem solving has been used that it is very difficult, if not impossible, to track them. The School of Natural Resources and Environment at the University of Michigan maintains one of the best databases on case studies of collaboration on natural resource issues. In addition, the Policy Consensus Initiative is developing a national database on the use of consensus-building processes to address a variety of public issues.[15] When it is complete, citizens and leaders interested in a particular issue will be able to search the database for cases in which people have used consensus-building processes to address that issue. Other databases are managed by the Community-based Collaboration Research Consortium and the Alliance for Regional Stewardship, the latter of which focuses on cases dealing with regional, transboundary issues.[16]

In the West, negotiation, mediation, and consensus building have been used to address issues revolving around nearly every natural resource, as well as in a variety of institutional settings, including site-specific disputes, administrative rules, management plans, intergovernmental coordination, legislation, and national policy. Examples are everywhere. Since the 1980s, efforts to resolve the senior but unquantified water right claims of Native American tribes have increasingly relied on negotiation and mediation, because litigating tribal rights in general stream adjudications proved too expensive and time-consuming and often led to needless conflict between tribal and nontribal communities.[17] Montana established a compact commission, a specialized agency to negotiate "sovereign-to-sovereign" with tribes and federal agencies. In Idaho, the governor appointed a special team to conduct negotiations. In Arizona, private water users have taken the lead in negotiating with the tribes and federal government. The results are impressive: seventeen completed compacts or settlement agreements involving tribes in eight states (and several other settlements involving federal agencies), all largely achieved through negotiation.[18] Often, these compacts or agreements include dispute resolution provisions to avoid litigation (for example, several Montana compacts provide for the appointment of a three-person dispute resolution board). These results demonstrate that interest-based negotiation can complement the strategy of first in time, first in right.

Other negotiations have been more difficult to conclude, and mediators are also becoming involved in some of these. In Arizona, tribal claims in both the Little Colorado River and the Gila River adjudications were turned over to a settlement judge. In Idaho's Snake River adjudication, a seasoned mediator is working with the parties to address the claims of the Nez Perce Tribe. Montana's compact commission has asked the Confederated Salish and Kootenai Tribes to agree to involve a mediator. In June 2000, stakeholders (including the Klamath Tribe) in Oregon's Klamath River basin adjudication attended a workshop to learn how mediation might help resolve that case. Workshops have even been conducted for judges to help them use mediation in their water law cases.

In another example, in 1989, the Forest Service and the BLM initiated a broad citizen participation process to set the scope of an environmental impact statement. The issue at hand was the impact of a private/federal land exchange that would allow development of a copper mine in the Prescott National Forest. The proposed mine had a history of deep conflict that began in the early 1970s and culminated in a public meeting in 1984 at which more than 800 people attended to hear from a panel of representatives moderated by Arizona congressman Bob Stump. The panel included the Forest Service, the BLM, Prescott County, and Phelps Dodge mining company.

The participants keyed on complaints about inadequate environmental information, collusion on the part of the federal agencies, and mistrust of the mining company.[19] Following the meeting, the Forest Service announced an agreement to require a full environmental impact statement (EIS) driven by a "comprehensive plan for citizen participation that would . . . permit all interested parties to have an opportunity to be informed . . . and to avoid public conflict."[20]

The scoping process, spanning four months, fostered dialogue between the citizens of Prescott and federal officials. Prior to public meetings, an independent facilitation team met with citizens and community leaders to understand local perspectives, build trust in the process, and establish an agenda for the scoping process. A program of public education was initiated about the issues, and public meetings were facilitated to set the scope of the EIS. Avenues were created for citizens to be actively involved in guiding the technical studies after the scoping process was complete.

The process culminated in an outline for the EIS that the citizens and public officials trusted and felt was legitimate. This early experience demonstrated how mining project proponents could be involved in open dialogue and face-to-face discussions with regulators and citizens, resulting in clear regulatory judgments. This case also shows that collaboration can be successfully integrated into the scientific management model of decision making and dispute resolution.

The timber/fish/wildlife (T/F/W) process that unfolded in Washington State in 1986 and 1987 was groundbreaking because it was both early and a large-scale effort. This multiparty, mediated negotiation resulted in revisions to Washington's Forest Practices Act. Although T/F/W was specifically about forest management practices, it was driven by concerns about habitat for salmon listed under the Endangered Species Act, specifically water quality and riparian integrity.

Mapping out the stakeholders in T/F/W was a daunting task. The forest products industry and private forest owners were represented because of the obvious impact the process would have on forest management practices. Native American tribes were included because federal court decisions from the mid-1970s granted them rights to salmon for traditional activities. The organized environmental lobby was involved because its litigative strategy over forest practices created the policy logjam that catalyzed the collaborative process. In addition, regulation of natural resources in Washington is divided among four agencies—the Departments of Ecology (water), Fisheries (anadromous fish), Natural Resources (public forest lands), and Wildlife (fish and wildlife)—and all of them were involved. In all, some two dozen representatives from various organizations participated.

The process, which was mediated by the Northwest Renewable Resources Center, began with a two-and-a-half-day session in July 1986 to discuss the problem and the potential value of a negotiated approach. This meeting at Port Ludlow ended with a commitment by all participants to pursue negotiation. The negotiation process operated at two levels: a series of technical working groups addressed specific issues, and the policy group addressed issues that could not be resolved by the technical specialists.

The various groups met intensively over the next four months, and an agreement in principle was crafted in a marathon sixteen-hour session in early December 1986. The agreement was presented to the Board of Forestry, which had the legal authority to draft regulations consistent with the agreement. When the final T/F/W agreement was published in February 1987, it distilled discussions and agreements that had occurred in more than 100 meetings.

Of course, negotiation, mediation, and consensus building are not always successful. The decades-long battle over wilderness in Idaho is an excellent example. Statewide wilderness bills had been the accepted way to resolve disputes over designating wilderness, and every state except Idaho, Nevada, and Montana had successfully crafted such legislation through a process of intense negotiation between interested parties and state, congressional, and other leaders.

In Idaho, Governor Cecil Andrus and Senator James McClure attempted to negotiate a statewide wilderness bill in the late 1980s, but several proposals died in Congress. In 1991, the Idaho legislature then tried mediation to resolve the issue, enlisting a professional facilitator, commissioning studies, and bringing federal agencies, conservationists, and Idaho citizens to the table. A BLM study recommended designating just under 1 million acres as wilderness in Idaho, but a proposal generated by environmental groups targeted more than 5 million acres. After more than two years of negotiations, the parties at the table had hammered out several incremental agreements, but national environmental groups voiced their opposition, threatening to derail any proposal sent to Congress. In short, the mediation among statewide stakeholders neglected the interests of national groups, who held veto power where the decision would ultimately be made—on Capitol Hill.

Challenges and Obstacles in the West

The use of negotiation, mediation, and consensus building to resolve natural resource disputes in the West faces a number of general and region-specific challenges and obstacles. Professors Steven Yaffee and Julia Wondolleck have summarized a common set of obstacles and challenges to the use of collaborative approaches to decision making and dispute resolution in natural resource contexts.[21] Box 7.4 summarizes their work.

In addition to these more general challenges, collaboration and consensus building also face some unique challenges in the West. In part, they have run head-on into the other strategies for resolving disputes—first in time, first in right; expert decision making; public participation; litigation; citizen initiatives; and devolution. These strategies are not exclusive to the West, but they are more firmly and prominently embedded there than in other re-

Institutional and Structural Barriers

- Lack of opportunities or incentives
- Conflicting goals and missions among stakeholders
- Inflexible policies and procedures
- Organizational norms and culture—an adversarial or "expert-ise" mind-set translates to a lack of support for collaboration
- Limited resources
- Lack of "collaborative" leadership, in contrast to "command-and-control" leadership[1]

Barriers Caused by Attitudes and Perceptions

- Mistrust or distrust
- Entrenched positions (for example, private property rights or wilderness preservation)
- Conflicting values
- Personality issues
- Group attitudes about one another
- Participating in bad faith

Problems with the Process of Collaboration

- Unfamiliarity with the process
- Lack of process skills
- Inability to identify stakeholders or representatives
- Inability to represent constituent interests (because of lack of internal communication and decision-making procedures)
- Technical complexity of the issues
- Lack of a common set of facts
- Managing the tension between collaborative problem solving and other issues and forums that constituents have in common
- Linking the process to formal decision-making arenas

Resistance of Public Officials

- Fear of losing status by sharing the power of policy making with citizens.

• The blind spot—an unthinking assumption that the public's views are so ill informed, narrowly self-interested, unrealistic, and moralistic that they cannot add anything of value to the decision-making process

1. See Daniel Yankelovich, *The Magic of Dialogue: Transforming Conflict into Cooperation* (New York: Simon & Schuster, 1999).

gions. Given this menu of strategies to satisfy their interests, not everyone agrees with the promise of collaboration.[22] Moreover, some (perhaps many) of the disputes over natural resources in the West revolve around fundamental ideological beliefs, such as the sacrosanct value of private property rights and the appropriate role of government in owning, managing, and regulating land, water, and other resource uses. When disputants frame their interests and concerns in these terms, collaboration and consensus building help build a better understanding of diverse views and interests—and thereby help reframe the debate. However, it may be difficult to help such people reach agreement, because their ideologies are so embedded into their culture or subculture that they would rather "fight the good fight" (even if it is not in their best interest) than admit that there might be a different way of understanding the world. In short, in some parts of the West, stubborn adherence to tradition is still celebrated, and the "independent operator" is seen as a hero, particularly when he or she refuses, on principle, to cooperate with "outsiders."

For purposes of clarity, we distinguish between arguments against devolution, which are addressed in chapter 6, and arguments about collaboration and consensus building. Box 7.5 summarizes the arguments against collaboration and consensus building.

George Coggins, a professor specializing in public land policy at the University of Kansas, declares that "devolution, collaboration, community dialogue, and consensus are the latest buzzwords in federal land management policies. They join a list of other indefinable if not undecipherable concepts such as multiple use, biodiversity, and ecosystem management in the pantheon of panaceas."[23] Some environmental groups, such as Montana Ecosystems Defense Council, believe that collaboration is a waste of time and that their time is better spent filing appeals.[24] Others are concerned that national

---

BOX 7.5   Arguments against Collaboration and Consensus Building

- Collaborative problem solving (CPS) delegitimizes conflict as a way of dealing with issues and mobilizing support.
- CPS places more emphasis on local interests than on national interests.
- CPS does not provide any way for distant stakeholders or the national interest to be effectively integrated.
- CPS does not account for the disparity among participants in terms of their experience, training, skills, or financial resources.
- CPS is neither faster nor less expensive than traditional processes.
- CPS is time consuming; it leaves little time for traditional advocacy and education.
- CPS results in outcomes defined by the "lowest common denominator."
- CPS holds a danger in developing a norm that decisions are only legitimate when they are acceptable to all stakeholders.
- CPS allows established policies and standards to be weakened or negotiated away.
- CPS allows public officials to abdicate their responsibility (by "passing the buck" and avoiding controversial decisions) when they delegate authority and power to CPS groups.
- CPS is often presented as a substitute for traditional public decision-making processes—without the same safeguards and forms of accountability (for example, public notice, open meetings, right of appeal).
- CPS fosters a redistribution of power away from national environmental groups (largely urban memberships) to local, place-based groups (largely rural).

---

interests are not adequately integrated into local, community-based discussions over the future of federal lands.[25]

Multiple-use advocates have suggested that collaboration is "an ingenious process . . . widely used by government and non-governmental organizations . . . to impose a previously determined position on an unsuspecting community." They go on to argue that collaboration "bypasses elected officials; removes accountability . . . and shifts governance from the people governed to the enlightened elite."[26] People from many walks of life wonder if consensus or broad-based agreement is even possible, or if such processes simply wear people out and result in watered-down, compromised solutions. These people also question the on-the-ground success of collaborative processes. In what must be one of the broadest and most scathing indictments of consensus building, former British prime minister Margaret Thatcher has said that "consensus seems to be the process of abandoning all beliefs, principles, values and policies in search of something in which no one believes, but to which no one objects."[27]

To thoughtful practitioners, these criticisms reveal a degree of misunderstanding about collaboration and consensus building that could be alleviated with better information and public outreach. They also expose deeply felt concerns about the fundamental shift in power that occurs when traditional decision makers share their authority with other stakeholders. People on all sides of natural resource issues wrestle uncomfortably with the riddle of who should be given decision-making responsibility. Such concerns should make us all refocus on best practices (ensuring that all affected interests are represented, that everyone is given a chance to participate, and so forth). Finally, these criticisms raise the question of scale. Some people would argue that collaboration is best suited to resolving issues at the local or subregional level. They say that such processes are not appropriate for tackling issues of national concern, including most broad policy decisions about federal lands and resources. We agree that integrating national interests within regional or community-based forums can be difficult, but it is not impossible. In chapter 4, we explored several methods (such as citizen juries and collaborative polling) for engaging "unaffiliated" citizens, including a broader cross section of the American public.

Citizens and interest groups are not the only people who question the value of collaborative problem solving. Public officials are also often skeptical. Their willingness and ability to engage in collaborative processes seem to be colored by the history of their relationships with other stakeholders, which are often characterized by mistrust and misunderstanding. Public officials also often lack experience with collaborative problem solving and are unfamiliar with how to integrate it into existing public participation and decision-making protocols. Many officials cite inflexible policies and procedures, particularly the Federal Advisory Committee Act. They raise concerns about increasing the visibility of the problem, generating more controversy, creating expectations that cannot be met, abdicating their decision-making responsibility, and compromising their ability to make science-based decisions.

While most of these concerns raise practical issues that might be addressed through education and demonstration projects, Daniel Yankelovich, in *The Magic of Dialogue*, suggests that there is a deeper, more disturbing reason that public officials resist meaningful public dialogue.[28] He says this resistance comes from two sources. One is a fear of losing status by sharing the power of policy making with citizens. The second is the assumption that citizens are so ill informed, narrowly self-interested, unrealistic, and moralistic that they cannot add anything of value to the decision-making process. Even if these claims are only partially true, they help explain the inertia of public institutions in the West in responding to natural resource and environmental problems and in incorporating more meaningful approaches to public participation.

Evaluating Success

Partly in response to these concerns, scholars and practitioners are developing different ways to evaluate the success of collaborative problem-solving processes. Most evaluation frameworks build on the basic ideas articulated in *Getting Disputes Resolved*.[29] The authors argue that dispute resolution or decision-making processes are better or worse to the degree that they increase the satisfaction of outcomes, minimize transaction costs, maintain (if not improve) relationships, and result in durable or sustainable outcomes. Although these four criteria were developed in reference to dispute resolution, they seem to apply equally well to public participation and collaborative problem-solving processes. The theoretical and conceptual basis for this simple framework, particularly as it applies to collaboration and consensus building, has been more fully developed by Judith Innes.[30] Using the same basic framework, the Montana Consensus Council has developed a simple, user-friendly "scorecard" (see appendix) for participants to evaluate the success of collaborative problem-solving processes .[31]

While the number of anecdotal stories about the success of collaborative processes is increasing, very little systematic, empirical analysis of a large number of cases has been performed.[32] To help fill this gap, the Consensus Building Institute, in cooperation with the Lincoln Institute of Land Policy, conducted a survey and set of interviews with participants in over 100 cases in which a facilitator or mediator assisted in the resolution of a land use dispute.[33] The researchers asked participants to compare what they had achieved with what they thought would have occurred otherwise.

In sum, 77 percent of the cases were settled, meaning the participants reached agreement. In these cases, 75 percent were implemented as intended by the parties. Ninety-two percent of the participants believed that their own interests were well served by the settlement, and 86 percent believed that all parties' interests were served by the agreement. Eighty-one percent of the respondents said the negotiation took less time and money compared to their next-best alternative to resolve the dispute, and 85 percent said that the assistance of an impartial facilitator or mediator was crucial or important. Even in the cases that were not settled, participants agreed that the process helped achieve minor agreements, improved relationships, clarified the interests of the stakeholders, and increased knowledge and understanding of the issues. Overall, 85 percent of the participants were satisfied with the process and its outcomes.

In a more recent study, the Western Consensus Council and the Consensus Building Institute, with support from The William and Flora Hewlett Foundation, examined participants' satisfaction in forty-eight cases of community-based collaboration on federal land and resources in the intermountain West. More than 90 percent of respondents ranked "quality of the process" and "working relationships" as important indicators of success, while only 70 to 80 percent of the respondents ranked "outcomes" as important. Some of the collaborative groups in the study are ongoing, so not everyone responded to the outcome questions. Nevertheless, the findings suggest that while outcomes are important, they are not the only indicators of a successful process. Many people seem to believe that the values of civic engagement—defined by the indicators included under "quality of the process" and "working relationships"—are as important as, if not more so than, the outcomes of such processes. If this is true, then it is inappropriate to determine the success of collaborative, consensus-oriented processes solely by the degree to which they achieve certain outcomes. If the participants convene and participate in such processes for purposes of civic engagement as well as achieving outcomes, it is only fair to evaluate the processes based on the objectives defined by the participants, not some preconceived objectives articulated by an interest group or the academic community.

As researchers and practitioners continue to develop and test methods to evaluate the success of collaborative processes, it will be important to develop criteria that allow us to compare the results of collaboration against other processes for public participation and public decision making. Such a framework, combined with empirical studies, will provide better information on the relative merits of the different approaches to resolving natural resource disputes. It would be practically and intellectually unfair to hold one process (such as collaboration or consensus building) to a higher or different standard than other processes.

Researchers and practitioners also raise concerns about who should evaluate such processes (the participants themselves, decision makers, citizens, or experts) and when such evaluation should take place (ongoing to allow for midcourse corrections, at the end of the process, or retrospectively—say, five years after implementation). Some debate also exists over how such evaluations should be conducted—through surveys, interviews, round-robin discussions, or some combination.

Despite these ongoing debates, it's not unusual to read or hear comparisons of collaboration and consensus building with other forms of dispute resolution (such as litigation). For example, conventional wisdom holds that collaboration is more cost effective than litigation. In reality, such a comparison is difficult because the processes are very different from one another and a great many variables must be considered. Nevertheless, evidence is beginning to mount that alternative dispute resolution is indeed less costly than litigation. A study by the Oregon Department of Justice found that the average monthly cost of resolving a dispute through a trial was $60,577, while mediation for similar disputes averaged $9,537 a month. The Florida Department of Environmental Protection estimated that parties in mediation saved a median of $75,000 each when compared to the costs of litigation. With at least two parties in any dispute, that's a minimum median savings of $150,000. In one western case, Kansas, Colorado, and Nebraska settled a four-year-old lawsuit over use of water from the Republican River through mediation. The Colorado Attorney General's Office estimated that the mediation saved $5 million in litigation costs; similarly, Kansas's attorney general said that her state avoided the $1 million a year it typically costs to litigate a water case.[34]

The use of negotiation, mediation, and consensus building over the past thirty years to resolve disputes over natural resources in the West and across the country demonstrates the value of this strategy. Although collaborative problem solving is not a panacea, the evidence seems to suggest that, relative to the other strategies that are commonly employed, integrating diverse interests through collaboration and consensus building tends to improve the satisfaction and durability of outcomes, as well as the quality of working relationships, thereby decreasing transaction costs.

Given this track record, one of the most compelling challenges and opportunities we now face is how to move beyond the use of collaboration and consensus building for addressing single issues on an ad hoc basis, to designing systems that can respond to the "stream of disputes" that characterize western natural resources. The long-term promise of collaboration and consensus building may be not only in resolving critical issues as they arise but also in improving the shape and function of governance in general.

In the next chapter, we examine a diverse portfolio of strategies to improve the governance of western resources by integrating the values and methods of collaboration and consensus building into processes for public participation, decision making, and dispute resolution.

NOTES

1. See Gail Bingham, *Resolving Environmental Disputes: A Decade of Experience* (Washington, DC: Conservation Foundation, 1986).

2. Contrary to the inclinations of some people, the Grazing Advisory Boards created to implement the Taylor Grazing Act of 1934 are not good examples of the type of collaborative problem solving we are describing here. The Grazing Advisory Boards, according to the legislative history of the act, were designed to invest local control of the range in the hands of people familiar with stock raising and the range. The boards were composed only of people grazing cattle, sheep, or both on the public domain, with the intent that the board would help the federal government determine the carrying capacity of the range, allocate range rights, and resolve any outstanding disputes. While this may have been an effective system of administrative in the 1930s and 1940s—and certainly required a degree of cooperation among stockmen and the federal government— it is a far cry from the type of collaborative forums that emerged in the 1970s in which people with a diversity of viewpoints and interests come together to solve a problem. The resource advisory councils, which took the place of the Grazing Advisory Boards beginning in the mid-1990s, more closely approximate the philosophy and strategy of collaborative problem solving.

3. For more on the rich history of cooperative approaches to decision making, see

E. Franklin Dukes, *Resolving Public Conflict: Transforming Community and Governance* (New York: Manchester University Press, 1996).

4. For more on biblical peacemaking, see Ken Sande, *The Peacemaker: A Biblical Guide to Resolving Personal Conflict*, 2nd ed. (Grand Rapids, MI: Baker Book House, 1991).

5. Perhaps the best place to gain an overview of the field of conflict resolution is the Web site of the Association for Conflict Resolution (http://www.acresolution.org), the premier professional association for practitioners, scholars, and people dedicated to promoting more cooperative ways to resolve conflict.

6. David D. Chrislip and Carl E. Larson, *Collaborative Leadership: How Citizens and Civic Leaders Can Make a Difference* (San Francisco: Jossey-Bass, 1994). The literature on and interest in social capital, civil society, and civic participation have mushroomed in the past five to ten years. For an introduction to these ideas, see Benjamin R. Barber, *A Place for Us: How to Make Society Civil and Democracy Strong* (New York: Hill & Wang, 1998); and Robert Putnam, "Bowling Alone: America's Declining Social Capital," *Journal of Democracy* 6, no. 1 (1995): 65.

7. See Dewitt John, *Civic Environmentalism: Alternatives to Regulation in States and Communities* (Washington, DC: Congressional Quarterly Press, 1994); John Dryzek, *Deliberative Democracy and Beyond: Liberals, Critics, Contestations* (Oxford: Oxford University Press, 2002); Philip D. Brick, Donald Snow, and Sarah Van de Wetering, eds., *Across the Great Divide: Explorations in Collaborative Conservation and the American West* (Washington, DC: Island Press, 2000); and Lawrence Susskind, Sarah McKearnan, and Jennifer Thomas-Larmer, eds., *The Consensus Building Handbook: A Comprehensive Guide to Reaching Agreement* (Thousand Oaks, CA: Sage, 1999).

8. For more information on the demographic and economic changes taking place in the West, see Katherine M. Albert, William B. Hull, and Daniel M. Sprague, *The Dynamic West: A Region in Transition* (San Francisco: Council of State Governments, Western Region, 1989); *The Western Charter Project* (Denver, CO: Center for Resource Management, May 2000); and William E. Riebsame, ed., *Atlas of the New West: Portrait of a Changing Region* (New York: Norton, 1997).

9. See William B. Meyer and Charles H. W. Foster, *New Deal Regionalism: A Critical Review* (Cambridge, MA: Environment and Natural Resources Program, John F. Kennedy School of Government, Harvard University, March 2000); and Charles H. W. Foster and William B. Meyer, *The Harvard Environmental Regionalism Project* (December 2000).

10. Charles H. W. Foster, "The Case for Environmental Conciliation" (paper

presented to the Annual Meeting of the American Institute of Biological Sciences, University of Vermont, August 19, 1969).

11. *Community-based Collaboration on Federal Lands and Resources: An Evaluation of Participant Satisfaction* (Helena and Cambridge: Western Consensus Council and Consensus Building Institute, October 2003).

12. See Daniel Yankelovich, *The Magic of Dialogue: Transforming Conflict into Cooperation* (New York: Simon & Schuster, 1999), for other ways to define deliberation, dialogue, and such.

13. See Lawrence Susskind and Jeffrey Cruikshank, *Breaking the Impasse: Consensual Approaches to Resolving Public Disputes* (New York: Basic Books, 1987); and Susskind, McKearnan, and Thomas-Larmer, eds., *The Consensus Building Handbook*. Other useful sources include Julia M. Wondolleck and Steven L. Yaffee, *Making Collaboration Work: Lessons from Innovations in Natural Resource Management* (Washington, DC: Island Press, 2000); and Society of Professionals in Dispute Resolution, *Best Practices for Government Agencies: Guidelines for Using Collaborative Agreement-Seeking Processes* (report and recommendations of the SPIDR Environment/Public Disputes Sector Critical Issues Committee, 1997).

14. Bingham, *Resolving Environmental Disputes*. This book is widely considered to be the standard evaluation of the first ten years of experience in negotiating and mediating land use, natural resource, and environmental disputes in the United States.

15. School of Natural Resources and Environment, University of Michigan, http://www.snre.umich.edu/; Policy Consensus Initiative, http://www.policyconsensus.org/.

16. This database of the Community-based Collaboration Research Consortium (http://www.cbcrc.org) is managed by the Institute for Environmental Negotiation at the University of Virginia. For the Alliance for Regional Stewardship's database, see http://www.regionalstewardship.org.

17. See "The Winters (*Winters v. United States*, 207 U.S. 564) of Our Discontent: Federal Reserved Water Rights in the United States," *Cornell Law Review* 69 (June 1984): 1077.

18. See Elizabeth Checchio and Bonnie G. Colby, *Indian Water Rights: Negotiating the Future* (Tucson: University of Arizona Water Resources Research Center, 1993). This source lists fourteen settlements in seven states. To this list must be added recent settlements involving the Yavapai Prescott Tribe in Arizona, the Warm Spring Reservation in Oregon, and the Rocky Boys Reservation in Montana.

19. This case study is based on James R. Richardson, "Negotiating Community Consensus in Preparing Environmental Impact Statements," in *Mediating Envi-*

ronmental Conflicts: Theory and Practice, ed. J. Walton Blackburn and Willa Marie Bruce, 5–9 (Westport, CT: Quorum Books, 1994).

20. Richardson, "Negotiating Community Consensus."

21. Wondolleck and Yaffee, *Making Collaboration Work.*

22. The most systematic treatment of arguments against consensus building is Douglas S. Kenney, *Arguing about Consensus: Examining the Case against Western Watershed Initiatives and Other Collaborative Groups Active in Natural Resources Management* (Boulder: Natural Resources Law Center, University of Colorado School of Law, 2000).

23. George Coggins, "Of Californicators, Quislings, and Crazies," *Chronicle of Community* 2, no. 2 (Winter 1998): 27–33.

24. See quote by Steve Kelly in "Howdy Neighbor!: As a Last Resort, Westerners Start Talking to Each Other," by Lisa Jones, *High Country News,* May 13, 1996.

25. See Michael McCloskey, "Report of the Chairman of the Sierra Club to the Board of Directors" (November 18, 1995).

26. See *Multiple Land Use Review* (July 1997).

27. Margaret Thatcher, speech at Monash University, Melbourne, Australia (Sir Robert Menzies Lecture), October 6, 1981. Archived at www.margaretthatcher.com.

28. Yankelovich, *The Magic of Dialogue.*

29. William L. Ury, Jeanne Brett, and Stephen Goldberg, *Getting Disputes Resolved: Designing Systems to Cut the Costs of Conflict* (San Francisco: Jossey-Bass, 1988).

30. Judith Innes, "Evaluating Consensus Building," in Susskind, McKearnan, and Thomas-Larmer, eds, *The Consensus Building Handbook.*

31. For more information, see Montana Consensus Council, http://www.mcc.state.mt.us.

32. See, for example, the collection of stories originally published in *Chronicle of Community* and now captured in Brick, Snow, and Van de Wetering, eds., *Across the Great Divide.* See also selected issues of *High Country News* (based in Paonia, Colorado).

33. Lawrence Susskind, Mieke van der Wansem, and Armand Ciccarelli, *Mediating Land Use Disputes: Pros and Cons* (Cambridge, MA: Lincoln Institute of Land Policy, 2000).

34. Larry Parriman, "Legislative Request on Agency Legal Counsel/Litigation Expenditure," memorandum to Scott Seacat, December 17, 2002, MT Department of Administration; see also *ECR Cost-Effectiveness: Evidence from the Field* (Tucson, AZ: U.S. Institute for Environmental Conflict Resolution, February 28, 2003 [white paper]), 5. Also, *Cost Comparison of Settlement Techniques for Environmental Disputes* (Florida Growth Management Conflict Resolution Consortium, February 1994 [white paper]), 4.

8

A Changing Landscape

During the past thirty years, people with diverse viewpoints and interests have effectively used negotiation, mediation, and other consensus-building strategies to resolve a host of western resource disputes on a case-by-case basis. Individually, these efforts protected resources, invigorated economies, and sustained communities. Collectively, however, their impact may be far greater. The success of consensus-building forums suggests that the underlying values—inclusive participation, informed decisions, and deliberative dialogue—could be applied more systematically. Beyond resolving individual disputes as they arise, the full promise of collaboration and consensus building may lie in improving the shape and function of governance itself.

A quick scan of any western regional newspaper illustrates that the management of western resources is characterized by chronic, recurring disputes. As so clearly revealed by the Klamath River situation, existing institutional arrangements are insufficient for dealing with this stream of disputes. The organic emergence of watershed councils, forestry partnerships, and other community forums initiated by civic entrepreneurs reinforces this observation—existing institutions do not provide the type of public space or engagement that citizens want. At the beginning of the twenty-first century, the primary challenge of managing western resources is to move beyond the ad hoc resolution of disputes and instead refine and reform existing systems of governance to better cope with the stream of disputes. Standard operating procedures must change so that collaboration is the "forum of first resort," rather than the forum of last resort or merely an "alternative" strategy.

In this chapter, we suggest that such a transformation is under way. At local, state, and federal levels, government officials are fostering incremental change by integrating negotiation, mediation, and other forms of collaborative problem solving into established public decision-making systems. While this may be a step in the right direction, some people are concerned that such government-sponsored efforts will founder on the embedded rigidity of the current decision-making system. One of the more outspoken proponents of this view, Daniel Kemmis, argues that it is only through the devolution of power and authority that we can realize the true benefits of consensus building and community-based collaboration. Kemmis and others argue that the West should embrace a series of experiments in democracy in which we allow the communities most directly affected by natural resources to assume far more responsibility for devising, adopting, and implementing management plans. Through a series of experimental pilot projects, we should test different models of public engagement, decision making, and dispute resolution to better learn which models offer the most promise to improve our existing systems of governance.

Another indication that a transformation is under way is the emergence of a new model of leadership, a shift from the traditional command-and-control approach to a focus on building relationships through dialogue. This collaborative model of leadership is designed to build the capacity of citizens and officials to engage people with diverse viewpoints in constructive forums with good information. It assumes that the very people affected by resource decisions can work together to sustain the diverse social, economic, and environmental values of the West.

The move toward more collaborative forms of governance is both a regional necessity and a historic imperative. Interest-based problem solving represents the most recent response to the limitations of all the other decision-making and dispute resolution strategies that have emerged during the past 150 years. While it is not likely to replace other ideas or models of governance, it arguably provides the most effective means to engage citizens and leaders in the process of shaping public policy to sustain the communities and landscapes of the West.

Incremental Change

Collaborative problem solving is gradually being integrated into existing systems of public decision making and dispute resolution on many levels. Proponents of collaboration are achieving this integration through the following actions:

- Promulgating laws that encourage or require the use of negotiation and other forms of dispute resolution;
- Adopting policy statements that promote the use of collaborative problem solving;
- Creating instruments of government to build agreements and resolve disputes;
- Designing systems to resolve recurring disputes over land and water.

Laws That Encourage or Require Negotiation

Alternative dispute resolution (ADR) has been successfully institutionalized in many contexts, including family law, workers' compensation, and several court-connected programs.[1] Montana has more than thirty laws, administrative rules, and court procedures that promote or require the use of some type of ADR. In Texas, more than 150 bills with significant mention of ADR were introduced in the 1999 legislative session. Thirty-two of these bills became law. According to Nancy Rogers, a professor of law in Ohio, more than 2,500 laws nationwide promote the use of negotiation and mediation in different contexts.[2] No doubt there is much to learn from these experiences as officials, scholars, and others look for ways to incorporate collaboration into western resource policy.

Four examples illustrate the range of laws that require or promote the use of collaboration in public decision making. The first is the 1998 federal Administrative Dispute Resolution Act, which encourages federal agencies to use ADR in both internal and external relations. The second is the federal Negotiated Rulemaking Act (1990), which encourages federal officials to sit down with the diversity of stakeholders on any given issue to prepare a preliminary draft of a proposed rule or regulation. The draft rule is then subject to the formal public notice, review, and comment process, before it is adopted by the responsible agency.[3] Following the trend at the federal level, the legislatures in Idaho, Florida, Montana, Nebraska, Texas, and Washington have passed statutes encouraging negotiated rulemaking.[4]

The third example is the Clean Air Act, which allows a governor or tribal leader to request the U.S. Environmental Protection Agency (EPA) to enter into negotiations with the parties to resolve disputes over the potential impact of a new major emitting facility or the redesignation and protection of an airshed under the Clean Air Act.[5] If a negotiation process is requested by either the state or the tribal jurisdiction, the EPA is required to convene such a process to resolve the dispute and "protect the air quality related values of the lands involved." If the parties do not reach an agreement, the EPA must impose a solution; thus a clear incentive exists for the parties to work out their differences. Either way, the resolution becomes part of the applicable plan. This negotiation provision was recently activated in Montana over concerns about the environmental impacts associated with a proposed power plant near Roundup, which may diminish the air quality in and around the Northern Cheyenne reservation. As of this writing, three sovereign governments—the Northern Cheyenne tribe, the Montana Department of Environmental Quality, and the federal EPA—are negotiating, with the assistance of a professional mediator. According to some preliminary research, this provision has been used at least three other times.[6] Other state and federal statutes likewise incorporate requirements for negotiation and mediation.[7]

The fourth example is the Secure Rural Schools and Community Self-Determination Act of 2000, otherwise known as the "County Payments Bill," which requires the Forest Service to create resource advisory committees (RACs) to provide early and ongoing input from citizens, organizations, tribes, land management agencies, and other stakeholders.[8] These RACs are modeled after the RACs created through administrative rule to provide more systematic and informed input and advice to the Bureau of Land Management (BLM) on planning and place-specific issues. A committee of scientists convened by the chief of the Forest Service in 1997 to propose changes in Forest Service operations recommended that collaborative management become the driving force for planning and management.[9] Before the proposed rules could be adopted, however, the Bush administration put a hold on revising the forest planning regulations.

How well are these efforts working? It is a basic lesson of public policy and administration that a wide, obstacle-filled gap exists between enacting a law and implementing it on the ground. To provide at least a partial answer to this question, consider the implementation and use of Montana's Negotiated Rulemaking Act.[10] The act was passed in 1993. In 1998, the Montana Consensus Council distributed a survey to the directors of twenty-one state agencies; nineteen agencies returned a completed survey. The survey found a total of five negotiated rulemaking proceedings in the first five years since the law was passed. In three of these cases, the legislature mandated the use of negotiated rulemaking. Two of these cases resulted in partial agreement, while the other resulted in a consensus package of proposed rules. The two proceedings that were initiated at the discretion of the state agency both resulted in consensus proposals.

Sixty-nine administrative rules were promulgated as a result of the five negotiated rulemaking proceedings. Fifty of the rules are new, and nineteen repeal existing rules. During this same five-year period, more than 10,000 administrative rules and regulations were promulgated by Montana state agencies. Of this total, nearly half focused on routine agency matters, such as the repeal of existing rules and the transfer of rules from one agency to another. In these situations, negotiated rulemaking is probably not appropriate. It isn't clear how many of the remaining rules were challenged through administrative or legal channels, or how many were adopted with no opposition.

Based on interviews with a number of stakeholders involved in the five cases, it appears that the law, at least in its current form, is not very user-friendly. According to state officials, negotiated rulemaking is not used more frequently for three primary reasons: (1) officials prefer to rely on informal consultations to obtain the input of interested parties, (2) they find the procedural requirements of the negotiated rulemaking process cumbersome, and (3) they claim that the right situation has not presented itself.

To improve the use of negotiated rulemaking, at least in Montana, it may be valuable to clarify the objectives of negotiated rulemaking—and to increase people's awareness and understanding of the place of negotiated rulemaking within the spectrum of approaches to involve citizens in administrative rulemaking in general. Negotiated rulemaking, like other forms of collaboration, is not a panacea and is not appropriate in all cases. Public officials, in particular, need guidelines or a set of best practices to match the most appropriate citizen involvement process to particular situations. Last but certainly not least, the process should be streamlined to make it more efficient.

At a more general level, the difficulties of implementing negotiated rule-making suggest that it would help to conduct more research on the implementation of other state and federal laws designed to promote collaboration.[11] Are these laws being used, and do they improve citizen participation and the quality of decisions? Or is the idea of collaboration being co-opted by public officials with little regard for actually engaging citizens in public decisions? Without rigorous follow-up and monitoring of implementation, we cannot know what refinements or adaptive measures may be needed to achieve the laws' intended outcomes.

Policy Statements That Promote Collaboration

In 1993, President Bill Clinton signed an executive order directing federal agencies to explore and, where appropriate, use consensus-building processes to develop regulations. Numerous memoranda of understanding (MOUs) among local, state, and federal agencies promote collaboration to achieve the goals of ecosystem management, resolve transboundary disputes, and make the best use of limited resources.[12] The U.S. Forest Service adopted a policy statement encouraging the use of "collaborative stewardship" in 1997.[13] Recently, Secretary of the Interior Gail Norton articulated her "4 C's" policy: conservation through communication, consultation, and cooperation. And in the spring of 2003, the U.S. Department of the Interior announced Water 2025, a comprehensive new federal water policy initiative. One of its key themes is to remove institutional barriers to increase cooperation and collaboration among federal, state, tribal, and private organizations.[14]

Governors have also encouraged the use of collaboration. The Montana Consensus Council, which is designed to build agreements and resolve disputes on natural resources and other public policy issues, was originally created by executive order.[15] In Massachusetts, the governor recently signed an executive order to "integrate dispute resolution into state government." It calls for the directors of state agencies to appoint ADR coordinators, develop an ADR plan, and submit annual reports. Several other states have passed similar executive orders.[16]

In 1997, the Western Governors' Association (WGA) passed a policy resolution encouraging the use of consensus-building approaches to shape public policy and resolve public disputes.[17] WGA also passed a policy resolution in 1998 endorsing the Enlibra principles for environmental policy in the West. Among other things, these principles, which were adopted by the National Governors Association, encourage greater public participation and collaboration in decision making. Three other regional political associations—the Council of State Governments–WEST (legislators), the Western Interstate Region of the National Association of Counties, and the Western Municipal Conference—have adopted a joint policy resolution on the role of collaborative problem solving in western natural resources.[18]

While most of these executive orders and policy statements are symbolic, they raise awareness, foster understanding, and help establish the legitimacy of collaboration in public decision making. Depending on how the policy statements are framed, they can also provide a springboard for action. The recent report to implement the 4 C's, for example, calls for a series of pilot projects. The Enlibra principles have guided projects to improve air quality on the Colorado plateau and wildlife habitat in the Great Plains. Under an MOU with the U.S. Forest Service and the BLM to "promote the use of consensus building processes for federal land management," the Montana Consensus Council has conducted educational workshops, assessed the potential for mediating disputes related to snowmobile use and wilderness management, and facilitated a dialogue among tribal, state, and federal governments to develop a reclamation plan for the Zortman-Landusky mine in north-central Montana.[19] It has also helped citizens, stakeholders, and government officials design and coordinate a public participation process to update the region's resource management plan.[20] The council has also provided advice to forest supervisors and district rangers, as well as their staff, on how to more meaningfully engage citizens in preparing travel management plans and revising forest management plans.

Instruments of Government to Build Agreements and Resolve Disputes

The close of the twentieth century saw a surge in the creation of local, state, and federal programs to promote collaborative approaches to public participation and public dispute resolution. Since 1984, when the National Institute for Dispute Resolution sponsored the creation of the first four offices in Hawaii, Massachusetts, Minnesota, and New Jersey, more than thirty state offices of dispute resolution have been created across the country. At least seven states west of the 100th meridian now have some type of program or state office of dispute resolution and consensus building, some of which specialize in natural resources and public policy.[21] (Unfortunately, when states reduce spending, many of these programs are the first to feel the pinch. During western states' recent budget slashing, several such programs were forced to cut back services and seek other funding streams, including grants.)

In addition to these state offices, several federal land management agencies have institutionalized the use of community-based collaboration, negotiation, mediation, and even joint fact finding. In 1999, Congress created the U.S. Institute for Environmental Conflict Resolution to promote the use of negotiation and mediation to resolve environmental disputes involving one or more federal agencies. The institute maintains a roster of experienced facilitators and mediators, provides a number of training programs, supports selected projects through grants, and otherwise provides a clearinghouse for information, advice, and assistance to federal agencies.[22]

In addition to using regionally based RACs, the U.S. Bureau of Land Management also relies on community-based partnerships to provide input and advice on specific land or resource-related issues at the field level.[23] While the RACs are appointed by the secretary of the interior in consultation with the governor of the respective state, the community-based partnerships are much more ad hoc and may vary in purpose and structure. The BLM has also created an Office of Collaboration and Alternative Dispute Resolution to promote the use of negotiation, mediation, and other collaborative problem-solving strategies throughout the agency's jurisdiction.

Although the Committee of Scientists's recommendation to adopt new administrative rules that encourage the use of advisory committees and other types of community-based groups in revising and updating national forest management plans has been put on hold, the Forest Service has created dozens of RACs to recommend stewardship and maintenance projects for federal funding. The Forest Service has also created a number of new programs—such as the Collaboration Service Team—that help the Forest Service and other agencies design and guide collaborative efforts.

Several other federal agencies have also created programs and initiatives to promote the appropriate use of collaboration and consensus building. For example, the EPA's Center for Conflict Prevention and Resolution emphasizes the use of negotiation and mediation in resolving disputes over Superfund and enforcement issues. The EPA's Community-Based Environmental Protection program is designed to bring public and private stakeholders together to integrate social, economic, and environmental values and generate place-based solutions.[24] The EPA has also adopted an agency-wide policy on public participation that encourages early, ongoing, and frequent opportunities for citizens to participate in environmental decisions. The U.S. Geological Survey created the Center for Science Policy to, among other things, encourage and support experiments in which citizens work side by side with scientists to identify what scientific and technical information is needed to address particular issues and how to jointly learn what they want to know.[25]

Taken as a whole, these programs and initiatives play a number of critical roles. They establish legitimacy and credibility for the idea of collaboration and its role in governance. They provide information and advice on different approaches to public involvement and public dispute resolution. They help build the capacity of citizens and leaders through education and training. Many of these programs provide staff who assess conflicts, design processes, and facilitate and mediate complex, multiparty dialogues. Finally, some of the programs produce publications to help raise awareness and understanding. Depending on staff, location, and politics, some of these efforts are more effective than others.

To help clarify the value of these different instruments of government, several people representing consensus councils met in the fall of 2002 to explore the degree to which consensus councils represent a unique type of institution. The first consensus council was created in 1990 in North Dakota and continues to operate as a not-for-profit organization. Shortly thereafter, the Montana Consensus Council was created by executive order in 1993 and was statutorily authorized in 2003. The Western Consensus Council was created as a regional not-for-profit organization in 1996, working with citizens and leaders throughout the American West. The Sonoma County Consensus Council, located in northern California, was created in 2001; it represents the first community-based consensus council. In 2002, Congress first considered a proposal to create a U.S. Consensus Council. At the time of this writing, a bill to create the U.S. Consensus Council is making its way through both the Senate and the House of Representatives. Several other jurisdictions—including the community of Bozeman, Montana, and the states of Idaho, Kansas, New Mexico, Utah, and Washington—are currently considering the possibility of creating consensus councils.

Consensus councils are unique in that they provide a permanent impartial and nonpartisan forum to support the legislative, executive, and judicial branches of government. As such, they serve as advocates for all interests and viewpoints, and for fair, deliberative problem-solving processes. They are not simply a provider of facilitation and mediation services but, perhaps more importantly, also represent a symbol of democracy in the twenty-first century—an essential forum for public participation, pubic decision making, and public dispute resolution.

The consensus council appears to be a uniquely western phenomenon. Even the proposal to create the U.S. Consensus Council is based largely on the model provided by state councils in the West. Why? The simple answer would be that other states in the region followed North Dakota's lead. But these states also share a number of characteristics that consensus councils are well suited to address: a preponderance of public lands and issues that cross jurisdictions; traditional, commodity-based economies struggling to compete in an increasingly complex and expanding market; a strong split between urban and rural populations (and values); rapid growth and changing demographics; and a grassroots awareness that existing institutions need help to successfully meet these challenges.

Systems to Resolve Recurring Disputes

Increasingly, institutions governing western resources are becoming more collaborative and less adversarial by employing dispute resolution "systems." Unlike most collaborative processes that emerge in response to a particular dispute or issue, the systems perspective is built on the observation that many policy arenas, political jurisdictions, and communities are faced with a stream of disputes. While many disputes can be anticipated and resolved through opportunities for meaningful public participation, others cannot. Some stakeholders feel that their interests are often best met through adversarial dispute resolution processes, such as administrative appeals and litigation.

Taking the time to design or redesign the system for resolving the stream of public disputes faced by an organization—rather than trying to resolve individual, ad hoc disputes—can save time and money, improve the efficiency and effectiveness of staff resources, and improve the organization's reputation and relationships with constituents. In their book *Getting Disputes Resolved*, William Ury, Jeanne Brett, and Stephen Goldberg provide a practical framework for designing dispute resolution systems.[26] Box 8.1 builds on their work by summarizing a set of principles for designing effective systems of public participation and dispute resolution to deal with western resource issues. The premise of this model is that an effective system for public engagement begins with opportunities for meaningful public participation. Where disputes cannot be anticipated and resolved proactively, the

---

BOX 8.1   Principles for Designing Effective Public Participation and Dispute Resolution Systems

- Put the focus on interests.
- Build in loop-backs to negotiation.
- Provide low-cost fallback procedures.
- Build in consultation before the process, and feedback after it.
  - Prevent unnecessary conflict by asking people how they want to be involved.
  - Learn from the experience, and adapt the system as needed.
- Arrange procedures in a low- to high-cost sequence.
  - Prevention procedures
    - To inform and educate
    - To seek input and advice
  - Interest-based procedures (to build agreement)
    - Unassisted negotiation
    - Facilitation
    - Mediation
    - Joint fact finding
  - Loop-back procedures (to keep the focus on interests)
    - Special master
    - Settlement conference
    - Nonbinding arbitration
  - Low-cost fallback procedures
    - Binding arbitration (rights-based)
    - Voting (power-based)
    - Litigation
- Provide the necessary motivation, skills, and resources.

---

system provides opportunities for negotiation and mediation prior to adversarial dispute resolution processes. In other words, it is better to anticipate and resolve issues through low-cost procedures—such as public consultation, negotiation, and even mediation—before resorting to procedures—such as lobbying and litigation.

Consider an example from north of the forty-ninth parallel, the Alberta Environmental Appeal Board (EAB), which hears all appeals on the comprehensive provincial environment law.[27] EAB hears cases on permit approvals, enforcement actions, land reclamations (associated primarily with gas and oil drilling), administration penalties, and contaminated sites. After inception, however, the board was soon inundated with cases. From 1994 to 2001, EAB received a total of 810 appeals. The vast majority of these appeals (83 percent) related to permit approvals of one kind or another. To ease this burden, EAB added a mediation program to the formal appeals process. The program included the setting of clear intake procedures; policies and guidance; a consumer guide; intensive training for board staff serving as mediators; and a monitoring and evaluation program. Since 1996, seventy-seven cases (or about 10 percent) have been mediated; 75 percent of those cases were settled in mediation.

From June 1999 through December 2001, EAB surveyed seventy-five people who had just completed a mediation. The survey asked participants whether they were satisfied with the mediation process, what they learned from it, what they thought of its efficiency, and if they would engage in it again. Most respondents (75 percent) said they would participate in mediation again, and 71 percent thought the process took less time and cost less money than going before the board for a formal hearing. Most respondents (71 percent) thought the mediation process encouraged them to consider various options. About 29 percent of respondents did not reach agreement in the mediation process, but only 14 percent said they would not participate in mediation again under similar circumstances. This means that even though some participants did not reach agreement, they still found the mediation process worthwhile. Also, more than half the respondents thought that the mediation process resulted in an agreement that satisfied them; improved their understanding of the other parties' concerns and interests; helped them to develop clear, reasoned explanations for why they might or did reach agreement through the mediation process; and was efficient and was time and money well spent.

Some dispute resolution systems target specific resources. Land use decisions, for example, are often fraught with disagreements. At least six communities and seven states have developed dispute resolution programs to cope specifically with land use issues.[28] In 1992, the Albuquerque city council created a Land Use Alternative Dispute Resolution Program, funded from city coffers. The program deals primarily with zoning and site-specific development issues and to date has handled 400 cases. The city doesn't track how many of these cases are settled without going to court, but program staff report that developers now reach out to stakeholders before submitting their building applications. Dialogue on land use issues in Albuquerque, they say, has shifted from narrow concerns to broader community interests. In 1998, the cities of Denver and Colorado Springs contracted with a mediation provider to address disputes over land use variances and planned unit developments. Soon, more complex and contentious issues were directed toward mediation. Today, the contractor mediates an average of thirty-five cases a year, with about 75 percent of those ending in signed agreements.[29]

Western states with statewide land use dispute resolution programs include California, Colorado, Idaho, Oregon, and Washington. Most of these programs focus on appeals brought against land use decisions made by the state or counties. Colorado's program addresses only disputes between government agencies. Although data on success rates are scarce, in large part because the initiatives are so new, most of these programs report that they have effectively reduced caseloads in the courts.

Negotiation and mediation are also being slowly integrated into systems to manage western water and to resolve the inevitable disputes that arise over water allocation. In at least one western state, Montana, the legislature created a water mediation program to help resolve disputes related to the adjudication of water rights. Montana also has a unique, statutorily created institution, the Reserved Water Rights Compact Commission, whose mission is to negotiate the resolution of water rights among state, tribal, and federal governments. In contrast to the more adversarial and prolonged litigious approach in many other western states, the commission has successfully negotiated compacts with five of the seven tribal nations in Montana as well as three compacts with the federal government.[30] Negotiations are moving forward or pending on reserved water rights held by other tribes and federal agencies.

The Montana legislature also directed the Department of Natural Resources and Conservation to design and implement a dispute resolution system for water policy and management. Under this system, the department has convened forums to build agreement on such statewide issues as water information management, agricultural water use efficiency, instream flow protection, and federal hydropower licensing and state water rights. The department has also increased its participation in watershed councils across the state.[31]

The systems approach can also be applied across state boundaries. In 1996, Montana and Wyoming incorporated a dispute resolution system into the Yellowstone River Compact, which provides an institutional framework for managing this interstate river.[32] The dispute resolution system moves from unassisted negotiation to facilitation before the states can resort to voting and then litigation to resolve disagreement over river management.

A brief consideration of any aspect of western resource policy suggests that ample opportunity and need exist to apply, test, and refine the principles of systems design presented in box 8.1. The process of designing an effective system for public participation and dispute resolution generally involves seven steps (as shown in box 8.2).

Proposals for Reform

Despite significant progress in the integration of consensus building and negotiation into existing institutions, some forward-thinking people envision reforming resource governance in less incremental, more fundamental ways. Many recommend giving control over planning and management for selected resources (such as specific federal lands or water) to local collaborative groups. Not surprisingly, westerners tend to support that idea. As Daniel Kemmis points out: "The grass-roots movement is irresistibly vibrant and growing, while the old system is increasingly paralyzed." Grassroots collaboration, he says, is "fundamentally at odds" with top-down, national, bureaucratic governance. The question, says Kemmis, is not whether the old system will be replaced but how to make the transition constructively.[33]

Wittingly or not, the Bush administration endorsed the ongoing conversation about restructuring the federal resources bureaucracy when it announced its Charter Forest proposal. This proposal called for certain national forests, or portions of them, to be managed on an experimental basis by alternative governing structures, including local trusts. A similar idea arose when foresters and researchers met at the University of Montana's Lubrecht Experimental Forest in 1998. They suggested that Congress designate a "virtual" region 7 of the national forest system to test collaborative governance structures and other mechanisms to provide regulatory flexibility.[34] An advisory committee would hold a national competition to select pilot projects across a range of administrative and geographic scales. The secretary of agriculture could waive unduly burdensome rules or regulations, and any projects would be carefully monitored—for both procedural efficacy and results—against established baselines. Similar proposals have also come from the Idaho Federal Lands Task Force and the Forest Options

---

BOX 8.2   Seven Design Steps to an Effective Public Participation or Dispute Resolution Process

Step 1. Identify and characterize a stream of disputes according to the source of disagreement (for example, disputes over values, policies, scientific and technical information, procedural issues, or relationships).

Step 2. Examine existing protocols, anticipating controversial situations and providing opportunities for meaningful public participation and—where disputes cannot be resolved proactively—the processes for how disputes are handled (for example, through avoidance, informal negotiation, formal grievance procedure, administrative proceedings, or litigation).

Step 3. Evaluate the performance of the current public participation and dispute resolution system in terms of transaction costs (time and money), satisfaction of outcomes, durability of outcomes, and impact on relationships.

Step 4. Design or redesign the system to provide more inclusive, informed, and deliberative opportunities for public participation and dispute resolution.

Step 5. Involve staff and stakeholders in evaluating and refining the existing system.

Step 6. Implement new protocols through demonstration and pilot projects.

Step 7. Monitor, evaluate, and refine the effectiveness of the new protocols.

Group. Pilot forests, they suggest, could test such strategies as entrepreneurial budgeting, forest trusts, rate boards to set forest user fees, and collaborative planning and governance, wherein broad-based boards of stakeholders would write forest plans and make on-the-ground management decisions.[35]

The concept has created a buzz in other resource arenas as well. In 1998, the Western Water Policy Review Advisory Commission—which consisted of eight citizens appointed by the U.S. president, twelve members of Congress, and the secretaries of the Department of the Interior and Department of the Army—said the federal government should initiate a series of pilot projects to restructure the water management bureaucracy, capitalizing on the strengths of watershed councils already established throughout the West. The pilot projects would test a variety of approaches to engage water users in governing at the local community level, such as basin-level cooperatives and strategies to sustain funding at the watershed level. Unfortunately, this "nested" approach has not been implemented as the commission intended and was replaced in favor of a more top-down model, undermining the original intent of the proposal.

Both the Center for the Rocky Mountain West and the U.S. Institute for Environmental Conflict Resolution have called for pilot projects to test alternative governance strategies for activities regulated by the National Environmental Policy Act. In 2001, the Foundation for Research on Economics and the Environment solicited proposals exploring alternative institutional arrangements for the protection of the Wild and Scenic portion of the Missouri River, now included in the Missouri Breaks National Monument. Top-ranked proposals recommended alternative management under a trust organization and by a citizen management committee.[36]

More recently, a consortium of policy centers in the West has suggested an even broader approach. They would enlist experts to report on opportunities for improved governance of the public lands and also initiate interviews with a broad spectrum of stakeholders to identify areas of difference and potential areas of agreement on public land governance. If the interviews revealed sufficient interest, the consortium would then convene a policy dialogue among a broad diversity of people and organizations to clarify the problems and explore the options to improve the governance of federal lands.[37]

From even a cursory review of these proposals, several common themes and principles become clear. Proponents of experimentation (and others) agree that the existing bureaucracy is dysfunctional and in need of a major overhaul. But they also recognize that dramatic, wholesale changes to the system could destabilize it beyond repair and create serious, unintended, unforeseeable problems. Experimentation, they say, allows us to test and learn from different models before completely transforming existing institutional arrangements. The time is ripe, they agree, because gridlock and acrimony have generated a growing civic will for more decentralized, participatory forms of decision making. A national competition for new models of governance would encourage entrepreneurialism, diversity, and excellence. It's time for public leaders to create the necessary "transitional legal space" to allow experiments to proceed (bearing in mind the limitations of devolving authority under existing law as explained in chapter 6).

Most of these proposals endorse a principled approach to experimentation. An overview of the various proposals suggests that, at a minimum, pilot projects should:

- be encouraged across a range of issues, administrative jurisdictions, and geographic scales;
- be governed by the principle of "accountable autonomy" (see chapter 6);
- promote "adaptive management," under which a plan is monitored and lessons learned are incorporated into future management on an ongoing basis;
- ensure that all decisions and actions are open and transparent.

New Models of Leadership

Incremental change and proposals for bolder systemwide experimentation are both essential in transforming the governance of western resources, but such efforts will land short of their promise without informed, active leadership. The responsibility to resolve disputes over natural resources and sustain communities and landscapes throughout the American West ultimately falls on the backs of individual civic leaders and citizens. To make the type of changes contemplated above, resource managers and decision makers must have both the will and the skills to meaningfully engage diverse interests, advocate for better processes (rather than lobbying for preconceived outcomes), and share power without abdicating authority.

In recent years, a library of books and articles has articulated new concepts of leadership. This new vision or model of leadership is variously referred to as facilitative, collaborative, servant, transforming, and relational. According to Daniel Yankelovich in *The Magic of Dialogue:* "The main difference between the older command-and-control and the new leadership models lies in the assumptions each makes about the best way to mobilize people to achieve an institution's objectives."[38]

In the command-and-control model, power is a zero-sum game—when you share power or give it to others, you diminish your own power. In this traditional model, "leaders" set objectives and strategies and then try to create a set of incentives and consequences to motivate people. This pattern of leadership is deeply entrenched in many institutions but is increasingly ineffective in situations that require innovation, a quick response to change, and the commitment of people with diverse viewpoints.

Managing natural resources in the twenty-first century requires a new style of leadership (see box 8.3). In contrast to exercising authority by taking unilateral action, today's effective leaders cross jurisdictions, disciplines, and cultures to forge alliances with diverse interests and viewpoints. They invite people to take ownership of a shared vision and values, and they work hard to bridge differences and nourish networks of relationships. To move in the desired direction, they share power and mobilize people, ideas, and resources. In the midst of this action, today's leaders provide integrity and credibility, and advocate for the integrity of the decision-making process.

BOX 8.3 Traits of Collaborative Leadership

- Focus on change
  - Tolerate complexity and uncertainty
- Facilitate the development of a shared vision by
  - crossing boundaries (jurisdictions, sectors, disciplines, cultures)
  - forging alliances with diverse interests and viewpoints
  - bridging differences
  - sustaining networks of relationships
  - model commitment to the shared vision
- Mobilize the people, ideas, and resources needed to move in the desired direction
  - Invite people to take ownership of a vision, strategy, and set of values
  - Empower others to contribute
- Create a forum to share power
  - Promote and safeguard the process
  - Provide credibility and integrity
  - Foster mutual respect and trust
  - Form partnerships with other leaders

They also show a high tolerance for complexity, uncertainty, and change. The new "collaborative" model of leadership emphasizes dialogue and building relationships. It begins by respecting the diversity of ideas and viewpoints. Respect builds trust, which in turn fosters communication, understanding, and eventually agreement. These are the cornerstones of effective leadership, and they are best accomplished through dialogue.

This new model of leadership is slowly being incorporated into the training and education of future resource managers and decision makers. As natural resource professionals have spent more time grappling with conflicting interests and fending off criticism—and less time managing their assigned resources—they have responded by rethinking the tools of their trade. In a survey of employers of entry-level foresters, for example, researchers found that it is increasingly important for all resource managers, including those in entry-level positions, to be able to effectively communicate and interact with the public.[39] A report by the Pinchot Institute for Conservation supports this, indicating that natural resource businesses, agencies, and nongovernmental organizations consistently place public participation, team building, and communication skills near the top of their wish list when hiring employees.[40]

In a survey of natural resource schools accredited by the Society of American Foresters, thirty-six of forty educators said natural resource professionals needed more training in public involvement, dispute resolution, and "relational" skills, and 96 percent of respondents said such training was "important" or "essential."[41] Despite budgetary and staff constraints, the number of schools offering specific courses on these topics has grown dramatically, from a reported three schools in 1992 to fourteen in 1997.[42] At most schools, these topics have been incorporated into already required courses on policy, planning, and management. In the West, nine professional natural resource schools now offer specific courses on public involvement, collaboration, and public dispute resolution—compared to only four in 1992.

Midcareer professionals are also finding more opportunities to reflect on their work and develop the relational skills required for collaborative problem solving. In response to gridlock over natural resource issues, the Montana Consensus Council convened a Natural Resources Leadership Forum in 1996 as a pilot project. Based on the positive feedback from this original forum, the council revised the course and convened the Montana Natural Resources Leadership Institute in 2001 and 2002. The objectives of the institute are to:

- foster a common understanding of key natural resource issues facing the state, including the history, law, policy, and science governing the issues;
- examine a variety of strategies, including prior appropriation, scientific management, public participation, litigation and ballot initiatives, collaboration and consensus building, localism, and citizen-driven collaboration, and refine skills for when to use what strategy;
- strengthen working relationships among individuals and organizations within the natural resources community;
- develop leaders who see beyond single disciplines and sectors and who possess the necessary skills to help Montanans shape public policies that integrate concerns for economy, environment, and quality of life.

The institute is designed for citizens and leaders who have a stake in the use and conservation of Montana's natural resources. Each year's class of the institute is designed to include participants representing the diversity of viewpoints on natural resource issues in Montana, including professionals from resource-based industries, environmental and conservation organizations, and resource management agencies, as well as people who own and manage land, educators, elected and appointed officials, and people who are concerned about the way our resources are managed.

Several agencies and organizations involved in shaping and implementing natural resource policy cosponsor the Montana Natural Resources Leadership Institute, including the Office of the Governor and several state agencies; the Environmental Quality Council of the Montana legislature; a number of university programs and departments; professional associations such as the Montana Association of Planners; interest groups ranging from the Montana Association of Realtors to the Montana Environmental Information Center; local government, including the Montana Association of Counties and the Montana League of Cities and Towns; and several federal agencies, including the Forest Service, the BLM, and the EPA.

In addition to participating in four monthly seminars, participants prepare a leadership action plan, which allows them to work independently or in small groups to apply the skills and knowledge gained during the seminars. Each seminar includes a mix of sessions on particular natural resource issues (such as energy, federal land management, wildlife, or water), the social and political context of natural resource management, and strategies to shape effective policy. Several other states, including Florida, Kentucky, North Carolina, and Virginia, convene similar leadership institutes, all of which are modeled after the leadership institutes convened by the Kellogg Foundation years ago (see www.wkkf.org).

Along with natural resource leadership institutes, several professional development courses are available to help midcareer professionals build skills. The International Association for Public Participation offers a series of courses on how to meaningfully engage the public in public decisions. The Consensus Building Institute and the Western Consensus Council teach skill-building workshops around the West, focusing on when to engage in a collaborative process, how to effectively participate in such a process, and how to design and manage a productive dialogue. The target audience for these workshops is process sponsors and stakeholders; the workshops are not intended to train additional facilitators and mediators. One of the greatest barriers to using collaboration is not the lack of skilled facilitators or mediators, but the lack of understanding and skills among stakeholders, including public officials. The goal is to bring together the diversity of stakeholders in a particular community or around a specific issue. This type of dialogue fosters a common understanding of the process, teaches skills in collaborative problem solving, and begins to develop a sense of respect, trust, and common purpose among the participants. Also, nearly all of the federal natural resource agencies, and the U.S. Institute for Environmental Conflict Resolution, offer courses in alternative dispute resolution strategies.

The Lincoln Institute of Land Policy, an educational organization located in Cambridge, Massachusetts, has developed similar courses tailored to particular issues. For example, after a comprehensive evaluation of the effectiveness of mediating land use disputes, the Lincoln Institute, in cooperation with the Consensus Building Institute, developed two courses on land use disputes. The first course is designed to raise awareness and understanding of the role of negotiation in resolving land use disputes, while the more advanced course is designed to improve people's ability to facilitate and mediate such disputes. The Lincoln Institute, working with the John F. Kennedy School of Government at Harvard University and the Western Consensus Council, has also developed a course on regional collaboration. This course is designed to help citizens and leaders deal more effectively with such transboundary, multijurisdictional issues as sprawl, water use, transportation corridors, and wildlife management.

The indicators examined in this chapter suggest that the values, principles, and strategies of collaboration and consensus building are both a regional necessity and a historical imperative. More and more frequently, westerners are turning to collaboration to accommodate differences and resolve on-the-ground problems that cannot be resolved by simply relying on the dispute resolution strategies that emerged during the past 150 years. Its rising popularity suggests that collaboration fills a need that is not met in other types of public forums or dispute resolution strategies. For many people, collaborative problem solving provides a more meaningful, more satisfying way of engaging one's neighbors—friends and rivals, stakeholders and decision makers alike—to solve shared problems and shape a common future.

Equally important, it is becoming more apparent that the ideas of collaboration and consensus building are slowly taking their place among the other paradigms for managing western resources. Based on the region's experience since the first environmental mediation in 1973, citizens and leaders are now moving beyond the ad hoc resolution of disputes and are refining and reforming existing systems of governance to better cope with the stream of disputes that characterizes the use of land, water, and other western resources. As this chapter illustrates, we can see positive signs that the ideas and strategies of collaboration are being institutionalized into western resource policy and management. However, people who care about the West have a long way to go and are engaged in an ongoing experiment to shape a more effective political culture, revitalize the role of citizenship, and improve existing institutional arrangements for governing western resources.

NOTES

1. Nancy H. Rogers and C. A. McEwen, *Mediation: Law, Policy, Practice* (Rochester, NY: Lawyers Co-operative, 1989).

2. See Montana Consensus Council, *Public Participation and Alternative Dispute Resolution Provisions in Montana* (2001); Center for Public Policy Dispute Resolution, University of Texas Law School, *Newsletter* 5, no. 1 (Fall/Winter 1999); and Rogers and McEwen, *Mediation*.

3. *Alternative Dispute Resolution Act, 28 U.S. Code* 651 (1998); *Negotiated Rulemaking Act, 5 U.S. Code* 561-570 (1990).

4. For more on the use and success of negotiated rulemaking, see Matthew McKinney, "Negotiated Rulemaking: Involving Citizens in Public Decisions," *Montana Law Review 60*, no. 2 (1999): 499–540.

5. *Clean Air Act,* 42 *U.S. Code* 7401-7671, sec. 164(e).

6. Maureen Hartman and Matthew McKinney, "Resolving Disputes under Section 164(e) of the Clean Air Act: Experience and Lessons Learned" (unpublished manuscript, September 3, 2003).

7. See Rogers and McEwen, *Mediation.*

8. *Secure Rural Schools and Community Self-Determination Act of 2000,* P.L. 106-393.

9. Committee of Scientists, U.S. Department of Agriculture, *Sustaining the People's Land: Recommendations for Stewardship of the National Forests and Grasslands* (March 15, 1999).

10. See McKinney, "Negotiated Rulemaking."

11. See, for example, Philip J. Harter, "The Actual Performance of Negotiated Rulemaking: A Response to Professor Coglianese" (unpublished, undated article on file with the authors).

12. Two examples of such collaboration are the Southwest Strategy (http://www.swstrategy.org) and the Greater Yellowstone Coordinating Committee.

13. See "Sustaining the Health of the Land through Collaborative Stewardship: Message to All Forest Service Employees from Mike Dombeck on His First Day as Chief" (January 6, 1997); see also Jim Burchfield, "Abandoned by the Roadside: The Long Road Ahead for Collaborative Stewardship," *Chronicle of Community* 3, no. 1 (1998): 31–36.

14. The 4 C's Working Group, *Leaving a 4 C's Legacy: A Framework for Shared Community Stewardship* (report to the assistant secretary of land and minerals management, July 2003); U.S. Department of the Interior, "Water 2025."

15. For a copy of the executive order, see http://www.mcc.state.mt.us.

16. Chris Carlson, "Executive Orders: How Governors Can Promote Collaborative Processes and Dispute Resolution for More Effective Governance," in *Solutions* (Policy Consensus Initiative, September 2000).

17. See Western Governors' Association, Policy Resolution 97-024 on "Consensus Building" (December 5, 1997), and Policy Resolution 99-013 on "Principles for Environmental Management in the West" (June 15, 1999).

18. *The Role of Collaborative Problem Solving in Western Natural Resources* (joint policy resolution of the Council of State Governments–WEST, the Western Municipal Conference, and the Western Interstate Region, National Association of Counties, 2000), http://www.mcc.state.mt.us.

19. MOV USFS/BLM MCC.

20. The Dillon Field Office's resource management planning process is well documented at http://www.mt.blm.gov/dfo/rmp/mccassesment.html.

21. The following organizations are connected in some way to state government,

and some of them receive at least a portion of their funding from the state's general fund: Resource Solutions, University of Alaska; Udall Center for Public Policy, University of Arizona; Common Ground, University of California; Montana Consensus Council, Office of the Governor; Oregon Dispute Resolution Commission; Texas Center for Public Policy Dispute Resolution, University of Texas; and the Institute for Environment and Natural Resources, University of Wyoming.

22. For more information on the U.S. Institute for Environmental Conflict Resolution, see http://www.ecr.gov/.

23. For more information on the BLM's community partnerships, see http://www.ntc.blm.gov/partner/community.html.

24. For more information on the U.S. EPA's Center for Conflict Prevention and Resolution, see http://www.epa.gov/adr/; for more information on the EPA's Community-Based Environmental Protection program, see http://www.epa.gov/ecocommunity/.

25. See Center for Science Policy, U.S. Geological Survey, http://www-wmc.wr.usgs.gov/csp/.

26. William L. Ury, Jeanne Brett, and Stephen Goldberg, *Getting Disputes Resolved: Designing Systems to Cut the Costs of Conflict* (San Francisco: Jossey-Bass, 1988).

27. For more information on the Environmental Appeal Board, see http://www3.gov.ab.ca/eab/.

28. *Integrating ADR Strategies into Land-Use Decision-Making: Guidelines for Public Officials* (Western Consensus Council, Consensus Building Institute, Pace University Land Use Law Center, April 28, 2003).

29. *Integrating ADR Strategies into Land-Use Decision-Making.*

30. MCA 85-5-11 (1989); MCA 2-15-212 (1979). See also Montana Reserved Water Rights Compact Commission, http://www.dnrc.state.mt.us/rwrcc/index.htm.

31. Matthew McKinney, "Designing a Dispute Resolution System for Water Policy and Management," *Negotiation Journal* (April 1992): 153–63.

32. *Yellowstone River Compact,* Subchapter 1, Dispute Resolution, *Administrative Rules of Montana* 36-5907 (September 30, 1996).

33. Daniel Kemmis, "Rethinking Public Land Governance for the New Century" (Pinchot Institute for Conservation Distinguished Lecture, February 11, 2000).

34. Center for the Rocky Mountain West, *Region 7: A Legislative Framework for Testing New Approaches to Public Land Stewardship* (April 25, 2002).

35. "Options for the Forest Service, 2nd Century: A Report to the American People from the Forest Options Group," www.ti.org/2c.html; Idaho Federal Lands Task Force, http://www2.state.id.us/lands/LandBoard/fltf.htm.

36. Foundation for Research on Economics and the Environment, "The Missouri

River Project: Exploring Alternatives for Lewis and Clark's Missouri River: Preservation, Restoration, Education," http://www.free-eco.org/rfp/index.html.

37. "Letter of Inquiry to the William and Flora Hewlett Foundation from the Natural Resources Law Center, O'Connor Center for the Rocky Mountain West, Ruckelshaus Institute of Environment and Natural Resources, Western Consensus Council, Kennedy School of Government, Andrus Center for Public Policy, Stegner Center for Land, Resources, and Environment, and Center of the American West" (April 23, 2003).

38. Daniel Yankelovich, *The Magic of Dialogue: Transforming Conflict into Cooperation* (New York: Simon & Schuster, 1999), 172.

39. T. L. Brown and J. P. Lassoie, "Entry-level Competency and Skill Requirement for Foresters: What Do Employers Want?" *Journal of Forestry* 96, no. 2 (1998): 8–14.

40. V. Alaric Sample et al., *The Evolution of Forestry Education in the United States: Adapting to the Changing Demands of Professional Forestry* (Washington, DC: Pinchot Institute for Conservation, 2000).

41. William J. Harmon, Matthew J. McKinney, and James A. Burchfield, "Public Involvement and Dispute Resolution Courses in Natural Resources Schools," *Journal of Forestry* (September 1999): 17–23.

42. Harmon, McKinney, and Burchfield, "Public Involvement and Dispute Resolution Courses"; see also Matthew J. McKinney, "Dispute Resolution Courses in Natural Resource Schools: Status and Needs for the Future," *Renewable Resources Journal* (Summer 1993): 6–13.

9

The Architecture of Dialogue

The decision-making and dispute resolution strategies described in this book evolved over the course of 150 years of western exploration, settlement, and continued growth. Each strategy developed in response to a particular need, and each has its peculiar strengths and weaknesses. All of these strategies continue to be available to citizens and leaders today, and that is both a blessing and a curse.

On the one hand, some issues are readily resolved by a single given strategy. All you have to do is choose the best one for your needs. Need more water for your crops? Buy senior rights from a willing seller, and you're set. Tired of seeing pop bottles and cans littering the roadside? Draft a "bottle bill" ballot initiative to encourage recycling. Time to update the district weed management plan? You might carefully combine a couple of strategies—the staff's scientific expertise and a well-designed public participation effort.

On the other hand, many western resources issues are not so simple. Complex, multiparty issues can seem intractable, leaving a trail of failed strategies and weary adversaries in their wake. Sometimes, as illustrated by the situation in the Klamath River basin, a number of strategies are brought to bear on the problem simultaneously, only to end up working as cross-purposes. Rather than resolving anything, the resulting scrum intensifies the conflict and frustration.

In either case, the questions are the same: How do you prevent an impending decision or emergent issue from flaring into a blazing hot dispute? And how do you select the most appropriate strategy (or strategies) for a given situation?

Obviously, it helps to understand each of the available strategies and to recognize their relative strengths and weaknesses. We hope this book has provided that understanding and context. In chapter 1, we introduced the following four criteria to help determine which strategy or problem-solving process might be most effective in addressing a particular issue or situation:

- How satisfied are the stakeholders likely to be with the outcome of a particular process?
- What is the chance that the issue will be resolved—and not recur—through one process or another? How sustainable is the outcome likely to be?
- What are the likely costs—time, money, and emotional energy—of relying on one process rather than another?
- How will the use of one process over another impact the relationships among stakeholders?

These four criteria are related. Dissatisfaction with outcomes may lead to the recurrence of disputes, which strains relationships and increases transaction costs. Because these four different costs typically increase or decrease together, we refer to them collectively as "the costs of disputing."

Applying these criteria, table 9.1 summarizes in broad terms the relative merits of the dispute resolution strategies examined in this book. Given the variability and complexity among natural resource disputes in the West, it is unrealistic to expect one strategy to be the best for every situation. But if you accept the above four criteria as valid measures of a strategy's effectiveness, then it follows that, in many situations, integrating diverse interests through negotiation and mediation tends to be less costly overall than strategies designed to determine who is right (for example, public interest litigation), which in turn cost less than processes that determine who is more powerful (for example, markets, professional expertise, and citizen initiatives). Integrating interests may not always be better than focusing on rights or power, but it does tend to result in greater and broader satisfaction with outcomes, lower recurrence of disputes, lower transaction costs, and less strain on

TABLE 9.1 A Comparative Assessment of Dispute Resolution Strategies

Model	Date	Strategy	Who Decides?	On the basis of?	Inclusive?	Deliberative?	Costs
Privatization	1855	First in time, first in right	Private individuals	Rights	No	Limited	Historically—low; Twenty-first century—high
	1980s	Free market environmentalism	Private individuals	Rights Power	Maybe	Limited	High to moderate
Delegation	1900	Scientific management	Experts	Power	No	Limited	High
Participation	1900	Citizen initiatives	Citizens	Power	Yes	Limited	Moderate
	1969	Public participation	Experts	Interests Power	Maybe	Limited	High to moderate
	1970	Public interest litigation	Courts	Rights	No	Limited	High
	1973	Negotiation, mediation, and consensus building	Stakeholders	Interests	Yes	Yes	Low
Devolution	1979	Sagebrush Rebellion	State officials	Power	Maybe	Limited	Moderate
	1990	Citizen-driven collaboration	Citizens	Interests	Yes	Yes	Low
	1991	County supremacy movement	County officials	Power	Maybe	Limited	Moderate

TABLE 9.2 Rethinking the Governance of Western Resources: Toward
More Inclusive, Informed, and Deliberative Processes

Traditional Strategy	Options for Improving the Governance of Natural Resources
First in time, first in right	Market-based mechanisms Public trust doctrine
Scientific expertise	Regional collaboration Joint fact finding Adaptive management
Public participation	Clarify roles of public officials Negotiated rulemaking Engage unaffiliated citizens
Citizen initiatives	Reform initiative process Deliberative democracy
Litigation	Negotiation Mediation Arbitration
Devolution	Federalism Intergovernmental compacts Trust arrangements
Interest-based negotiation Collaboration Consensus building	Best practices Situation assessment Systems design

relationships. Table 9.2 summarizes the options for rethinking and improving the governance of western resources, based largely on the findings of the situation assessment.

The First Step to a "Healthy" Process—
Assess the Situation

If table 9.1 helps us understand the relative merits of the various strategies, it also reveals only half of the picture. To determine the most effective process for a particular issue or situation, we also must understand the interests, concerns, and expectations of the people involved. Too often, decision makers assume they already have a finger on the public's pulse, and so they neglect one simple step—asking the stakeholders themselves to help define the problem and describe possible outcomes.

Imagine you're a doctor with the Centers for Disease Control and Prevention, and you've just landed in Yuma, Arizona, where a flulike illness has killed six people and sent thirty more to local hospitals. Your job is to control the outbreak and, if possible, prevent more deaths. The minute you arrive, you order antiviral drugs for anyone showing upper respiratory symptoms, and you set up medical teams to begin inoculating the entire population of Yuma with a new fast-acting flu vaccine. A week later, twelve more people have died of apparent pneumonia, hospitals are full, and the outbreak is spreading east, on direct course for Phoenix. What's gone wrong? (In this hypothetical case, the culprit wasn't influenza but the soil fungus *Coccidioiomycosis* carried into the air by a strong dust storm.)

Natural resource and dispute resolution professionals don't typically deal with such alarming emergencies, but like doctors, they must be master diagnosticians if they hope to see favorable results. Designing a dispute resolution process and convening the "right people" without first understanding the problem and people's needs and interests is akin to treating an illness before you have identified its cause. The basic principle here is timeless: as Aristotle said, most disputes can be deflated into a single paragraph if the disputants dare to define their terms.

To make an accurate diagnosis and define the terms of a dispute or public issue, dispute resolution professionals commonly recommend conducting an assessment. Variously referred to as a conflict assessment, situation assessment, conflict analysis, or stakeholder analysis, the assessment's objectives are to identify the people interested in or affected by an issue or situation; to clarify their interests and concerns (or the issues they care about); to analyze the real-world options people have to pursue their interests; and to determine the feasibility of moving forward with some type of collaborative or consensus-oriented process.

These objectives are based on the premise that no single model or approach to public participation, collaborative problem solving, or dispute resolution exists. As explained throughout this book, people have choices; many different ways are available to engage citizens, resolve disputes, shape public policy, and foster social change. Since each natural resource or public policy situation is unique, the process for engaging citizens and officials to build agreements and resolve disputes should be tailored to the specific needs and interests of the people involved in a particular situation. The best way to ascertain those needs and interests is to conduct an assessment, to talk with—and listen to—those people.

An assessment allows a convener—the person or organization interested in potentially convening a collaborative or consensus-seeking process—and all stakeholders to begin developing a common understanding of the substantive issues, the diversity of viewpoints and interests, and peoples' "best alternative to a negotiated agreement." An assessment helps people understand the history and dynamics of a particular issue or situation and clarifies the incentives of the various parties to engage in some type of negotiation.[1] It can also be a vehicle to help people critically examine the costs and benefits of alternative public participation or dispute resolution strategies. People often learn more about one another as a result of an assessment, which can help build respect, trust, and working relationships.

Some decision makers argue that assessments are unnecessary, time-consuming, and expensive. In certain situations, where the key issues and stakeholders are well defined and agreed upon by all parties, an assessment may not add much value. However, natural resource disputes are rarely that easy to pigeonhole. More often, as explained in chapter 1, such issues are defined by multiple parties, issues, and jurisdictions; scientific and technical uncertainty; and a range of potential public participation and dispute resolution strategies—all of which create different views on what is important, relevant, and compelling. The risks of proceeding without an assessment are that key parties may be left out of the process (and may later undermine it), that the right issues may not be addressed or framed appropriately, and that the process chosen may not be appropriate for the situation.

Assessments have been used to help people design effective public dialogues since the early 1970s.[2] In fact, Gerald Cormick completed something like an assessment in 1973 before initiating what he says is the first formal environmental mediation in the United States. In the early 1980s, a mediator interested in negotiated rulemaking articulated for the first time the philosophy and methods used to conduct assessments. In 1990, the Administrative Conference of the United States recommended that assessments be conducted for all prospective negotiated rulemakings.[3] Other dispute resolution professionals further refined the idea of conducting assessments in the late 1980s.[4] The Society for Professionals in Dispute Resolution adopted a set of best practices for convening collaborative processes, including the use of assessments, in 1997. Professor Lawrence Susskind, founder of the MIT-Harvard Public Disputes Program, and his colleagues articulated the definitive text on completing assessments in 1999 as part of *The Consensus Building Handbook,* the most authoritative guide on consensus building available today.[5] Given the history of strategies to resolve natural resource disputes in the West, assessments are a relatively new phenomenon. Dispute resolution professionals may consider assessments to be a best practice, but it will no doubt take time for decision makers, natural resource managers, and citizens to better understand the role and value of assessment in designing effective public dialogues.

The process of conducting an assessment typically follows the steps outlined in figure 9.3. Our intent here is not to examine the details of how to conduct an assessment; for more specific information, we recommend *The Consensus Building Handbook.* For our purposes here, we want to provide a general description of the assessment process and then illustrate that with a few examples.

To initiate an assessment, a sponsor—typically a government agency or decision maker, or any person or group interested in a particular issue or situation—decides that an assessment would be useful and retains a credible impartial assessor. The assessor should be viewed by all stakeholders as impartial and nonpartisan and should have some understanding of the issues at stake and the institutional context of the issue—including the range of dispute resolution strategies available to the parties. The assessor should be an effective interviewer and a discerning listener, since interviewing is the primary method of gathering information during the assessment. The assessor should have a clear mandate from the sponsor, including an understanding that the assessor operates autonomously and will make recommendations based on his or her best judgment.

Working together, the sponsor and assessor make a preliminary list of stakeholders to interview, develop an interview protocol, and invite stakeholders to participate. The assessor typically reviews appropriate documents to learn more about the issues and parties and then conducts interviews either one-on-one or in small groups of people with similar interests. Most assessors prefer to conduct interviews face-to-face, but sometimes it is more practical to interview people by telephone. Once the interviews are complete, the assessor prepares a report that synthesizes the findings and conclusions of the interviews, along with one or more options on how the

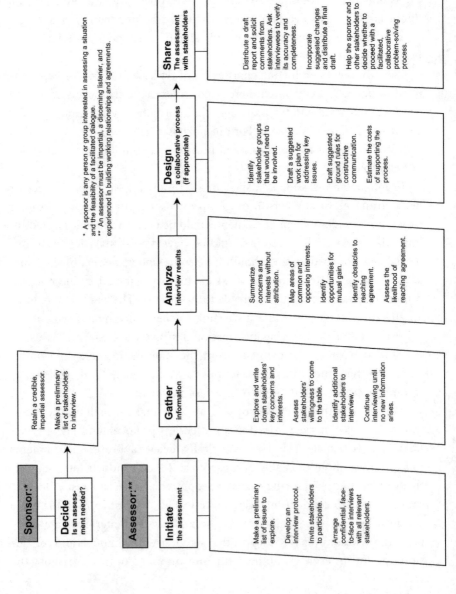

Sponsor:*

Retain a credible, impartial assessor.

Make a preliminary list of stakeholders to interview.

Decide
Is an assessment needed?

* A sponsor is any person or group interested in assessing a situation and the feasibility of a facilitated dialogue.
** An assessor must be impartial, a discerning listener, and experienced in building working relationships and agreements.

Assessor:**

Initiate
the assessment

Make a preliminary list of issues to explore.

Develop an interview protocol.

Invite stakeholders to participate.

Arrange confidential, face-to-face interviews with all relevant stakeholders.

Gather
information

Explore and write down stakeholders' key concerns and interests.

Assess stakeholders' willingness to come to the table.

Identify additional stakeholders to interview.

Continue interviewing until no new information arises.

Analyze
interview results

Summarize concerns and interests without attribution.

Map areas of common and opposing interests.

Identify opportunities for mutual gain.

Identify obstacles to reaching agreement.

Assess the likelihood of reaching agreement.

Design
a collaborative process (if appropriate)

Identify stakeholder groups that would need to be involved.

Draft a suggested work plan for addressing key issues.

Draft suggested ground rules for constructive communication.

Estimate the costs of supporting the process.

Share
The assessment with stakeholders

Distribute a draft report and solicit comments from stakeholders. Ask interviewees to verify its accuracy and completeness.

Incorporate suggested changes and distribute a final draft.

Help the sponsor and other stakeholders to decide whether to proceed with a facilitated, collaborative, problem-solving process.

FIGURE 9.1. How to Conduct a Situation Assessment. (Adapted from "How to Conduct a Conflict Assessment," developed by the Consensus Building Institute, Copyright 1998, and published in *CBI Reports* Spring 1998.)

stakeholders might proceed. Depending on the scope of the issue and the number of people involved, the reporting format may be a conference call, a two-page memo, or a twenty-page analysis. The report is typically distributed to the people interviewed and to anyone else who might be interested in the issue.

The objective of this reporting function is twofold: to validate that the assessor has accurately captured the needs, interests, and options as articulated by the interviewees, and to determine how, if at all, to move forward. The information gathered during the assessment allows stakeholders, including the decision makers, to tailor a process to match the situation. The resulting process may include any of the strategies described in this book. If certain criteria are met, it may be appropriate to convene a consensus-building process. Table 9.3 presents criteria to determine whether a consensus building process is appropriate.

To illustrate the value of an assessment in designing the appropriate architecture for a constructive public dialogue, consider the following examples. In 2001, the Montana legislature passed HB 397, which required the governor to create a task force to prepare a water management plan for the Clark Fork River basin in western Montana. The legislation was drafted in response to years of chronic drought in the basin and increasing concerns over water allocation and use. According to HB 397, the water management plan should include strategies to protect existing water rights, foster the orderly development of water, and promote conservation.

The governor asked the Montana Consensus Council to assume responsibility for convening and coordinating the task force. The council mailed questionnaires to more than 130 people and organizations interested in or involved with water management in the basin. This survey was designed to identify people's interests and concerns about water management in the basin and to determine who should participate on the task force. The council also conducted interviews with key players around the basin. While the number of interviews was limited because of initial funding constraints, more than 75 percent of interviewees and questionnaire respondents agreed that there was a need for the task force and a basinwide water management plan. People also identified a laundry list of issues that should be addressed in the plan.

The council prepared and distributed a report summarizing the findings and suggested a two-pronged approach for moving forward. The first was to convene a series of educational forums, and the second was to help

TABLE **9.3** A Checklist to Determine If Consensus Building
Is Appropriate

Necessary Conditions for a Consensus-building Process	Assessment and Comments		
Is There a Constituency for Change?			
Do people have a common concern over a reasonably well-defined issue?	❑ Yes	❑ No	❑ Maybe
Are people frustrated with the status quo? Do they truly want something to change?	❑ Yes	❑ No	❑ Maybe
Do people believe that the issue is timely and compelling?	❑ Yes	❑ No	❑ Maybe
Are people uncertain about their best alternative to a negotiated agreement?	❑ Yes	❑ No	❑ Maybe
Do people believe that the issues are negotiable (that is, there are no strongly felt issues involving a fundamental principle, right, value, or precedent)?	❑ Yes	❑ No	❑ Maybe
Do people desire more control over the outcome?	❑ Yes	❑ No	❑ Maybe
Do people want to avoid an adversarial situation?	❑ Yes	❑ No	❑ Maybe
Are people concerned about the costs of a prolonged dispute?	❑ Yes	❑ No	❑ Maybe
Do people desire a sense of closure?	❑ Yes	❑ No	❑ Maybe

TABLE 9.3 Continued

Necessary Conditions for a Consensus-building Process	Assessment and Comments	
Is There Sufficient Stakeholder Capacity?		
Are stakeholder groups clearly organized? Do they have clear lines of communication and decision making?	❏	Yes
	❏	No
	❏	Maybe
Can legitimate, credible representatives be identified, and are they willing to participate?	❏	Yes
	❏	No
	❏	Maybe
Are stakeholders willing to articulate their interests and seek solutions that accommodate the interests of other stakeholders?	❏	Yes
	❏	No
	❏	Maybe
Are public officials and decision makers committed to the process?	❏	Yes
	❏	No
	❏	Maybe
Are there sufficient resources to support the process (time, money, information, and so forth)?	❏	Yes
	❏	No
	❏	Maybe
Final Analysis		
Do people believe that they are likely to get more out of a consensus-building process than they are likely to get out of their alternatives for addressing the issue(s)?	❏	Yes
	❏	No
	❏	Maybe

interested parties in the Flathead Basin above Flathead Lake form a watershed council. The council convened an organizational meeting based on the report, and after a thorough discussion, the various interests groups and watersheds agreed to select their own representatives to serve on the task force. Participants agreed on a preliminary scope of work and began meeting in summer 2002 to build a common understanding of water availability and water rights in the basin. They continue to meet once a month and hope to complete the water management plan by summer 2004.

A situation assessment doesn't always lead to full-blown collaborative problem solving or consensus building. The issue at hand may not be ripe, or stakeholders may prefer to first try other avenues to address the situation. For example, after successfully building and implementing an agreement on sanitation standards for subdivisions in Montana, participants in one working group decided they wanted to sustain a dialogue among all stakeholders on issues related to land use and growth management in the state. With the assistance of the Montana Consensus Council, they created the Montana Growth Policy Forum, designed not as a formal agreement-seeking process but as an educational forum and policy dialogue—an opportunity to exchange ideas, examine policy options, and build a common understanding on land use and growth-related issues.

The forum met regularly from October 2000 through 2002. Participants included builders and developers; realtors; city, county, and state governments; conservationists; advocates for smart growth; advocates for affordable housing; ranchers and farmers; other landowners; surveyors, engineers, and planners; contractors; and transportation interests. The forum evolved into a place where citizens and leaders with diverse viewpoints could exchange ideas, seek input and advice from one another, and develop options to effectively respond to land use and growth in Montana. Although the forum did not result in any proposals for public policy, the participants overwhelmingly agreed that it fostered working relationships and a better understanding of the complicated system governing land use.

In other situations, assessments lead in very different directions. In 2000, the Dillon Field Office of the U.S. Bureau of Land Management (BLM) asked the Montana Consensus Council to design a public participation process for its four-year resource management planning effort. Interviews with local, state, and national stakeholders, including the BLM, made it clear that people were leery of the enormous time commitment that would be required by a full-scale consensus-building process overlapping the four-year planning effort. Instead, they wanted to participate in more focused bursts, targeting the issues that most affected their interests. With the help of the BLM and a unique coordinating committee that focused solely on public participation strategies, the council designed and convened a series of subgroups under the resource advisory council, a federally appointed group. Different subgroups addressed Wild and Scenic River designation, areas of critical environmental concern, and travel management. In addition to the subgroups and the coordinating committee on public participation, the BLM is also relying on information fairs, an interactive Web site, a newsletter, and press releases to encourage public participation as the planning effort moves forward.

Situation assessments provide the foundation for meaningful, effective public dialogue. They help sponsors, conveners, stakeholders, and process managers design the appropriate architecture for public participation and public dispute resolution. In the context of the 150-year history of strategies to resolve natural resource disputes in the West, assessments are a very recent development. Assessments are likely to become more important as people, including decision makers, demand more efficient and more effective approaches to shaping public policy and resolving public disputes.

Toward an Ethic of Sustainability

While different strategies may be useful in different circumstances, the basic proposition of this book is that the best way to sustain communities and landscapes in the West is to reconcile or integrate interests. Based on our experience as dispute resolution practitioners, and our interpretation of the history of natural resource policy in the West, integrating interests tends to be less costly than determining who is right, which in turn is less costly than determining who is more powerful.

Unlike other strategies, negotiation and mediation—the primary ways to integrate interests—allow the stakeholders themselves to make decisions. (Of course, negotiated agreements typically must be implemented through the appropriate legislative or administrative policy-making process.) In this respect, these two strategies offer a sense of self-determination—the people most affected by the issue or situation are meaningfully involved in the decision-making process.

Negotiation and mediation, including collaboration and consensus building, also tend to be more inclusive than other dispute resolution strategies. Inclusive participation means that an effort is made to meaningfully engage all viewpoints and interests. It implies that participants are empowered by the expectation that the decision maker will consider their input and advice, which will influence the outcome. Negotiation and mediation are also more deliberative than other strategies. Stakeholders have an equal opportunity to share views and information. These processes also foster mutual learning, common understanding, and consideration of a variety of options; people seek to understand the reasons (or interests) behind different viewpoints. Finally, the process is transparent and accountable to constituents, to the public, and ultimately to the issue or situation at hand.

These advantages move us one step closer to implementing Aldo Leopold's "land ethic" and achieving the "ethic of place" articulated by Charles Wilkinson. In 1949, Aldo Leopold argued: "A thing is right when it tends to preserve the integrity, stability, and beauty of the biotic community. It is wrong when it tends otherwise." This land ethic, according to Leopold, is based on the premise that the individual is a member of a community of interdependent parts. It provides moral direction on relationships between individuals and society, and between humans and the biophysical community—including soil, plants, animals, air, or—collectively—the environment. Building on Leopold's vision of a land ethic, Charles Wilkinson argues that we need to develop an "ethic of place." Such an ethic, according to Wilkinson, "respects equally the people of a region and the land, animals, vegetation, water, and air. [It] recognizes both that western people revere their physical surroundings and that they need and deserve a stable, productive economy."6

With this encouragement to move beyond an ethic of self-interest, we suggest that our prescriptive framework fulfills the requirements of Leopold's and Wilkinson's ethic of community and place. While it acknowledges the self-interests of people who care about the West, the framework calls for an approach that includes *all* interests and viewpoints. In this respect, the "community of interests" is, or at least should be, inclusive—it should include the life support, economic, recreational, aesthetic, scientific, historical, cultural, religious, and intrinsic values associated with the western landscape.

The challenges of integrating this diverse set of values come together in the idea of sustainability. According to the World Commission on Environment and Development: "Sustainable development meets the needs of the present without compromising the ability of future generations to meet their own needs."7 This principle implies that each generation inherits a natural and cultural legacy from its ancestors and holds it in trust for its descendents. It acknowledges the need for economic development but asserts that such development must maintain the integrity of the other values provided by nature.

Achieving sustainability is not primarily a scientific or technical challenge, nor is it simply about managing natural resources more effectively and efficiently. Rather, at its core, sustainability is about integrating people's diverse needs, interests, visions, and cultures.[8] As this book reveals, the cumulative effects of the approaches that have been used to resolve these differences in the West have become so evident and unacceptable that reform and the search for new approaches to building agreement and resolving disputes are well under way. Various forms of negotiation, mediation, consensus building, and collaborative problem solving provide better ways to address differences among people and to help build agreement on what should be sustained and how.

To paraphrase Leopold, the ethic of sustainability, including the role of interest-based approaches to dispute resolution, is not only an evolutionary possibility but also a practical necessity. Continuing to pit jobs against wildlife, growth against habitat, and economics against nature only ensures that the side with the most power wins. But power, like politics, swings back and forth on the pendulum of time. To genuinely resolve the issues facing the West will require integrating competing interests. We believe that interest-based negotiation and public dialogue offer the best hope to achieve livable communities, vibrant economies, and healthy landscapes in the West.

Beyond the West

Our analysis of the history of strategies to resolve natural resource disputes in the American West suggests several lessons that are applicable to other regions and countries:

- Ideas and strategies become embedded in policy and institutions; they are used as the default procedure even when they are not working.
- To overcome this inertia, it is important to have a vision of how the governance system could be improved and to then provide adequate space within existing policies and institutions to allow for experiments in public participation, public decision making, and public dispute resolution.
- Our prescriptive framework is adaptable to any governmental structure; it is applicable throughout the world. Of course, its application needs to be sensitive to the history and culture of public decision making in different regions or countries, but the basic ideas can be adapted to any system of governance. The general goal is to promote multiple approaches that provide

inclusive, informed, deliberative dialogue. The more specific goal
is to tailor processes to the needs and interests of a particular
situation.

- Similarly, the idea of conducting a situation assessment is an independent, objective method that is applicable across regions,
cultures, and governance systems.

- The most effective decisions integrate the best-available science
with the values and interests of the people affected by the
decisions.

- Increasingly, people around the globe are recognizing that natural resource issues tend to cross borders—city/rural lines, agency
jurisdictions, even national boundaries. The principles and
strategies of collaboration are ideally suited to engaging people
across such divisions and resolving transboundary issues.

- Well-designed public participation or collaborative processes
offer opportunities to hear from "forgotten" interests, such as
unaffiliated citizens—people who don't belong to a cohesive
stakeholder group. A safe and welcoming forum can draw their
participation.

In addition to offering some lessons to others, the West might also learn
from the experiences of others. Realizing that cultures and governance systems vary, it is possible to harvest lessons from others by focusing on specific
issues. As the West continues to struggle with rapid growth, sprawl, and
water supply issues, the policies and best practices from other countries can
serve as useful models. Such efforts are already under way in Maryland,
which agreed to work in a collaborative partnership with the German state
of Schleswig-Holstein, exchanging data and technical expertise in the areas
of smart growth, green buildings, and renewable energy.[9] Based on this
working relationship, Maryland is now planning to develop two wind farms.
Climate protection strategies from Sweden and Denmark are being implemented in Portland, Oregon, and car-sharing programs in Seattle, Portland,
and Denver are modeled on German and Swiss efforts to reduce rush-hour
traffic and pollution. Park managers the world over are watching Africa's
ambitious plans to create a series of international wildlife parks through
transboundary collaboration.[10]

The rise of collaboration and consensus building in the West, and their integration into more traditional decision-making processes, reflects a renewal of citizenship and a return to governance by and of the people. We believe that this form of direct democracy complements the efforts of government officials to convene collaborative forums on resource decisions. We encourage both citizens and public officials to initiate collaborative forums, but we caution all involved that if their intent is to influence public policy, they need to link their efforts to formal decision-making processes.[11]

But we should also take care that collaboration doesn't become just another layer of bureaucratic red tape in an already matted knot of procedures and decision-making processes. In the Klamath River basin, for example, it may be too soon to begin large-scale negotiations. Water rights are still being adjudicated, so it remains unclear which users will receive enough water to meet their needs and which ones will go wanting. Tribal and federal reserved rights also remain unquantified, and it seems that the federal agencies responsible for fish and wildlife need to clarify and reach agreement on the effects of Klamath Basin stream flows and lake levels on the various populations of threatened and endangered species. Until these steps are taken— possibly with some collaborative elements—larger negotiations would only generate more frustration and perhaps ill-timed backlash against future collaboration.

Yet it's never too early—or too late—to invite people to communicate and cooperate on a common problem. We see opportunities in the Klamath situation to gradually turn warring interests into a community of diverse but cooperative interests. Living far from the basin, and without the luxury of talking to all of the affected people, we can't pretend to understand the situation well enough to design a specific problem-solving process at this time. But in the spirit of applying the principles explained in this book, we can suggest one possible course of action as an example of how collaborative problem solving might improve the situation in the Klamath River basin.

While the water rights adjudication process proceeds, it may be useful to focus on the disagreement over water flows and levels and their impact on threatened and endangered species. An impartial third party could conduct a situation assessment on that issue, interviewing the key stakeholders and decision makers about their interests and concerns and their willingness to collaborate and negotiate. Interviewees should include—at a minimum— biologists and administrators with the U.S. Fish and Wildlife Service (both endangered species and refuge branches), the National Marine Fisheries

Service, and the U.S. Bureau of Reclamation; officials with the California and Oregon fish and wildlife agencies; irrigation districts throughout the basin; fisheries advocates and other conservation organizations; the Klamath, Yurok, and Hoopa tribes; dam operators and utility companies; the Federal Energy Regulatory Commission; commercial fishery operations; and recreational anglers and river users.

Based on the results of the interviews, if people are willing to work together, a principled process could be designed to build a common understanding and seek agreement on the water needs of the relevant species. Such a process should be facilitated by an impartial third party and might include joint fact finding, collaborative work groups on specific issues, and public forums to exchange information. Participants would draft and adhere to ground rules and a work plan, cooperating in good faith and staying focused on the task at hand. It would also be important to engage the ultimate decision makers—perhaps as high up as the governors of Oregon and California, the secretaries of the interior and agriculture, and the White House—or at least keep them updated and well informed as the process unfolds. A variety of media contacts could be invited to cover the process, and all meetings should be open to the public (with clear protocols for public comment and participation).

Ideally, the process would result in a concise, plainly written report outlining the best-available knowledge on the effects of water flows and levels on the relevant species. Participants would sign off on the report as a statement of agreement on the contents.

If such a process proved fruitful, it would provide far more than a single agreement on the biological questions currently muddying the waters. Participants will have developed trust, a shared understanding of the issues and one another's interests, and perhaps even the kernels of a shared vision for resolving the larger issues facing the basin. Assuming the adjudication is complete, participants could build on their work together, inviting other stakeholders in the basin to join the dialogue and broadening the scope to address the larger issues of basinwide water allocation and drought response. Again, it would be valuable to enlist an impartial facilitator and to interview stakeholders before beginning negotiations.

We don't pretend that interest-based negotiation and collaboration are panaceas; a thorough assessment of the Klamath situation may reveal irreconcilable values, overwhelming distrust, or other insurmountable barriers to collaboration. Clearly, however, the Klamath's troubles remain unresolved, despite ample doses of scientific expertise, litigation, public participation, and power mongering. Perhaps it's time people sat down to talk—and listen—to one another.

The Klamath situation is representative of many contentious natural resource issues and disputes across the West. But these same disputes present us with an opportunity. History has brought us a number of dispute resolution strategies. Experience has taught us their strengths and weaknesses and has led us toward more collaborative and consensus-oriented processes. The field of public dispute resolution has recently delivered the essential theories and best practices for addressing the challenges that lie before us. Understanding our arrival at the confluence of these various currents should embolden us to chart a new course for natural resource decision making in the West.

NOTES

1. Richard Nevstadt and Ernest R. May, *Thinking in Time: The Uses of History for Decisionmakers* (New York: Free Press, 1986).
2. This discussion of the history and purpose of conflict assessments is based on Lawrence Susskind and Jennifer Thomas-Larmer, "Conducting a Conflict Assessment," in *The Consensus Building Handbook: A Comprehensive Guide to Reaching Agreement,* ed. Lawrence Susskind, Sarah McKearnan, and Jennifer Thomas-Larmer (Thousand Oaks, CA: Sage, 1999).
3. Gerald W. Cormick, "Mediating Environmental Controversies: Perspectives and First Experience," *Earth Law Journal* 2 (1976): 215–24; Phillip J. Harter, "Negotiating Regulations: A Cure for the Malaise," *Georgetown Law Journal* 71, no. 1 (1982): 1–113; David M. Pritzker and D. S. Dalton, *Negotiated Rulemaking Sourcebook* (Washington, DC: Government Printing Office, 1990).
4. See Christopher W. Moore, *The Mediation Process: Practical Strategies for Resolving Conflict* (San Francisco: Jossey-Bass, 1986); and Susan L. Carpenter and W.J.D. Kennedy, *Managing Public Disputes* (San Francisco: Jossey-Bass, 1988).
5. Lawrence Susskind, Sarah McKearnan, and Jennifer Thomas-Larmer, eds., *The Consensus Building Handbook: A Comprehensive Guide to Reaching Agreement* (Thousand Oaks, CA: Sage, 1999).
6. Aldo Leopold, *A Sand County Almanac and Sketches Here and There* (New York: Oxford University Press, 1949), 224–25; Charles F. Wilkinson, "Law and the American West: The Search for an Ethic of Place," *University of Colorado Law Review* 59, no. 3 (1988): 401–25.
7. World Commission on Environment and Development, *From One Earth to One World* (New York: Oxford University Press, 1987).

8. Gerald Cormick et al., *Building Consensus for a Sustainable Future: Putting Principles into Practice* (Ottawa: National Round Table on the Environment and the Economy, 1996).

9. Dale Medearis, Brian Swett, and Marrylin Zaw-Mon, "International Best Practices and Innvoation—Strategically Harvesting Environmental Lessons from Abroad" (unpublished, undated manuscript on file with the authors).

10. Peter Godwin, "Without Borders: Uniting Africa's Wildlife Reserves," *National Geographic,* September 2001.

11. This is one of the key ingredients for success that has emerged from over twenty-five years of experience in public dispute resolution. For more, see Lawrence Susskind and Jeffrey Cruickshank, *Breaking the Impasse: Consensual Approaches to Resolving Public Disputes* (New York: Basic Books, 1987).

Acknowledgments

During the past 15 years, we have had the opportunity to work with a number of citizens and leaders throughout the American West. We have helped diverse groups of people, representing every conceivable viewpoint, shape public policy to foster livable communities, vibrant economies, and healthy environments. Based on these experiences, we conclude that although there are myriad ways to foster social change, resolve public disputes, and shape public policy, the most likely way to produce wise, durable decisions over the use of natural resources is to bring together the right people with the best available information in constructive forums that focus on the places and issues people care about. This book explains why we believe this conclusion is a historical imperative and a regional necessity.

Several people and organizations made this book possible. For starters, we would like to thank Patrick Field, Sarah Van de Wetering, Keith Allred, Cathy Barbouletos, Mike Harper, Steve Hartmann, and John Freemuth, all of whom read various drafts of this manuscript and provided valuable feedback on the history of natural resource policy, the theory and practice of collaborative problem solving, and the politics of the American West. We also greatly appreciate the time and perspective contributed by Charles Wilkinson in the foreword.

We are also grateful to the many people we have worked with over the years, and from whom we have learned much about human nature, politics, and the governance of natural resources. The staff, consultants, and board of directors of the Montana Consensus Council provided an ever-present sounding board for 10 years, during which many of the ideas in this book were developed and refined. While less frequent, we also benefited from many insightful dialogues with Kent Briggs, Daniel Kemmis, Terry Minger, Don Snow, and Larry Susskind. We have been very fortunate to be able to draw on their experience and wisdom and appreciate the time they have dedicated to our work.

We also recognize the many students in Matt's Natural Resource Dispute Resolution course at the University of Montana. This course regularly includes students in law, forestry, conservation, environmental studies, and the humanities (literature and philosophy). It has provided an opportunity to help organize our thinking, test ideas, and clarify our understanding of the history of governing natural resources.

Finally, a special thanks to several institutions that have supported our work over the years, including the University of Montana, the William and Flora Hewlett Foundation, and the Lincoln Institute of Land Policy. Matt would also like to thank Carroll College for providing a quiet place to write major portions of this book during the spring of 2003.

Appendix
Project Evaluation Form

Please help us improve the services we offer. As participants, your comments and suggestions are the most important measure of our performance. Please complete both parts of this form.

1. What was the name of the project you participated in?

2. Was the facilitator helpful? If so, how? If not, please explain.

3. Did the facilitator fulfill his or her responsibilities? (Check all that apply.)

_____ impartiality
_____ enforcing ground rules
_____ encouraging participation
_____ helping group invent solutions
_____ implementing agreement

_____ keeping confidentiality
_____ staying on schedule
_____ promoting civil discussion
_____ documenting agreement and
_____ build agreement

_____ process design
_____ keeping group focused
_____ coordinating meeting logistics

4. Did you encounter any specific problems during the process? (Check all that apply.)

Unrealistic expectations: _____ mine _____ others'
No compelling reason to reach agreement: _____ me _____ others'
Stakeholder groups: _____ too many _____ too few
Available information: _____ too much _____ too little
Deadlines: _____ too soon _____ too distant
Other (please explain):

5. How could this process be improved?

6. What process would you have used to address this situation if you had not participated in this collaborative process?

_____ No action   _____ Direct discussion with decision maker(s)
_____ Litigation   _____ Lobbying
_____ Proposed legislation   _____ Citizen initiative
_____ Citizen petition   _____ Other (please describe)

7. Compare this collaborative process to your next best option (from #6 above). Which of the two would most likely:

Cost less?   _____ collaboration   _____ other option
Take less time?   _____ collaboration   _____ other option
Improve communication
among participants?   _____ collaboration   _____ other option
Improve trust among participants? _____ collaboration   _____ other option
Produce a more effective,
lasting outcome?   _____ collaboration   _____ other option

8. Would you recommend a collaborative process to address similar issues?

Participant Satisfaction Scorecard

Please circle the number that best matches your level of agreement with each statement. Also check whether you think that aspect of the process is important or unimportant. 1=completely disagree, 2=strongly disagree, 3=disagree, 4=indifferent, 5=agree, 6=strongly agree, 7=completely agree.

	Important	Unimportant	Circle One
THE OUTCOME			
An agreement was reached.	θ	θ	1 2 3 4 5 6 7
The agreement was ratified by everyone needed to implement it.	θ	θ	1 2 3 4 5 6 7
The agreement is adaptive to new information, interests, and ideas.	θ	θ	1 2 3 4 5 6 7
The underlying issue was resolved; the problem will not likely recur.	θ	θ	1 2 3 4 5 6 7
I trust the people who will implement the agreement.	θ	θ	1 2 3 4 5 6 7
The outcome satisfies my basic interest.	θ	θ	1 2 3 4 5 6 7
The overall situation is better than before.	θ	θ	1 2 3 4 5 6 7
The outcome is better than what I could get from another process.	θ	θ	1 2 3 4 5 6 7
WORKING RELATIONSHIPS			
The process helped build trust among participants.	θ	θ	1 2 3 4 5 6 7

The process improved communication among participants. ⊖ 1 2 3 4 5 6 7

I gained insights about the issues and others' views and values. ⊖ 1 2 3 4 5 6 7

I would negotiate other issues with the same participants. ⊖ 1 2 3 4 5 6 7

The process improved my ability to resolve public issues. ⊖ 1 2 3 4 5 6 7

QUALITY OF THE PROCESS

Everyone who wanted to participate had a fair chance to do so. ⊖ 1 2 3 4 5 6 7

Everyone's concerns were respected. ⊖ 1 2 3 4 5 6 7

Everyone had access to the information needed to make good decisions. ⊖ 1 2 3 4 5 6 7

Information we used was relevant and up to date. ⊖ 1 2 3 4 5 6 7

The process fostered information gathering and learning as a group. ⊖ 1 2 3 4 5 6 7

The group considered different options for resolving the issue. ⊖ 1 2 3 4 5 6 7

People at the table were accountable to their constituencies. ⊖ 1 2 3 4 5 6 7

There was a way to raise due process complaints during negotiation ⊖ 1 2 3 4 5 6 7

Gains and losses were fairly distributed among all participants. ⊖ 1 2 3 4 5 6 7

The public was able to review and comment on the process and outcome. ⊖ 1 2 3 4 5 6 7

The process was efficient. It was time and money well spent. ⊖ 1 2 3 4 5 6 7

About the Authors

Matthew McKinney is director of the Public Policy Research Institute at the University of Montana. The institute helps citizens and leaders shape public policy to sustain communities and landscapes. Prior to this, he served as the founding director of the Montana Consensus Council for ten years. During the past eighteen years, he has designed and facilitated nearly fifty multiparty dialogues related to such diverse issues as federal land management, water policy, fish and wildlife, land use planning and growth management, and public health and human services. He is a senior lecturer at the University of Montana's School of Law; a faculty associate at the Lincoln Institute of Land Policy; and a partner with the Consensus Building Institute. He received his Ph.D. in natural resource policy and conflict resolution from the University of Michigan and was a research fellow at the John F. Kennedy School of Government, Harvard University. Matthew lives with his wife and three daughters in Helena, Montana.

William Harmon is a freelance writer specializing in natural resource management, recreation, mental health issues, and collaborative problem solving. He has served as the communications coordinator for the Montana Consensus Council since its inception in 1993. He is the author of eight books and numerous published articles. He received a B.A. in English from the University of Montana and has worked as a writer and editor for the U.S. Forest Service and for the Montana Department of Natural Resources and Conservation. He lives in Helena, Montana, with his wife and family.

Index

DATE DUE